SCHOOL FINANCE POLICIES AND PRACTICES
AND PRACTICES
The 1980s: A Decade of Conflict

Edited by

JAMES W. GUTHRIE

University of California, Berkeley

**First Annual Yearbook of the
American Education Finance Association**

BALLINGER PUBLISHING COMPANY   WITHDRAWN

Cambridge, Massachusetts

A Subsidiary of Harper & Row, Publishers, Inc.

This book is printed on recycled paper.

International Standard Book Number: 0−88410−195−9

Library of Congress Catalog Card Number: 80−19707

Printed in the United States of America

Library of Congress Cataloging in Publication Data

Main entry under title:

School finance policies and practices.

(First annual yearbook of the American Education Finance Association)
Includes index.
1. Education−United States−Finance−Addresses, essays, lectures.
2. United States−Social policy−Addresses, essays, lectures. I. Guthrie, James W. II. Series: American Education Finance Association. Annual yearbook of the American Education Finance Association ; 1st.
LB2825.S337   379.1′1′0973   80−19707
ISBN 0−88410−195−9

CONTENTS

LIST OF FIGURES

LIST OF TABLES

FOREWORD
Equity, Liberty, and Efficiency

H. Thomas James
President, The Spencer Foundation

I am pleased to assess the first yearbook of the American Education Finance Association and I wish to begin with the chapter by Kirst and Garms. Their view of the school system as a dependent variable is a sound one, and their consideration of the power of demography, the economy, and polity in shaping schools provides a useful framework in which to ponder fiscal problems of public education in the 1980s.

I have no quarrel with their thoughts on demography. Barring war or other calamities, their predictions should hold reasonably well. We can look for continuing decline in the school age population through the decade ahead, dropping by 1990 to about the same enrollment level as in 1960.

On the second independent variable, the economy, Garms and Kirst are virtually silent. Noting that demographic projections are risky, they might well have said that forecasting the economy is sometimes downright foolhardy. While writing this foreword I was privileged to hear an internationally respected panel discuss the economy. The only panel member willing to bet on economic indicators gave slightly favorable odds on gold hitting 1000 before the Dow-Jones Industrial Average, but his odds were even on which would

This paper was initially delivered as a major invited address before the 1980 American Education Finance Association conference in San Diego.

reach 500 first—on the way down! We have come through a decade characterized by "stagflation," and nothing approaching consensus seems to favor a brighter view for the 1980s; Kirst and Garms, if we may interpret their estimates for expenditures on education as at least in part an index of general economic conditions, expect it to be worse in the 1980s.

It is in the realm of polity, the third independent variable, that these authors develop their most sophisticated analyses. Arraying many of the complex social forces that shape political decisions, they note that segments of our population with increasing enrollments, such as Hispanics and low income people generally, have little political influence over budgets, whereas older people who are politically active and have little direct interest in education are on the increase. Such a divergence bears watching, for if such imbalances become great, they breed revolution—and revolutions are never started, nor are they ever won, by the elderly.

Returning to another facet of demography, Kirst and Garms predict that migrations from north and northeast to south and southwest will continue as a social phenomenon, exacerbated by declines in cheap fuels and the search for softer lifestyles. Areas in decline are placed in a double bind. The elderly affluent, decamping with their capital, reduce the tax base needed to support the elderly poor who must perforce remain. The young who leave to pursue new opportunities, for which frequently their education qualifies them, are precisely the ones most needed to remain as a balance for the less mobile, the less able, and the less educated. Shorter but similar migrations from central city to suburb in the Northeast and Middle West have had a comparable effect, withdrawing the wealth and talent needed to make cities function while leaving behind disproportionately large numbers of those most needing social services of all kinds and least able to afford them.

Putting their variables together, Kirst and Garms paint a dismal picture of the future for American schools. With urgent demands for defense, health, and welfare, they see little hope of large-scale federal increases for education. The best hope seems to be for continued increases in state support, which should ease the need for local increases, hard to come by in any event. The implication, of course, is that power and authority over education will continue to wax at the state level and wane at the local.

This is a bleak assessment, yet it is no bleaker than one that Garms, Kelly, and I made fourteen years ago, after completing a study of the large cities:

> In our society the educated are capital assets to a community, and the uneducated are liabilities. As long as a city either has empty spaces within its boundaries, or can extend its boundaries, it matters little that educated citizens who are able to win social and economic privileges move out to the edges of the city and those who cannot remain at its core. It is when the educated cross the boundary and leave the city, subtracting their productive skills and their capital wealth from the pool in the city, and adding both to another civil division, that the city is weakened. If for each educated person it loses, the city must accept in exchange an uneducated person, then as long as that pattern of exchange persists the decline of the city is inevitable. (James, Kelly, and Garms 1966: 16)

Kirst and Garms now seem to see that generalization as applicable to states as well.

Yet, despite these bleak outlooks and the doom and gloom literature with which we are all too familiar, there are hopeful signs that need to be held in mind. Let me emphasize four:

1. Declining numbers of students to be educated in most places will contribute to decline in relative spending for schooling and should to that degree make resources relatively easier to come by.

2. In most places, declining numbers will reduce crowding and interpersonal conflict that for several decades have made school attendance and teaching an unhappy experience for many. This will doubtless improve the quality of education, as well as the quality of school life, in the decade ahead.

3. From researchers devoting close study to urban schooling, those willing to listen are hearing good news about successes in city schools. Chase says, "Urban education has an inner vitality which is generating innovative programs and strategies of great potential even in the midst of extremely diverse conditions" (1978: 35–36). Clark, who has reviewed urban elementary schools and programs achieving unusual success, described these schools and programs as "neither so surprising nor so different as to be considered unattainable by large numbers of urban

schools" (1980: 467–70). Furthermore, in that same *Phi Delta Kappan* issue, Harold "Doc" Howe reminds us, as he has so often before:

> When we overemphasize our problems, it is easy to forget our achievements. In my view that is what has happened to the public image of American education. For a country where each succeeding generation has for 100 years been more literate than the preceding one, we have an unbalanced view that places our educational problems, of which we have plenty, on center stage and shoves our achievements into the wings. There is not a country in the world with as complex a society and as tumultuous a history that can point to an education establishment as open, as diverse, and as excellent as ours. (Howe 1980: 446–47)

4. Pressure groups and voluntary associations supporting public schools, which fragmented and quarreled during the 1950s and 1960s, seemed toward the end of the 1970s to be reforming in useful alliances and showing new strength in the political arenas. If continued into the 1980s, these trends could reduce much of the popular malaise about schooling.

Let me turn now to two of the large issues dealt with in this volume—liberty and equality—and appeal to those concerned with school finance to press for the involvement of more philosophers in a continuing dialogue. We have heard frequently about freedom of choice and about equity. I have written before about liberty and equality, trying to disentangle two terms that are as slippery as any in our civic language. They are also the most basic among that broad and deep set of values that has bound our society together and made it recognizable for 200 years as a nation demonstrably different from all others. Libertarian views, with their high regard for freedom, derive from the English Revolution of 1688 and the writings of John Locke; notions of equality derive from the French Revolution and the writings of Jean-Jacques Rousseau. Both are built solidly into the fabric of our government and into the institutions we have devised to increase knowledge, morality, and civility.

However, liberty and equality are ever in conflict, and that conflict has provided much of the dynamic tension that has maintained this nation's vitality. These two basic values stood at the head of the list compiled by President Eisenhower's Commission on National Goals. They are deeply identified with our political parties. President Eisenhower always listed liberty first (as did the commission he created). President Kennedy always listed equality first. Yet we know that they are interdependent in our lives; the rejection of one or the other is not an option open either to individuals or to institutions in our society.

After the early years of this century, liberalism as a political movement began with concern for the protection of individual liberties, rights of property, and civil rights. Subsequently, it turned to favoring government growth and government remedies for social and economic reforms. Equity considerations bulk large in the school finance literature, going back to Cubberley's dissertation at Teachers College in 1905, and concerns for equity have energized the great reform movements in school finance down to and including the current one stemming from *Serrano* (1971). In the 1970s, however, we saw increasing signs of liberalism swinging back to its traditional concerns with curbs on government; protection of individual liberties, property rights, and civil rights; and freedom from government and corporate intrusion and, more especially as the decade drew to its close, from the raging inflation for which government is blamed. What this means in terms of education, and specifically for financing education, is not yet clear, but it needs to be talked about, and I argue that the readers of this book would do well to persuade more philosophers to join in the discussion, for philosophers can help such talk to be more orderly in form, more cumulative in its effects on knowledge, and more civil in tone than is likely to be the case without them. More important, philosophy can discipline us to ask the right questions and to recognize right answers when we find them.

The libertarian standard is raised high by advocates of vouchers, with their emphasis on freedom of choice. Such advocacy draws followers, for that standard is very old and very powerful, and it is difficult in the attendant uproar to weigh the consequences as carefully as need be.

The libertarian flag is also waved by the new populists such as Paul Gann and Howard Jarvis, in their drives to limit taxation and government spending. Here too, supporters rally to the libertarian standard, and it is difficult in the uproar to emphasize that when the Constitution was written, we opted for representative government because we were convinced that deliberative bodies would be better able to weigh benefits of taxes against their burdens. Gann and Jarvis are probably right in their estimate that they will continue to carry popular majorities as long as government employees spearhead the opposition. Eventually, however, citizens must carefully analyze the benefits to be foregone in years—perhaps generations—to come if arrangements for schooling are disrupted, as now threatened by severe fiscal containment proposals.

Concerns for efficiency and productivity are relative newcomers to discussions of schooling, dating from what has been called the scientific management movement in the second decade of this century. Again, we need to be careful about clarity in the definition of these terms. Efficiency, as the term is used in school finance and in economics, means making the best use of resources to achieve specified aims. The problem economists have in applying this proposition to education is that the aims are not clear, and when they settle for surrogates, like the level of schooling in the international studies or achievement-test scores, educators protest that such trivia cannot stand for the grander aims of schooling.

If I understand correctly the interests of fiscal containment proponents, they intended neither harm nor help to public education. They mean to see property and property taxes cut. An unintended consequence of such actions is to force financing and administration of schools into sharply altered patterns. State and federal governmental agencies come to play an increased role. However, I would be greatly surprised if anyone could find hard evidence that it has improved school efficiency. My own expectation would be quite the contrary: systems under great stress usually lose efficiency.

I expect difficulties to persist in applying the efficiency criterion to schools, and I consider this problem primary for scholars interested in the financing of education through the 1980s. It would be useful to find better ways of stating the aims of education in quantifiable terms and of specifying what could be accomplished at varying levels of spending. It would be especially useful to a state facing an intense tax-cutting campaign to specify the losses that the state would suffer at reduced levels of funding in terms of valued aims of education that must be foregone or, conversely, what additional valued aims could be accomplished if present levels of funding were increased. We are fortunate to have useful work going forward on this subject in several of the school finance study centers, and I have no doubt that progress will continue to be made in the 1980s.

Similarly, it has been hard to estimate educational production or the effects of schooling, and lack of such estimates hampers applications of economic models. Here again, useful work is progressing, with close cooperation between educators at several school finance study centers, though many important issues remain to be resolved. If progress continues to be made on such promising variables as time on task, separation of institutional functions from socialization functions, individual attainment, analysis of resources by classrooms, and many others, we may finally be ready for the heady task ahead, perhaps in the 1980s, of estimating the effects of substituting technology for personal services on the costs and benefits of schooling. For in the 1980s we shall be seeing the long-heralded entry of technology as an important component in the school finance equation.

It would also be useful, as we look forward to studies of school finance in the new decade, to be more concerned than we appear to be about the quality of the data upon which much of our work is based. Many of the data of interest to scholars in our field derive from accounts kept at the local school level. Rules observed by the keepers of these accounts derive not from immutable laws, but from a set of agreements that are themselves sensitive to (and can be changed by) the political process. We have seen more than enough macrostudies of data accumulated in this way. A few case studies, carefully chosen and carefully designed, might be particularly useful at this time for shifting our attention from old (and probably wrong) answers now accepted to some new questions that need to be asked.

I look toward the future with wary optimism. I go on expecting improvement during the decade ahead, especially in the quality of education and the quality of life in our schools. Perhaps we can all work together more closely in the 1980s to make that hope come true.

REFERENCES

Chase, Francis S. 1978. *Urban Education Studies: 1977–78 Report.* Dallas: Council of the Great City Schools, May 4.

Clark, David L. et al. 1980. "Factors Associated with Success in Urban Elementary Schools." *Phi Delta Kappan*, March, pp. 467–70.

Cubberley, Ellwood Patterson.

Howe, Harold, II. 1980. "Two Views of the New Department of Education and Its First Secretary." *Phi Delta Kappan*, March, pp. 446–47.

James, H. Thomas; James A. Kelly; and Walter I. Garms. 1966. *Determinants of Educational Expenditures in Large Cities of the United States.* U.S. Department of Health, Education, and Welfare, Office of Education, Cooperative Research Project No. 2389. Stanford, California: School of Education, Stanford University.

Serrano v. Priest, 96 Cal. Rptr. 601, 43T P. 2d 1241 (1971).

ACKNOWLEDGMENTS

This first yearbook represents the fulfillment of a hope long held by many individuals associated with the American Education Finance Association (AEFA). This organization has consistently served as a means of communication, an arena for public policy debate, and a mechanism for educating policymakers, professional educators, and interested members of the lay public. Until this point, however, the only avenue available to AEFA for pursuit of its purposes was its annual convention. The conventions have been thoughtfully designed and well attended. However, by their nature they seldom permit the intense concentration upon a major issue or set of issues necessary for complete understanding. With the addition of a major annual publication, AEFA expands its ability to accomplish its objectives.

Numerous individuals contributed to the completion of this project. The AEFA is governed by a sixteen member board of directors, eight selected annually to serve two terms. This project was firmly endorsed by the AEFA board both in 1979 and 1980. A complete list of directors for these two years appears elsewhere in this volume. At this point the editor wishes to express his appreciation for their support and counsel. Also, two AEFA presidents, Alan Odden and Richard Rossmiller, respectively, director of the School Finance Project at the Education Commission of the States and professor, School of Education, University of Wisconsin, Madison, have provided useful assistance on literally dozens of dimensions.

Each of the volume's thirteen contributors is due a special note of praise. Authors were generous in contributing their time and knowledge. Each chapter was solicited with no promise of remuneration. Each author was willing simply to assist in expanding the marketplace of public policy ideas. The editor is particularly grateful for the willingness of authors to shape their contributions so as to conform to the book's conceptual structure of involving three of American society's major value streams.

Two of the chapters have been previously published and the editor wishes to express his gratitude to Kern Alexander of the *Journal of Education Finance* and J. Gallagher and R. Haskins, editors of *Care and Education of Young Children in America*, and the Ablex Publishing Company for the appropriate permissions.

Several individuals proved crucial in ensuring the transformation of this volume from a simple set of ideas into a concrete publication. Among these were Jane Beaumont, Viviane Dutoit, Chris Endo, and Judy Snow, all of whom participated in the correspondence, communication, conversations, copying, typing, and revising entailed by such an undertaking. Also, Anne Just, Pearl Mitchell, Tom Timar, and Ina Spinka, as research assistants in the Program in Policy Analysis at the Graduate School of Education, University of California, Berkeley, assisted frequently in criticizing ideas, making arrangements, identifying citations, and the myriad of other seemingly small but underrated tasks involved with editing a volume such as this.

To all the foregoing, and probably to countless others whose names may have slipped my memory, I want to acknowledge my indebtedness. My most fond hope in this connection is that my successors in editing subsequent volumes will have similar unselfish assistance.

James W. Guthrie
Berkeley, April 1980

INTRODUCTION

James W. Guthrie

The years from 1955 to 1980 encompass the most intense and far-reaching period of school finance reform in the history of the United States. Propelled variously by judicial decisions, legislative enactments, federal and philanthropic foundation incentives, powerful political interests, academic arguments, and altruism, the overwhelming majority of states undertook a substantial revision of the means by which they generated and distributed revenues for public school support.

Chapter 3 contains a thorough assessment of these revisions. Suffice it to state here that the reforms are completely satisfying to only a few. Proponents of greater equity contend that the alterations have been insufficient to achieve the resource parity necessary for true equality. Fiscal guardians have been distressed by increased spending and taxes precipitated by the equity reforms. Similarly, defenders of liberty or choice have been disturbed by alterations in conventional local school district decisionmaking arrangements that have frequently accompanied finance reform. This latter group desires a return to "local control" that characterized United States school policymaking in the earlier portion of the twentieth century.

Each reform appears to contain within it the seeds for yet another reform. In a society possessed of heretofore unmatched complexity, it is nearly impossible to alter one major policy component without provoking reverberations throughout other segments as well. Thus efforts to achieve greater equality have provoked concern on the part of those whose primary value emphasis is liberty or efficiency. The prospect of continued tension between equality, efficiency, and liberty and a desire better to understand the consequences that such tensions might have for future school finance policy prompted the American Education Finance Association to focus upon this topic in this its initial yearbook. However, before undertaking this description, we offer a preview of the contents of the entire volume.

PREVIEW

The yearbook Foreword is by H. Thomas James, one of the most respected scholars in the history of school finance. Indeed, James, now president of the Chicago-based Spencer Foundation, is one of three or four persons largely responsible for shaping school finance into a respectable field of academic inquiry. From his perspective of forty years of practical and professional experience, he describes the potential conflict between equality, efficiency, and liberty; analyzes the history of each value stream; and posits several predictions regarding the future of school finance policy. It is his observation that school finance has matured as a technical field and that greater precision has resulted from utilization of econometric techniques, computer simulations, and public finance concepts. However, major clarification regarding the nexus between public school finance and public values is badly needed, and this is a task that would be greatly assisted by the involvement of philosophers. This book is in part philosophical for precisely this reason. The editor and contributors also believe strongly that the future direction of school finance policy should be guided by a substantial concern for values.

In addition to public values, the direction of public policy is also shaped by historic events and contemporary demographic, economic, and social trends. Consequently, before paying particular attention to the potential practical school finance conflict between equality, efficiency, and liberty, we devote Section I to a discussion of past and future policy environments. Chapter 1, by the volume's editor, James W. Guthrie, describes the school-finance-related reforms that took place between 1955 and 1980. Chapter 2 is by Michael W. Kirst, professor at Stanford University Graduate School of Education and president of the California State Board of Education, and by Walter I. Garms, dean and professor at the School of Education, University of Rochester. Each has a long record of scholarship regarding educational policy generally and school finance particularly. Their chapter describes demographic, economic, and political data dimensions and deduces from them conditions likely to influence school finance policymaking in the decade of the 1980s. Whereas educators were able to capitalize upon favorable political and economic conditions in the 1960s and shape them to the benefit of education generally, an opposite condition is developing in the 1980s. It would appear that contemporary trends are more likely to influence policy to the disadvantage of education and professional educators.

Section II contains two chapters concerned with the value of equality. In Chapter 3, K. Forbis Jordan, senior specialist in Education, Congressional Research Service, United States Library of Congress, joins with Mary P. McKeown, a finance analyst with the Maryland State Board of Higher Education, to summarize literature regarding the definition and measurement of finance equality and then undertake an assessment of the progress over the last two decades in achieving school finance "equality."

Chapter 4 addresses James' earlier plea for the greater involvement of philosophers. The author is John E. Coons, and the chapter poses the question, "Can education be equal and excellent?" Coons sensitively probes proponents of equality regarding their ultimate values. He asks, "Equality for what?" Is equality valuable for its own sake or because approaching it would facilitate progress toward another and perhaps higher value? Coons is a professor of law at the University of California, Berkeley. Ironically, as a law professor, initially untrained in school finance matters, he perhaps is more responsible for recent school finance reform than any other single individual. He, in conjunction with William H. Clune and Stephen D. Sugarman, developed the legal logic that eventually proved persuasive in many of the state level equal protection suits seeking finance reform. Despite such successes in law and school finance, Coons may eventually draw equal or greater notice for his clarity as a public policy philosopher. In addition, his use of the English language comes closer to poetry than almost anything else currently being written about matters of public policy.

Section III is concerned with a discussion of "efficiency." The initial chapter, Chapter 5, is by J. Alan Thomas, professor in the

Department of Education, University of Chicago. Thomas' credentials regarding education and efficiency extend over a substantial period. He was among the first to apply econometric techniques in a scholarly search for components of efficient schools. He is currently engaged in an intense assessment of classroom and household practices and their contributions to productive instruction. His academic contributions neatly reflect progress that has been made since the mid-1960s in developing greatly more sophisticated models of educational processes. Thomas' chapter itself describes conventional models of school efficiency, summarizes their limitations, and suggests classroom and household components that must be added for more complete understanding.

Chapter 6 is a joint contribution led by the doyen of school finance economists, Charles S. Benson, professor at the Graduate School of Education, University of California, Berkeley. Benson is assisted by Stuart Buckley and Elliott Medrich, research associate and project director, respectively, of the Children's Time Study Project, University of California, Berkeley. Benson has long been noted for his ability to contribute new insights to important policy areas that previously have been trivialized by conventional models and techniques. In this chapter, he and his colleagues once again turn the tables on those who believed that the last research word on school efficiency had already been written. They concentrate on the consumer — school children — and concern themselves with the interaction between children's and parents' time, a resource that heretofore has generally been omitted from considerations of educational efficiency. They then contrast the impact on student school achievement of parent-child interaction relative to the socioeconomic climate of the school student body. By asking new questions, they throw new fuel on an old fire.

Section IV is devoted to two views of the link between school finance and the value of liberty or choice. Chapter 7, by Jacob Michaelsen, professor of economics, University of California, Santa Cruz, and a former school board member, develops a new justification for greater utilization of market mechanisms and consumer choice in the provision of schooling. Michaelsen's argument is neither anti-public school nor overly simple. He contends that over time public schools share a tendency with other public services to become unresponsive to the clients they were established to serve. The impediments stem from reasons as diverse as inability to define goals precisely, professional dominance over client interests, and the absence of a production technology. Regardless, for the welfare of the broader public, Michaelsen contends that public schools badly need to strike a new balance between the search for equality and the desire for quality: voucher plans are one example of how such a new balance might be struck.

Chapter 8 disputes the utility of unfettered choice for school clients. The author, Henry M. Levin, noted economist on the faculty of the Stanford University Graduate School of Education, is far from being a complacent defender of public schools and their current mode of operation. Neither would he quickly condone conventional methods of financing public schools. However, aside from whatever other commitments Levin may have for radical school reforms, in Chapter 8 he contends that vouchers, as an expression of a free market means for school reform, pose a severe threat to societal integration and social equality. In his arguments he demonstrates a philosophic facility similar to John Coons, upon whose voucher plan he focuses. Both Coons and Levin are able to step outside their major academic roles, lawyer and economist, respectively, and concern themselves with the ends and values of public policy.

THE HISTORIC AND SOCIAL CONTEXT OF SCHOOL FINANCING

1 UNITED STATES SCHOOL FINANCE POLICY 1955–1980

James W. Guthrie
University of California, Berkeley

The years from 1955 to 1980 mark an unusually tumultuous time in education generally and in school finance and related policies in particular. It was a period during which proponents of greater equity, efficiency, and liberty mobilized political forces in frequent efforts to alter or protect school-finance-related arrangements. The result was a quarter century of change—perhaps greater change than at any other time in our nation's history—in the means by which resources for support of public schools are generated and distributed. However, to characterize this period as merely one of change is inadequate. Many of the policy proposals and legislative alternatives of the period were at odds with one another. It was also a time of substantial political conflict.

The probability is high that neither the changes from the past nor the resultant tensions have yet run their course. For many individuals, the nation's educational systems continue to be viewed as unequal, inefficient, restrictive of freedom, or any combination of the three. More reforms are desired and undoubtedly will be sought. Thus, the 1980s will be a period during which reform forces will continue to seek a new equilibrium.

The author wishes to acknowledge the assistance of Anne Just, Charles Benson, Walter Garms, and Henry Levin in the preparation of this chapter.

An understanding of the past is interesting in itself, and, additionally, may be instructive for those engaged in reform efforts in the future. Thus the purpose of this chapter is to describe the past twenty-five years of reform efforts, illustrate tensions between various value proponents, and distill whatever commonalities may exist from among the reform efforts and their effects. The chapter concludes by speculating regarding likely points of conflict during the coming decade.

BACKGROUND

Analyzing the roots of a reform often involves an infinite regress regarding cause. Pendulum swings of social change seem so inevitable that identification of the precise time when a movement began is virtually impossible. Such is certainly the case with school finance reform. Selection of a starting point necessitates an arbitrary choice. Our choice in this regard is the period beginning with the famous United States Supreme Court decisions in *Brown v. Board of Education* (1954, 1955). In the preceding quarter century, Americans had been preoccupied with economic instability and international warfare on a huge scale. The post–World War II period was possessed of sufficient tranquility to permit the nation to pay attention to a number of its long festering internal issues, equal educational opportunity among them.

It would be useful, at least for purposes of facilitating understanding, if social reforms could be encapsulated in easy conceptual compartments. For example, the period from 1955 to 1965 has been portrayed as the "Age of Equality," anchored by previously mentioned judicial desegregation mandates on the front end and on the other end by congressional and executive branch concern for breaking the cycle of poverty with the Elementary and Secondary Education Act (1965). The years from 1965 to 1975 have been described as the "Era of Efficiency," dominated by the so-called "accountability movement" and attendant efforts to render schools more productive. The time from 1975 to 1980 has been cast as a counter-struggle by those desirous of greater choice—for example, vouchers, school site management, tuition tax credit plans, and alternative schools.

Regrettably, such tidy chronological separations, however expedient, are overly facile and meaningless. Worse yet, their inaccuracy masks the kaleidescopic tensions that interact continuously to shape and reshape American policy. Not only do proponents of equality, efficiency, and liberty refuse to limit their efforts to specified time strata, but their endeavors are also uneven with regard to level and branch of government, geographic region, and policy focus. Even more confusing is the fact that a particular reform may be sought by proponents of more than one value stream, each doing so for reasons that, in the abstract, may be antithetical. For example, during the quarter century under consideration, so-called "alternative schools" were frequently sought by those who believed greater discretion for teachers and parents to operate outside conventional public school confines would enhance equality of opportunity. Other alternative school advocates favored the movement because of the expansion of freedom and choice that was expected to result.

This complexity is compounded by intra- and intergovernmental friction. It is possible within the same time frame to have federal policymakers mandating greater efforts at equality—for example, the Brown desegregation decisions—while almost simultaneously advocating greater attention to excellence—for example, the 1958 Sputnik-inspired National Defense Education Act (1958). Nor did the sometimes contradictory kaleidoscope freeze in the 1960s. Enactment of the 1965 Elementary and Secondary Education Act, with its substantial concern for equality, was followed closely by local efforts to achieve greater freedom of choice through "community control" of public schools (Levin 1970). Even in the late 1970s, Californians were attempting to implement equality features of Serrano [1] while simultaneously coping with the cost-cutting efficiency movement promoted by Howard Jarvis and Paul Gann, sponsors of widely publicized tax limitation initiatives. [2]

Because of this web of currents and countercurrents, untangling efforts to achieve greater equality from those directed at maximizing efficiency or liberty also involves a measure of arbitrary decision-making. Consequently, we begin our analyses with the mid-1950s attempts to achieve greater equality and then, in sequence, concentrate on efficiency and liberty. In such a contrived separation, readers should not be mislead into believing that these were separate movements. As suggested above, overlap, interplay, evolution, and opposition have been constant.

THE SEARCH FOR EQUALITY

The decisions in *Brown v. Board of Education* (1954, 1955) initially had little direct bearing upon school finance policy. However, these cases do mark the beginning of a renewed national concern for social equality. Implementation of these judicial mandates was slow and uncoordinated. Nevertheless, it did proceed, even when military force was required to ensure progress. Lower court decisions and the Civil Rights Movement that followed contributed to a national atmosphere of concern: public consciousness regarding inequalities had been substantially extended and heightened (Wirt 1971). A number of authors and social scientists began to describe the extent of inequality that then characterized schools. In 1961 James Bryant Conant, former president of Harvard University, published *Slums and Suburbs* and described the poverty of cities as constituting a keg of "social dynamite." In 1964 Patricia Cayo Sexton analyzed the intra-district spending disparity that afflicted Detroit's city schools. This new sensitivity was poignantly manifest in the mid-1960s proliferation of social legislation sponsored by the Johnson administration under the "Great Society" and "War on Poverty" banners (see Aaron 1978).

The 1964 Civil Rights Act broke new ground on two educational fronts. Perhaps most important for this analysis, it contained Section 601 prohibiting federal funding of activities tainted by racial discrimination. This provision pierced one of the major historical impediments to massive federal aid to education. Previously, northern and liberal members of Congress were reluctant to vote for large-scale federal aid bills unless funds were to be denied to or used as incentives to desegregate southern dual school systems. Just as resolutely, southern members of Congress were reluctant to support legislation containing such restrictive provisions. For a century, large-scale federal school aid bills were brought to a standstill by this conflict (see Guthrie 1968b). The 1964 Civil Rights Act cleared the path for what was to be the federal government's largest educational initiative, the 1965 Elementary and Secondary Education Act.

The 1964 Civil Rights Act also authorized a massive social science effort at assessing equality of educational opportunity. This assessment was directed by and eventually came to be named for the famous sociologist James S. Coleman. The Coleman (1966) report's major conclusions were not particularly satisfying to educators and proponents of greater efforts to achieve equaltiy. It documented the achievement gap between white and black students. It proceeded to assert that the gap was not accompanied by significant inequality of resources, at least within regions of the United States.[3] It added further that, once student social background factors were controlled, school variables showed little positive correlation with student achievement. This latter finding was widely interpreted to mean that schooling made little difference. Efficiency proponents were quick to utilize this as an argument against continued increases in school funding, a theme to be described more fully in the subsequent section. The report was released in December of 1966 and was immediately controversial. Researchers asserted that its data-gathering and analytic techniques were sufficiently flawed as to emasculate the policy utility of its conclusions.[4] Thus, aside from or despite its findings, the furor precipitated by the Coleman report intensified concern for equality.

The concern was elevated further by the 1967 release of the Civil Rights Commission report, *Racial Isolation in the Public Schools.* Though not directed immediately at school finance concerns, the Civil Rights Commission thesis included the view that resource equality was a necessary, even if not by itself sufficient, prerequisite for equal educational opportunity.

Concommitant with the excitement of federal legislation and research reports, two sets of scholars in Chicago began concentrating their analyses upon the inequality of United States school finance arrangements. Interestingly, one group (John E. Coons and his law student protegeés, William H. Clune and Stephen D. Sugarman) owed their introduction to the complexities of property taxation and school aid distribution formulas to desegregation research they conducted for the Civil Rights Commission. While Coons, Clune, and Sugarman were developing the embryonic ideas that eventually were to reach maturity in their 1970 publication *Private Wealth and Public Education,* another scholar—Arthur Wise (1968), whose doctoral dissertation research on the topic was eventually published as *Rich Schools: Poor Schools*—was also focusing upon potential legal remedies for the tax rate and expenditure disparities that then characterized U.S. school financing.

Wise and Coons' team had reached a conclusion in common. The pervasive inequalities of school finance arrangements in most of the fifty states were not likely to be remedied through the legislative process. For decades, districts rich in property wealth had been able legislatively to protect their taxing and spending advantages, and the probability appeared slender that a sufficient coalition of low property wealth districts would be able to overturn the situation. Thus, the more promising reform avenue was to seek judicial redress for the inequity.

Both Wise and the Coons, Clune, and Sugarman team grounded their arguments in the U.S. Constitution's Fourteenth Amendment and similar provisions, plus education sections of state constitutions. Each contended that education was of sufficient significance in twentieth century America as to have acquired the status of a fundamental interest and that it therefore was deserving not only of state but also federal constitutional protection. If education were a fundamental interest, then government would have to possess a compelling reason, not simply a rational one, for discriminating against individuals. Such strict scrutiny at governmental purposes is also triggered when suspect classifications such as race, income, or geographic residence are involved as recipients or objects of publically supported services.

In designing remedies both Wise and Coons, Clune, and Sugarman pursued a negative approach. However, over time, the Coons' team's formulation became more prominent. They formed the so-called principle of fiscal neutrality: "The Quality of public education may not be a function of wealth, other than the total wealth of the state" (Coons, Clune, and Sugarman 1970). A reconstructed state school finance plan that met this test would, presumably, be constitutional.

In order for the legal theories to be applied fully in courts, a factual case also had to be made. This involved three major steps. First, the extent of the inequality had to be documented; property tax rate differentials, school district spending differences, and state aid inequalities had all to be compiled for states in which a legal challenge was to occur. Second, an argument had to be framed linking these unequal resources to uneven student achievement. Last, uneven achievement might itself have to be linked to differences in student life chances or outcomes.

Research for the initial leg of this argument—unequal distribution of taxation and spending—had to be constructed individually for each state. This was true not only because each state's distribution pattern is unique with regard to details, but also because state constitutions differ sufficiently to make it necessary to frame variations of the basic legal argument accordingly. Numerous school finance re-searchers cooperated with attorneys in amassing the factual argu-ments. Joel Berke, Robert Goettel, and others compiled data for an important Texas case (see Berke 1974; and Moskowitz and Sherman 1979). Alan Thomas (1968) and Guthrie, Levin, Kleindorfer, and Stout (Guthrie et al. 1971) undertook the task in Michigan. Charles Benson and his colleagues performed a similar operation in Califor-nia. In other states, the operation was repeated.

The second and third legs of the argument were precipitated pri-marily by widespread secondhand interpretations of Coleman report findings. If, as Coleman was understood to mean, dollars spent on schools were not linked significantly to quality of schooling and if school quality did not influence student achievement, then perhaps existing school finance inequities were harmless. Why bother to re-form a system that was inflicting no damage; why not let is bumble along on its arcane course? Two strategies were undertaken to coun-teract this perception. Arguments were offered that not only were the Coleman data and techniques flawed, but also that the conclu-sions were simply inaccurate. Researchers such as Bowles and Levin (1968) demonstrated that by utilizing different techniques and mak-ing different assumptions, they could analyze Coleman data and obtain positive results—namely, that resources did make a difference in student achievement. In that such research efforts were handi-capped by the absence of data, other than previously collected Cole-man report survey results, these arguments were valiantly made but not always persuasive.

Attempts to dilute Coleman report interpretations ultimately proved more successful than those that strove to overturn them. Dilution was accomplished by reciting the report's methodological weaknesses in substantial detail. These weaknesses were alleged to include imprecise specification of the conceptual model and sample design; inappropriate survey techniques, inaccurate aggregation of data, and invalid statistical procedures. When experts completed their courtroom testimony with regard to such weaknesses, judges ap-peared to wear confused facial expressions. The attempt was to create a courtroom impression of staggering technical complexity. The hoped for effect was, at least, a neutralization of Coleman inter-pretations. In fortunate instances, courts were to view the question of school effectiveness as somewhat extraneous to the legal matter at hand, an academic exercise of little significance: the view was, "after all, if school dollars made so little difference, why were high spending districts engaged in such intense efforts to retain their spending advantage." One member of the California Supreme Court, now retired, was quoted as saying, "Everybody knows you get what you pay for, and I suspect schools are no different in this regard."

Reform efforts in the separate states did not proceed in isolation. Once the basic tenets of a legal attack had been formulated by Coons, Clune, and Sugarman and by Wise, they were honed by other legal scholars and shaped to the peculiarities of specific states. Also, school finance specialists from several major universities played an important role in developing data and compiling and presenting factual information in support of legal theories. The individuals involved in these efforts were drawn into a national network that facilitated cross-pollinization of ideas and provided actors in the various states with extraordinarily sophisticated technical assistance with regard to law, school finance, statistical analysis, school productivity, school management, testing, and data processing.

This network had several nerve centers from which connections spread to the states. One such center was the Lawyers Committee for Civil Rights Under Law. For a period, the National Urban Coalition played a significant coordinating role. In time, the School Finance Center of the Education Commission of the States came to be the hub of such informational and coordinating activities. Participants and organizations comprising this national network drew substantial financial support from major philanthropic foundations.[5]

The impression should not be gained that this network concerned itself only with legal efforts to achieve school finance reform. Numerous books and articles were written by network members that contributed to a reform climate and that generated numerous alternative solutions, such as taxation and finance distribution plans. Also, the network was comprised of individuals participating in state legislative committees and executive branch commissions. Reform contributions were made through such commission approaches in Florida (Governor's Citizens Committee 1973), New York (New York State 1973), California (Benson et al. 1972), and Oregon (Pierce et al. 1975).

Whatever the contributions of individual researchers and state legislative committees or executive branch commissions, the major medium of reform was the judicial system (*Hargrave* 1970). On occasion, a court case was not itself necessary: the threat of a well-formulated suit was sufficient to trigger legislative or executive branch consideration of reform (Education Commission 1979a). However, such threats would not have been as effective had not similar suits been tried and decided in behalf of plaintiffs elsewhere. Thus, the central reform role of courts justifies added description.

There are literally dozens of cases, covering thirty-six states, far too many to review here (Education Commission 1979b; School Finance Project 1980). Consequently, we comment on only six. The selection is based not so much on whether the case triggered a state's reform. Rather, the selection is justified more in terms of a case representing important and divergent points of view. The cases are described chronologically.

Hobson v. Hansen (1967, 1971)

This case was brought against the Washington, D.C. schools in the mid-1960s. Plaintiffs contended that black children were being denied equal protection in the delivery of school services. They proceeded to demonstrate that the district engaged in discriminatory practices—for example, "ability grouping"—and that spending was higher in predominantly white schools. The prime cause of the spending disparities was the district's personnel policy, which permitted more senior instructors, with higher salaries, to exercise contractual privileges to transfer to schools serving the districts' white students. A result was substantially higher spending per pupil in such schools.

Judge J. Skelly Wright ordered the district to remedy the imbalance, but four years later plaintiffs asserted that unjustified dollar disparities still existed. In 1971, Wright again heard the case and ordered strong remedial steps such as the transfer of high paid teachers to black schools so as more nearly to equalize spending patterns. Subsequently stories were frequently cited regarding teachers who were transferred in order to equalize spending but for whom there were no students to form classes in their specialty. The court order, in attempting to achieve greater equality, had on occasion to sacrifice substantially by way of efficiency (Horowitz 1977).

Hobson's principles were highly applicable to numerous other school districts. At the time teachers in most large city schools also had teacher transfer privileges based upon seniority. School administrators braced themselves for an onslaught of litigation in which teacher collective bargaining contract provisions would be pitted against the equal protection clause. However, change came through another avenue. The facts in *Hobson*, plus a significant set of research results simultaneously published by the NAACP Legal Defense and Education Fund (see Martin and McClure 1969), influenced Congress to alter the rules regarding ESEA Title I. Henceforth, to be eligible for Title I funds, school districts had to comply with so-called "comparability guidelines" (*National Journal* 1970). These regulations ensured that local school district funding per pupil was reasonably equal before Title I funds could be spent. It subsequently took several years to revise the regulations and guidelines so as to render them effective. Nevertheless, these federal government actions were remarkably quick to reduce intradistrict per pupil spending disparities. It is doubtful that a judicial strategy could have been equally effective. Certainly court action would not have been as quick.

McInnis v. Shapiro (1970)

This court case was based upon alleged inequities in the Illinois school finance system. It was tried in a three judge federal district court, and the 1968 decision favored the defendant, the state. Upon appeal, the U.S. Supreme Court upheld the initial decision without issuing an opinion. Despite an outcome unfavorable for plaintiffs, the case is of substantial importance because it was to determine the course of subsequent legal reform strategies. The court ruled in *McInnis* that the existing system would remain in effect because even if it was responsible for unequal provision of school revenues, there was no equal protection need for equal spending, and the remedy being sought by plaintiffs was judicially unmanageable.

Plaintiffs had sought redress of their grievances through redistribution of financial resources in accord with the educational needs of students. However admirable such a request, the court could not envision a means by which accurately to ascertain children's "needs." Hence, the unfavorable outcome for plaintiffs. The case was sent on appeal to the U.S. Supreme Court, which refused to grant a writ of certoriari, thus permitting the lower court decision to stand.

The significance of *McInnis* resides in its influence on subsequent plaintiff strategies. No longer would liberal-oriented remedies be sought that emphasized school financing in accord with student needs. This remedy was directed at the "equal school outcomes" definition of equality, wherein resources would be spent in inverse proportion to a student's disadvantaged status. Rather, following *McInnis*, the remedy subsequently to be sought was to be consistent with the Coons, Clune, and Sugarman principle of fiscal neutrality. This decision rule, while not specifying what the remedy should be, permits an assessment to be made of its judicial acceptability. Presumably, any remedy that does not link available resources to wealth, other than the wealth of an entire state, is acceptable. Also, the *McInnis* decision made clear the fact that cases had to undergo thorough preparation.

Serrano v. Priest

This is probably the best known of the school finance reform cases. Its roots extend to the late 1960s efforts of southern California resident John Serrano to obtain higher quality public school services for his son, Anthony. Through several stages, John Serrano came into contact with Coons, Clune, and Sugarman's legal theories, and a case was brought with Anthony Serrano as the lead plaintiff. Because the California legislature holds itself immune to suit, without its granting explicit permission, plaintiffs were left only with the option of suing a variety of state administrative officers who arguably possessed authority to redistribute state legislative appropriations for schools in a fiscally neutral fashion. Hence, the lead defendant was the California state treasurer, the now deceased Ivy Baker Priest. The state controller and chief state school officer were also named as defendants, even though they were at least partially sympathetic to plaintiffs' position.

Serrano had a particularly torturous judicial history (see note 1). There were several trial court opinions and two major state supreme court decisions; the latter are known as *Serrano* I and *Serrano* II. *Serrano* was one of the earliest equal protection school finance suits. This, when coupled with the duration and complexity of the issues and the fact that California is the nation's most heavily populated and largest spending state, probably accounts for the substantial national attention accorded the cases.

However, aside from its glamorous features, *Serrano* illustrates many conclusions that have emerged from the last quarter century of school finance reform efforts. Consequently, this description will accord the case what might otherwise appear as disproportionate emphasis.

The case was originally filed in 1968 in the Los Angeles County Superior Court. School finance conditions then existing in California were classic examples of the "evil" reformers desired to rectify. California had a conventional "Foundation Plan" whereby local school districts were mandated by the state to spend a minimum amount per pupil. There existed a state-enacted "computational" tax rate. If by taxing themselves at this rate, districts were unable to generate the minimal per pupil spending level, state equalization aid was available to make up the difference between the computed local contribution and minimal required local spending. The difficulty, at least for *Serrano* plaintiffs and their sympathizers, was that property-wealthy school districts could spend amounts in excess of the minimum at tax rates substantially lower than property poor districts. In *Serrano*, plaintiffs made much of the contrast between Baldwin Park, a property-poor Los Angeles suburb, and the property-wealthy and renowned Beverly Hills Unified School District. At the time of trial, the former had a property tax base of $16,000 per pupil while the latter enjoyed the benefits of $200,000 per pupil. Baldwin Park spent $595 per pupil in 1968, while Beverly Hills spent $1,244. The property tax rate in Beverly Hills was less than half that in Baldwin Park.

This system, similar to ones installed in the majority of states in the first quarter of the twentieth century, had initially been justified on grounds that it offered an incentive to local school districts to spend the amount per pupil necessary to guarantee an educational "foundation." Moreover, the plan equalized ability of low wealth districts to offer such a foundation. Last, local control was preserved because districts desiring to spend more than the minimum were free to do so. They needed only to make the added local tax effort necessary to fulfill their desire.

The facts regarding the California finance system were summarized quickly for the lower court in *Serrano*. However, defendants, then represented by attorneys from the Los Angeles County District Attorney's Office, sought a "demurrer." They contended that even if plaintiffs' facts were accurate, a position they did not concede except for purposes of arguing their technical point, no law was being violated. If Baldwin Park spent less at a higher tax rate, so what? What statute or constitutional provision prohibited such a condition? The initial lower court decision concurred with this position, and *Serrano* proceeded on appeal to the California Supreme Court in order to assess whether or not "Foundation Plan" funding arrangements violated state and federal law.

In the summer of 1971, the California Supreme Court issued its decision, a joyous day for plaintiffs and the reform network. The court concluded that if facts were as plaintiffs alleged regarding the unequal charters of local district taxing and spending, then both the U.S. Constitution and California's State Constitution were in violation. The case was remanded to the court of original jurisdiction for a trial on the facts. Completion of the subsequent trial phase was to occupy several years. During the interim, the California legislature enacted a school finance bill intended to meet a court equal protection challenge, Senate Bill 90. The new school finance plan imposed substantial limits on high spending school districts; however, it did not move quickly to narrow the gap between high and low wealth districts in terms of their ability to spend. Indeed, the trial court eventually found the new equalizing plan to be insufficient to meet the fiscal neutrality decision rule.

While *Serrano* was at trial, the U.S. Supreme Court issued its 1973 decision in *Rodriguez v. San Antonio*. This decision is described in greater detail later, but the point to be noted here is that it lifted the validity of the federal constitutional argument. Fortunately for *Serrano* proponents, the 1971 state supreme court case, *Serrano* I, had made it clear that the California constitution also encompassed authority to strike the alleged injustice under consideration.

In 1974 Judge Bernard Jefferson, then of the Los Angeles Superior Court, rendered his trial decision in favor of the plaintiffs (*Serrano* 1974). Jefferson, consistent with the constitutional template provided him by the state supreme court in its 1971 decision, found the California system to be in violation of the state constitution. He provided the legislature with five years in which to implement a reform system that constrained school district spending within a band of $100 per pupil.

The Jefferson decision was itself appealed to the state supreme court. After what seemed an interminable period, *Serrano* II was handed down on December 30, 1976. This decision reaffirmed the trial court action. The legislature then took the court mandate seriously and produced another "solution" in June of 1977. This statute, Assembly Bill 65, was extraordinarily complicated. It seemed like school finance had gone mad. It contained esoteric features such as "breakpoints," "squeeze" and "double squeeze" factors, "base revenue limits," and "adjusted base revenue limits." When enacted it was probable that more persons in California understood Einstein's theory of relativity than could comprehend AB 65.

The complexity was a necessary component of the political process. In order to gain a favorable majority, AB 65 supporters not only had to accept a complicated mechanism aimed at easing the pain of equalizing a heretofore quite unequal system, but they also had to accept added measures proposed by advocates for greater efficiency and liberty. If millions of additional school dollars were to be spent to obtain greater equity, then many legislators wanted to ensure that such funds were well spent. Hence the added provisions. In a sense, the pursuit of equity had itself evoked a demand for greater efficiency and liberty.

No sooner had Californians begun to understand AB 65 than the system underwent an even more radical transformation. On June 6, 1978, barely a year after enactment of AB 65, California's electorate enacted Proposition 13 limiting property taxation. This constitutional amendment triggered withdrawal from the public sector of $7 billion in local property tax revenues. Treasury surpluses permitted a state level "bail out" of local government, school districts included. The bail out was embodied in Senate Bill 154, containing yet another school finance distribution formula. This bill squeezed high spending districts even more tightly than its immediate predecessor, AB 65. However, it also signaled the death knell for conventional patterns of school district governance in California. Proposition 13 had the unanticipated consequence, at least unanticipated for many of the fiscal conservatives who sponsored it, of providing California with full state funding for its schools and simultaneously emasculating the state's historic local school district control. By 1979, the legislature was paying more than 80 cents out of every school support dollar. California had the reality, if not yet the mentality, of full state funding. Equity had been enhanced by *Serrano*. Efficiency was promoted through the fiscal containment outcome of Proposition 13. Liberty, of choice, proponents believed they had suffered at the hands of both. Their turn perhaps would come later.

Senate Bill 154, the Proposition 13 bail out, was a one year statute. It was replaced in 1979 by Assembly Bill 8. This statute was to be California's fifth school finance plan in a decade (Guthrie 1979).

It also triggered debate. *Serrano* advocates, or at least the more intense among them, asserted that there still existed high wealth school districts with spending advantages impermissible under Judge Jefferson's decision. This was the position of John McDermott, the lawyer who had successfully pursued the case throughout the major portion of its evolution.

McDermott's position was countered by state officials who argued that 85 percent of the state's students already fell within the $100 spending band and that within a reasonable number of years the band would encompass fully 95 percent of all California students. Moreover, they contended, after Proposition 13, taxes were no longer an issue. The property tax rate throughout the state was uniform, 1 percent of market value. They argued that little inequality remained and that the cost to the state and taxpayers of eliminating the last vestige of inequality would be too high. After all, California schools had already had to adjust to five different school finance plans in the 1970s. Such changes had occurred simultaneously with many other school reforms—namely, collective bargaining, aid to handicapped children, and a major bilingual education drive. There was a limit to the amount of change a system could absorb and still function satisfactorily. As if to emphasize the point, the 1979 legislature enacted a moratorium on major school legislation.

For their part, McDermott and his colleagues were reluctant to give up. They countered that whereas 15 percent of the student population may not sound like much, in reality that constituted 600,000 students, more than the entire school age population of many states (Rhoads, Frentz, and Marshall 1978). They threatened to take the case back to court, and Californians braced themselves for *Serrano* III.

Serrano had, and may continue to have, substantial national significance. Among other matters, it displayed that the equal protection argument could be made on state constitutional grounds, even if the federal argument was eroded. Second, *Serrano* made it clear that the principal of fiscal neutrality could be fashioned in a manner acceptable to courts in calculating a judicially manageable remedy. *Serrano* also reinforced the view that legislatures would respond responsibly to judicial school finance mandates. As will be seen from the New Jersey state legislature's reaction in *Robinson v. Cahill* (1973), such compliance could not be assumed automatically.[6]

Serrano underscored the significance of the national reform net-work. As heavily endowed with resources as California was, many of the ideas and strategies utilized both at trial and in the legislature owed much of their origin to the creativity and support of network participants. Also, *Serrano* illustrates the virtual impossibility of achieving major school finance reform without simultaneously ad-dressing demands from efficiency and liberty proponents. One wave of reform, as we stated at the beginning of this chapter, appears to contain within it the seeds of its successor. Last, *Serrano* makes it clear that reform, even through the judicial system, need not be quick. John Serrano's son Anthony was in junior high school when the case was initially brought to trial. He was a working adult in 1980, and the case was still perhaps not complete.

Rodriguez v. San Antonio

While *Serrano* was developing in California, a Texas case was perco-lating through the courts along remarkably similar lines. The issues were effectively the same. The Texas school finance system per-mitted the same spending and tax rate disparities found in California. If there was a difference, it was that Texas was characterized by even greater inequalities. However, Texas plaintiffs grounded their argu-ments exclusively in the U.S. Constitution, and thus, their case was tried only in a federal district court. The initial decision was favor-able to plaintiffs, but the appeal judgment was a disaster. For a while it appeared that the appeal would stymie the entire reform move-ment in states far beyond the borders of Texas.

In March of 1973, the U.S. Supreme Court issued its decision in *Rodriguez v. San Antonio.* The court was closely divided. By a five to four decision, the fragmented majority decided that education, not being explicitly mentioned in the Constitution, was not a "fun-damental" interest. Hence the appropriate judicial test was only that the Texas school finance system possess a "rational basis." Defend-ants contended that spending and taxing disparities were a conse-quence of the desire to preserve local control. Aside from the moral righteousness of the argument, regardless of whether local control or school spending and taxing equality is a higher value, the Supreme Court ruled that such was not the nature of the decision. There ex-isted a rational basis for the Texas system, and that sufficed to protect it. If the Court had found education to be a "fundamental interest," then a more severe constitutional test necessitating a compelling justification for governmental action would have been appropriate. Such an intense criterion might have overcome the rational basis trade-off for retention of local control.

The melange of opinions constituting the majority in *Rodriguez* contained other arguments used in overturning the lower court decision. The Court asserted that defendants did not readily constitute a suitable class: they were not uniformly poor, nor members of a racial group, nor from geographically identifiable areas. Thus, no so-called legally suspect classification appeared to be involved. Last, the Court was not persuaded that students in low wealth, low spending districts were being "damaged" as a consequence of financing disparities. Loosely translated, the Court was not convinced that dollars for schools were tightly tied to the quality of services made available to pupils. The efficiency argument originally raised in connection with the Coleman report had once again come to the surface and dramatically influenced public policy regarding school finance.

Reform proponents were deeply depressed by *Rodriguez*. Unless the Supreme Court should reverse itself, a highly unlikely situation except perhaps over the long run, hopes of achieving reform with a single slash of the public policy sword were eliminated. Worse, many feared that the entire movement would founder unless responses could be generated to the Court's three rejection arguments.

Robinson v. Cahill

This case was decided by the New Jersey Supreme Court in May 1973. Its prime significance initially was to buoy reformers whose spirits only a month earlier had been severely depressed by the previously described decision in *Rodriguez*. *Robinson* made it clear that school finance reform could take place at the state level, even if it necessitated separate suits tailored to the legal and factual details of each offending state. *Robinson* displayed that, however time-consuming and costly, *Rodriguez* could be circumvented.

In the time following the initial New Jersey Supreme Court decision in *Robinson*, the case began to assume additional significance, becoming something of a negative example. The legal framework for the case had never been clear, and as a consequence, court directives were complicated. The New Jersey legislature was reluctant from the outset to implement the court decree. At one point, the summer of 1977, the state supreme court had to resort to the unprecedented action of closing the state's public schools in order to force compliance. Only then did the legislature enact a state income tax providing the funds necessary to implement the court's decision.

Two other conditions served to render *Robinson* complicated. The case relied upon New Jersey's constitutional provision charging the state with responsibility for operating a public school system that was "thorough and efficient." Plaintiffs contended that the unequal distribution of taxing and spending authority under the old school finance plan impeded provision of "thorough and efficient" school services. The court concurred but found that more than school financing was at fault.

Remedy involved not only a revised flow of funds, but also a monumentally complex state management system requiring local school districts to specify curriculum objectives in more detail than generally possible and thereafter to allocate funds as though scientifically accurate educational production functions actually existed. Again, efficiency was made a partner with equality in order to build the coalition necessary to gain passage of a remedy. The result was incomplete equalization of financial resources and creation of a system of state-mandated paper work that threatened to drown whatever creativity remained in New Jersey's local schools. School finance and management in New Jersey underwent substantial change in the five years after the initial supreme court decision in *Robinson.* However, few if any reformers believed the system was made either more thorough or more efficient. (For further analysis, see Lehne 1978; Goertz 1978; and Goertz and Hannigan 1978.)

Levittown v. Nyquist

Unlike the previously described school finance court decisions, *Levittown* (1978) has not reached fruition. Nevertheless, the case contains an argument that heretofore has been omitted from the court cases. The state's largest city school districts intervened as plaintiffs. These cities contend that New York's state school finance plan is unconstitutional because it fails to consider adequately the added cost of city operation, an added cost that allegedly burdens city revenue services more heavily than suburban or rural property tax bases.

This "municipal overburden" argument is countered by several prominent economists who contend that cities spend more money because they choose to offer services in the public sector that are paid for privately or simply not provided elsewhere outside the city. (For an extended discussion, see Garms, Guthrie, and Pierce 1978: ch. 15; and Brazer et al. 1971.) For example, cities may subsidize rapid transit systems through property tax proceeds. Suburban residents may have to pay the cost of commuting from their own pockets. Why, municipal overburden opponents inquire, should noncity residents be asked to subsidize cities even further because the latter choose voluntarily to offer such a wide variety of public services? For their part, city advocates point to the wide array of city services provided for noncity residents—for example, museums, airports, and theaters. Regardless of the validity of either side's position, the initial lower court decision accepts the municipal overburden argument completely. It is not yet clear how New York's highest court will respond on appeal.

There remain many other school finance cases, some successful, others unsuccessful; some awaiting appeal, others not yet at trial. It may be that legal challenges to allegedly unfair school finance plans will maintain momentum throughout the 1980s. However, if such is the case, it will be against the substantial opposition of fiscal conservatives and proponents of added school efficiency and liberty. The dominant reform value throughout the 1970s has clearly been equality. Concerns for efficiency and choice made their presence felt, but they were generally subordinate to the major theme of greater financial equalization. However, as the 1970s concluded, it appeared that public support for school finance reform, narrowly defined, was declining relative to a concern for efficiency and fiscal restraint.

EFFICIENCY

Efforts to render schools more productive, to maximize output at a specified resource level, are not unique to the twenty-five year period under consideration in this chapter. Raymond Callahan (1962) and David Tyack (1974) have each written insightful descriptions of the

"Cult of Efficiency" that pervaded American education at the beginning of the twentieth century. This earlier effort assumed that adoption of scientific management principles would earn for schools the mantle of legitimacy then accorded private sector business endeavors. This more recent efficiency movement also attempted, in part, to pattern schools after business. However, in the struggle to make schools "accountable," contemporary reformers became frustrated with the inability of technocratic procedures to increase educational productivity and consequently evolved through two additional stages—testing and fiscal containment. This section traces each of the three stages, beginning with the technical-industrial accountability model.

The 1957 Soviet space success, Sputnik, triggered substantial criticism of America's public schools. They were tried quickly in the press and found guilty of defrauding the United States of technological supremacy. Congress responded by enacting the 1958 National Defense Education Act, intended to buttress instruction in science, mathematics, and foreign language. Cynics were quick to observe that America's schools were remarkably responsive: a year later, 1959, the United States launched its first successful space capsule. Whatever the objective performance of America's schools at the time, the seeds of public dissatisfaction had been widely sown. Moreover, as the space program began to accomplish ever more amazing feats, the question continued to be asked, How is it we can put a man on the moon while the student on the street cannot read, write, or count satisfactorily?

Against this backdrop of unfocused public dissatisfaction with school productivity, there appeared the previously mentioned 1966 Coleman report with its widely misinterpreted finding regarding school resources and student achievement. Whereas Coleman and his colleagues were careful to circumscribe their conclusion, intending only to say that schools appeared to have little influence on achievement, which was independent of the social class conditions of individual students, laymen frequently were quick to assume that this meant schools had no effect and that added dollars for schools would be wasted.

Technocracy

If student achievement was disappointing, and dollars spent in the conventional pattern had little influence, then the time had come for new strategies. Efficiency proponents were quick to suggest that many private sector management techniques, if appropriately applied to schools, could provide answers—by which they meant higher student performance and lower costs. Thus, the latter part of the 1960s and the early portion of the 1970s witnessed numerous efforts to apply technocratic management strategies to public education.[7] Techniques such as Program Performance Budgeting Systems (PPBS), systems analysis, Program Evaluation and Review Techniques (PERT), and Management by Objectives (MBO) had been honed during World War II, polished in the private sector during the postwar period, and propelled to their greatest prominence with the space program successes of the 1960s.

In 1967, the year following publication of the Coleman report and its conclusions regarding school effectiveness, President Johnson issued an executive order facilitating implementation throughout the federal executive branch of Program Performance Budgeting.[8] Johnson had been impressed with the manner in which his initial secretary of defense, Robert MacNamara, had imposed a measure of order on a previously unruly defense department by the use of PPBS. Indeed, MacNamara, a former Harvard Business School "whiz kid" and Ford Motor Company manager, had an intense understanding of the range and limitations of modern management techniques, and his Pentagon achievements were commendable. However, those who became advocates for the application of these same techniques to schools generally lacked MacNamara's balanced view.

America's education system has long been subject to the rapid adoption and subsequent dissolution of fanciful fads, and PPBS was to be no exception. If the Department of Health, Education, and Welfare,[9] including the Office of Education, had to implement Program Planning Budgeting, then surely so could school districts. Also, if it was good enough for the Pentagon and the federal government, then just as surely it would benefit schools. Education publications were quick to trumpet the virtues of the new management techniques.[10] Consulting firms rapidly packaged the new management tools for sale to local school district superintendents and school boards who, even if they did not know what PPBS and PERT were, certainly knew they needed them. It was difficult to resist such a popular steamroller.

Local school districts were not alone in their eagerness to promote more efficient schools. State legislatures also joined the technical-industrial school improvement bandwagon. In 1970, the California legislature mandated the implementation of Program Planning Budgeting systems in each of the state's more than 1,000 districts, and this was to be done within five years.[11]

Other states, frustrated at not being able to dictate increased school output, began legislatively to intrude on school processes. Competency Based Teacher Education (CBTE) became yet another crest on the accountability wave.[12] Literally dozens of states began requiring that teachers be trained with an eye toward those instructional techniques that were most effective with students. Once they had mastered these professional techniques, then they would be licensed to teach and certified as competent. The idea was badly flawed. There existed few scientifically proven instructional skills (Heath and Nielson 1974). Teaching continued to be far more of an art than a science. Despite the exaggerated claims of many teacher trainers and the impetus given to the idea by federal conferences on the topic, the scientific base of pedagogy was simply too thin to justify competency-based teacher education, and the idea generally was short lived.

Even the federal government was not immune from efforts to inject private sector management techniques into education. The Office of Economic Opportunity (OEO) sponsored several experiments aimed at elevating school productivity. Performance contracting was a federally financed scheme wherein private firms would be paid for instructing students in selected portions of the school curriculum. If student performance met or exceeded previously agreed upon levels, then the contractor was to receive a financial bonus. This payment for results strategy was also short lived after the uncovering of scandalous conditions in the Texarkana, Texas, schools wherein a contractor was alleged to be teaching students the answers to test questions in order to enhance achievement scores (Lessinger 1969). That was not the end, however. The Office of Economic Opportunity attempted other pay for results experiments wherein parents and teachers were paid for higher student achievement, and in another experiment, students were paid for higher performance.

Testing

For all the publicity, money, and effort, the technocratic accountability movement appeared by the early 1970s to have produced little by way of results. The scorecard used by the public continued to reflect failure. Standardized test results had been declining since the mid-1960s. Annually the College Entrance Examination Board reported that scores on Scholastic Aptitude Tests (SAT) were lower than the preceding year (James 1975, 1976, 1978). If the new management techniques could not reverse the sorry situation, then what could? One answer to the question was to utilize more tests. The assumption behind the strategy was that by measuring school output, focusing the glare of public scrutiny upon student performance, educators would be induced to work harder or more effectively.

Beginning in 1964, the federal government contributed to the testing movement by appropriating funds to a National Assessment of Education Progress (NAEP).[13] This nationwide testing program eventually was to be operated by the Education Commission of the States (ECS) in Denver, Colorado. The three year cycle of NAEP testing was administered in a fashion that discouraged comparisons between states and school districts. Nevertheless, even if not useful for purposes of holding a particular state or single school district accountable, it provided a baseline against which to judge education's future performance generally.

After the initiation of the NAEP, a number of states began mandating statewide testing programs. Frequently these tests were tied to the awarding of high school graduation certificates. Proficiency standards and minimal competences were important phrases frequently reflected in legislation. By the latter portion of the 1970s, thirty-five states had adopted a form of testing to encourage or ensure higher school productivity.[14] Educators resisted on grounds that the tests were insufficient to capture the full range of school purposes and that overuse of examinations would distort the ends of education. A backlash of sorts occurred, with consumer advocate Ralph Nader criticizing the national testing programs (Allan Nairn and Associates 1980). Several states, New York prime among them, enacted "truth in testing" bills.[15] Despite such criticisms, the public generally continued to believe that tests were accurate measures of school output. A Spring 1980 Gallop poll revealed that 75 percent of the public was favorably disposed to testing; an even higher proportion of minority group members hold such views.[16] Nevertheless, as the 1970s drew to a close, nationally administered test scores continued to reflect a decline.

Fiscal Containment

School districts have lived with taxing limitations for more than a century. Conventional school finance plans permitted local school boards to maintain taxing discretion only within a ceiling; if the tax rate were to be higher, it necessitated voter approval. Beginning in the 1970s, however, a new strategy began appearing with increasing frequency — limitations on spending. In 1972, in an effort to avoid a court ruling in the previously described case, *Serrano v. Priest*, the California legislature enacted Senate Bill 90. This legislation imposed a spending ceiling upon school districts. The bill's complicated formula resulted in a different ceiling for each district. This was intended to permit low spending districts to close the gap between themselves and their more fortunate counterparts. The result froze high wealth districts into a posture wherein they no longer could maintain their privileged spending patterns; indeed, many of them no longer could even keep up with inflation. This spending limit, when coupled with declining enrollments, meant that for the first time, some districts annually found themselves in the position of having the same or a smaller total operating budget than was the case for the previous year. Doctoral dissertations began to examine a relatively new phenomenon — organizational decline (Agee, in progress). Ten other states followed suit in adopting spending ceilings.

Efficiency proponents contended that if schools could not be made more productive, then at least it would be possible to limit the amount of public money wasted. The spending limit wave began to build and spilled over beyond the boundaries of public schooling. By the mid-1970s, spending limitation campaigns for all local public services had been organized and succeeded in twenty-five states. Several state governments had spending ceilings imposed upon them, and serious sets of proposals were made not only to require annually that federal spending be balanced against revenues, but also to limit federal spending to a specified proportion of the gross national product.[17]

The fiscal containment movement appeared to be fueled by public alienation from government following the Nixon administration Watergate scandals and by fiscally conservative arguments that government at all levels was characterized by waste. Also, inflation was boosting taxpayers into ever higher income brackets whereby their taxes were being increased, even though their buying power was not. Similarly, inflation pressures on the housing market were pushing property values to unheard of heights, and assessed valuations and property taxes were escalating along with them. Increasing numbers of homeowners became vocal regarding their distress over property taxes.

In California property owners found a hero in Howard Jarvis, a prime sponsor of Proposition 13. This latter was a publically enacted constitutional amendment that limited California's property taxes to 1 percent of market value. The measure prompted a 60 percent reduction in property taxes for many homeowners. The public treasury was deprived annually of $7 billion in property tax revenues. The measure passed easily, with 68 percent of those voting supporting the amendment.

Despite this attack by such an apparent fiscal meat axe, California's public services survived because an almost unknown $6.6 billion fiscal surplus enabled the state to bail out local governments, including school districts. Once learning of this huge surplus, many members of the public were infuriated and prompted to support even more stringent fiscal containment policies. Hence, in the subsequent year, 1979, Proposition 4 was enacted. This limited state spending increases to an amount equal to population growth and alterations in personal income and the federal consumer price index. As if this were not sufficient, Howard Jarvis returned in 1980 with Proposition 9, a proposal to reduce California's state income taxes by more than 50 percent. Apparently enough was enough, as voters rejected the measure soundly.

California appeared to occupy the extreme position on the fiscal containment pendulum. However, it did not represent an anomaly. A Rand Corporation survey revealed that total government spending as a function of gross national product grew steadily from 1929 to 1975. By that year government spending, including schools, equaled 35 percent of the total value of all goods and services produced in the United States. From 1975 to 1979 this percentage fell to 32.6 percent. Lower education's—that is, K–12—share of GNP also declined from its 1975 level, from 7 to 5 percent of GNP. As a percent of total government spending, education had fallen from 30 percent in 1956 to 27 percent by 1975 and even lower by 1979 (Pascal and Menchik 1979).

Proponents of greater school efficiency sometimes emphasize resource "inputs"—money, labor, time. Other advocates of greater educational effectiveness focus upon school "outputs"—academic achievement or similar measures of student performance. The quarter century under consideration began with an emphasis on "output" and shifted in time to a concern for processes. It evolved even further such that by 1980 the prime efficiency strategy was limitation of "inputs." To some degree efforts to achieve greater equalization need not directly conflict with reforms aimed at influencing school processes or outputs. At least occasionally, proponents of equality and a more rigorous school curriculum—for example, "back to basics"—can coexist and may even cooperate. However, attempts to achieve greater school efficiency by limiting inputs of school dollars are seldom compatible with equity reforms. School finance reform is difficult to impossible in an atmosphere of fiscal containment. States that undertook substantial alterations of their finance distribution schemes usually did so with the advantage of a treasury surplus (Kirst 1979; Shalala and Williams 1974). Without additional resources, equity necessitates a redistribution, taking from some to give to others. Fiscal containment policies militate against surpluses in the absence of which equity can come only from redistribution. Revisions of distributional arrangements are themselves almost always fraught with tension. Altering a plan to redistribute resources such that there are not simply winners and even bigger winners (or at least winners and those held harmless), but rather winners and losers, invites intense political conflict. It is such conflicts that frequently give birth to proposals for greater liberty or choice, the topic to which we next turn.

LIBERTY

Freedom to choose from among alternatives is a long-respected component of American culture, schooling included. Since its colonial inception, America's educational system has been characterized by substantial diversity. Choices existed whereby parents and citizens could satisfy their preferences for schooling. In *Pierce v. Society of Sisters* (1925), the U.S. Supreme Court affirmed the right of parents to select from among both public and private school alternatives. Even within the public school sector, efforts have consistently been made to ensure that even though schooling was compulsory, schools themselves were nevertheless responsive to the clients they served. Responsiveness was intended for public schools to facilitate choice, to be a proxy for liberty in a system that otherwise held a monopoly position for most parents and students.[18] Of course, it should be remembered that the substantial diversity characterizing American public education before and immediately after World War II was justified, at least in part, on grounds that differential taxing and spending for schools was a by-product of responsiveness. Through migration, a household, at least one able to afford the housing investment necessary, could presumably satisfy its tastes for schooling. The school finance equity reform movement began, in the last quarter century, to attack this assumption and the fiscal arrangements accompanying it. Once this attack began, proponents of liberty attempted to protect arrangements for diversity.

Efforts to ensure or enhance liberty for public schools have taken two primary forms—(1)·reforms intended to render public schooling more diverse and more responsive to clients and (2) proposals to encourage greater privatization of schooling. The twenty-five year period under examination here contains several efforts to achieve reform on both these dimensions.

Privatization

The mid–1950s Supreme Court school desegregation decisions precipitated numerous reactions. One outcome—white efforts to avoid racially desegregated schools—took various forms—violent resistance, civil disobedience, legal subterfuge, delay, and escape. This latter strategy resulted in the greatest surge in nonpublic school enrollments in the twentieth century. By 1968, the time by which court-ordered desegregation was at its most intense, nationwide nonpublic school enrollments climbed to 14 percent of the total school population (U.S. DHEW 1974).

This growth resulted primarily from the formation of hundreds of "white academies" in southern states. Prince Edwards County, Virginia, attempted to aid such segregated schools by closing its public schools (see *Griffin* 1964). Mississippi rescinded its compulsory school attendance law and attempted to arrange state tuition payments for students attending segregated private schools. These and similar efforts were eventually found to be illegal. Under the pressure of court decisions, Internal Revenue Service investigations, and sheer economics, white academies began to close.

By 1975, the nationwide proportion of students enrolled in nonpublic schools had been halved, to only 7 percent (NCES 1976). Undoubtedly white fears of racially mixed schools had been at least partially assuaged, and this accounted for the closing of many segregated private schools. However, inability of proponents to gain sustained public financing for the antidesegragation institutions also contributed significantly to their decline. Not only can school finance reform lead to change, it is also sometimes the case that the absence of a change in school finance policy can lead to reform.

No sooner had nonpublic school enrollments declined to 7 percent than they began once again to ascend. By 1980 it was estimated that nonpublic school enrollments had rebounded to between 10 and 11 percent of total kindergarten through twelfth grade enrollments. This time the movement did not appear to be fueled by white desegregation fears: something else was motivating parents and students.

While southern whites attempted to avoid racial desegregation by establishing private schools, private school clients in several northern states also sought public financial support. The loss of many instructors from religious orders, the unionization of lay teachers, and rising costs generally were creating intensified fiscal pressures upon private sectarian schools. Their legislative proponents in states such as New York and Pennsylvania enacted state aid provisions benefiting nonpublic schools. Such aid took various forms — direct aid to nonpublic schools for supplies and to cover costs of state mandated operations such as testing, transportation to students, and state income tax credits and deductions to households paying private school tuition. Whatever the political popularity or moral rectitude of such provisions, they systematically were found to be constitutionally unacceptable (Duffy 1972).

Nonpublic school advocates enjoyed, at least initially, greater success in their efforts to obtain federal financial aid. In an extraordinarily adroit move, Johnson administration education officials were able to fashion a compromise between the National Education Association and the National Catholic Welfare Conference (Guthrie 1968a) that permitted enactment of the 1965 Elementary and Secondary Education Act. Previously, major federal school finance bills had dissolved in Congress because of conflict over racial desegregation, aid to nonpublic schools, and fears of federal control. As previously mentioned, enactment of the 1964 Civil Rights Act diluted the issue of race. The landslide election of LBJ in 1964 provided political muscle sufficient to overcome the federal control argument.

The church-state compromise constructed by executive branch lobbyists over aid to nonpublic schools was of the following nature. Federal funds could be used for the purchase of instructional supplies, title to which was to remain, at least nominally, in the public sector (Meranto 1967). However, materials themselves would be made available to nonpublic school students in their schools. This was described by Johnson administration strategists as similar to the operation of public libraries. When a citizen checks out a library book, no one asks, What church do you attend? Why then, they contended, should it be different for educational materials? Additionally, nonpublic schools are entitled to benefit from publicly funded ESEA Title I services, but the personnel involved must be in the employ of the public schools of proximity. This executive-branch-initiated compromise was welded together with such authority that subsequent congressional consideration of the bill failed to ripple even a minor seam in the uniform interest group front.

Simultaneously frustrated by the inability to obtain judicial approval for a major state aid to nonpublic schools plan and heartened by the above-described federal assistance breakthrough, nonpublic school aid advocates subsequently attempted an even more dramatic strategy—congressionally approved tuition tax credits. A concerted tuition tax credit coalition effort was mounted in the 95th Congress. Proponents put forth a bill that would grant to households a federal income tax credit proportional to their nonpublic school tuition payments. The plan included higher and lower education and had a tax credit ceiling of 25 percent of school and college tuition payments. It was estimated that, if enacted, the plan would cost the federal treasury several billion dollars annually in foregone tax revenues. President Carter announced his opposition and his intention to veto the bill should it successfully navigate both houses of Congress. Carter's veto threat was sufficient to forestall Senate passage. However, the House of Representatives took an opposite stance and voted favorably, 209 to 194.[19] The absence of Senate concurrence, obviously, prevented passage of the bill. Nevertheless, the surprise to many was that tuition tax credit proponents had failed by so slender a margin. Clearly, another effort would follow.

There remains yet another avenue by which privatization proponents attempted to gain public financial support—voucher plans. Governmental aid to students, who then select the school of their choice, was popularized for higher education with the advent of the so-called "G.I. Bill" following World War II.[20] In 1955, Milton Friedman, the Nobel-Prize-winning economist, advocated a similar strategy for returning efficiency and responsiveness to lower education (see Friedman 1962: ch. VI). Friedman's idea began to receive greater attention during the onset of the efficiency movement in the 1960s. The previously mentioned Office of Economic Opportunity (OEO), organized under the Johnson administration, attempted a number of market-oriented education experiments, of which a modified voucher trial was a component. Following several widely publicized academic analyses (Cohen and Farrar 1977), the OEO attempted to persuade one or more entire states to experiment with a voucher plan. However, opponents prevailed. Finally, one small local school district, Alum Rock, in the area of San Jose, California, consented to undertake a diluted voucher trial.

The Alum Rock experiment limited choice to public schools. A segment of the district's elementary schools were themselves divided into a series of minischools, schools within schools. Each of these subunits adopted a different theme, style, or instructional strategy. Parents were provided with information regarding different attributes of schools and then permitted to select among them. A sophisticated accounting system was developed that permitted dollar resources to follow individual students with accuracy, even when students transferred schools several times in the course of an academic year.

The Alum Rock trial concluded with mixed reviews (Weiler 1974). Privatization critics asserted that vouchers were imperfect, and proponents contended that the experiment was flawed and that inability of private sector schools to participate rendered the experiment invalid.

Aside from the success, or lack thereof, in Alum Rock, voucher proponents made another California effort in 1979. Taking a lesson from fiscal containment successes through direct democracy, John E. Coons and Stephen D. Sugarman attempted to gain an amendment to the California Constitution that would have transformed the entire state into a voucher system. The Coons-Sugarman initiative was elaborately drawn in an effort to compensate for weaknesses of previous proposals and to balance the public's welfare with private schooling. Despite careful efforts, their petition failed to gain sufficient registered voter signatures to place the initiative on the 1980 ballot for electoral approval. As with tuition tax credit advocates, Coons and Sugarman also plan to try again. They contend that the manner in which legislatures respond to equal protection court mandates will interact with fiscal containment policies of efficiency advocates to damage the quality of public schooling. When this erosion is evident and substantial, the public will then be receptive to a voucher plan.

Responsiveness

The 1960s and 1970s encompassed a period of intense public school criticism. One dimension of these complaints was that schools were insensitive to the preferences of clients, parents, and students. Public policy diagnosticians attributed the illness to excessive influence by educational professionals, administrators, and teacher organizations. The prime remedy was judged to be a restoration of local control—greater citizen participation. Toward this end, four reform surges took place between 1955 and 1980: (1) the so-called "community control" movement, (2) efforts to establish "alternative schools," (3) administrative decentralization, and (4) school site management and parent advisory councils.

Community Control. In the early 1970s the Ford Foundation sponsored a study of New York City schools. The report, authored principally by Mario Fantini, was entitled *Reconnection for Learning* (New York City 1967), and it recommended that steps be taken to disaggregate the huge New York City school district into presumably more manageable subunits. Three experimental "community control" districts emerged and rapidly became the focus for substantial conflict. Whereas parents desired discretion over personnel evaluations and hiring as a crucial component of "community control," teachers' union officials desired retention of the civil service model that had long been in effect. Parents lost, leading to the eventual demise of the community control experiment in New York City, but not before the idea received widespread attention elsewhere (Levin 1970; see also Berube and Gittell 1969; and Gittell et al. 1971).

Eventually, the New York legislature enacted a bill that divided the city's schools into thirty-three elementary districts with elected boards subject to the overall authority of the city's central school board. Each of these subdistricts contained more pupils than the overwhelming majority of school districts throughout the United States. Community control proponents were dismayed that the new subbureaucracies would be touted as a way to return schools to the "people." Moreover, early political analyses asserted that the newly elected local boards were heavily dominated by citizens supported by teacher unions (Gittell 1967).

Alternative Schools.   This concept, much like accountability, was and continues to be a semantic umbrella of sufficient breadth to encompass numerous schooling ideas, some of them antithetical. In the 1960s, several notable authors wrote educational critiques and asserted that public schools were debilitatingly uniform, repressive, stifling of student and staff creativity, and administered in a mindless fashion (see, for example, Kozol 1967; Rogers 1968; Kohl 1967; and Silberman 1970). "Alternative" education was proposed as a reform. British primary schools were frequently cited as a model for students' early years, wherein relatively unstructured learning experiences would more easily assist in the transition from home to scholarly activities. Secondary students could benefit from "schools without walls," of which the Parkway School in Philadelphia was a much publicized illustration (see Cox 1969; Resnik 1970). Many parents removed their children from public schools to place them in private "alternative" schools. Public school systems themselves, unwilling to forego their market share easily, established public "alternative" schools. The Office of Education funded three large alternative school experiments in the public school systems of Minneapolis, Minnesota; Gary, Indiana; and Berkeley, California.[21] By the end of the 1970s, the movement had run its course, and several of its major ideologues had revised their opinions, confessed a change of heart, and advocated more structured schools (Kozol 1978).

Administrative Decentralization.   Large city school districts under-went a wave of decentralization during the 1960s and 1970s. The general justification was that disaggregation would permit schools to be more responsive to clients and employees. The typical pattern was to divide the district into several administrative subunits, each with an administrative officer nominally in charge of all the schools in the subdistrict. Districts varied with regard to the degree of decisionmak-ing discretion permitted these subunits. In most instances, fiscal authority continued to be centralized. Personnel administration also typically remained a central office function. Curriculum planning and instructional emphasis were often permitted to vary in accord with the tastes of the subdistrict administrator. Only in New York City was disaggregation accompanied by political reform—namely, the election of subdistrict school boards. In other cities, the central school board continued to be the policymaking body for the entire district. Consequently, critics contended that decentralization accom-plished little more than added costs and the insertion of yet another bureaucratic layer between local schools and "downtown" decision-makers. It was difficult, outside of city school central offices and subdistrict administrators, to identify those favorable to the reform (LaNoue and Smith 1973).

School Site Management.   The relative failure of community con-trol, alternative schools, and administrative decentralization encour-aged yet a fourth effort to infuse schools with greater citizen partici-pation. This additional reform was described in detail initially by a New York State reform commission that utilized the label "school site management" (Guthrie 1976). The plan intended both to gain a greater measure of lay control and to provide more "accountability" by using the school, rather than the district, as the basic decision-making unit for personnel and curriculum. School district central offices would continue to handle fiscal and business matters and serve as planning, coordinating, and record-keeping bodies. A parent advisory council (PAC) at each school would be responsible for selec-tion and evaluation of the school principal and for advising that officer on curriculum, instructional, and personnel matters. Princi-pals were envisioned as being on multiyear contracts, the renewal of which was subject to parent advisory committee approval. Within specified boundaries, the principal and parent advisory council would have discretion over funds budgeted for the school by the central office. Each school's budget allocation was to be determined by a set of uniform decision rules, including criteria such as number, grade level, and achievement records of pupils assigned to the school. The parent advisory council would issue an annual evaluation report including plans for the subsequent year.

The school site management idea was not particularly well received in New York State, but the Florida legislature was favorably impressed. As a component of a statewide school finance reform plan enacted in 1972, the Florida legislature adopted school site management and a statewide testing program (see Governor's Citizens Committee 1973). Several other states adopted parent advisory council components for their state categorical aid programs. Portions of the idea also were favorably received by federal authorities, which began to include parent advisory council requirements for schools receiving categorical aid funds under programs such as ESEA Title I, Emergency School Assistance Act (ESAA), and bilingual categorical funds. The idea became so pervasive that school administrators were soon to ask that the parent advisory councils undergo consolidation lest principals' nights consist of one council meeting after another and little else.

Aside from the widespread adoption in form, there is slight evidence regarding the effectiveness of the idea. In many instances, little budget discretion was ceded to parents, collective bargaining agreements with teachers continued to render most decisions a central office matter, parents claimed they were too easily coopted by administrators, and few principals were attracted to the idea of their job security being tied to parental approval. These factors inspired the impression that the reform was widely adopted but not yet of consequence (see *Improving Education* 1967).

CONCLUSION

What can be concluded from a quarter century of school-finance-related reform efforts? Reform proponents cite a series of statistics from which they infer success. For example, between 1969 and 1978, school operating expenditures increased by 23 percent in real terms—that is, after controlling for inflation's erosion of the dollar. In 1969, state revenue contributions accounted for but 39 percent of school spending. By 1978 this figure had risen to 51 percent. Supporters also point to development of new constitutional standards by which to judge school spending equality, favorable lawsuits in thirty-six states, constraints on spending disparity within states and within individual school districts, and substantially revised taxing structures in many states (Kelly 1980).

There are critics who put forth a contrary view. They assert that employment has been forthcoming for numerous attorneys and analysts, but it is not yet clear from achievement measures that children have benefited from the court decisions. They contend further that efforts to achieve equality have required so many political side payments to efficiency proponents that schools are now deluged with unproductive technocratic accountability freight. Indeed, given the tendency to rely upon state revenues more and local property taxes less, some cynics assert that the system of education has become more bureaucratized, rule bound, and lacking in local responsiveness than before the reform period began.

Whether reforms have borne fruit is not yet easily answerable. The jury would appear to need a longer period in which to hear the evidence and deliberate. Nevertheless, aside from the presence or absence of immediate benefits to students, the reform movement has had describable effects. School finance reform appears to have been closely linked with state tax restructuring. Use of the judicial system as a component of the reform strategy is worthy of assessment. Last, linkage between the three values—equality, efficiency, and liberty—deserves some concluding comments.

Taxation

In that a major portion of the equal protection suits regarding school finance alleged disparities in the effort needed by local school districts in generating school revenues, it is no surprise that state and local tax schemes have undergone substantial revision in the effort to fashion remedies. Moreover, even attempts to rectify spending disparities typically have taxation consequences, as legislatures have a predilection for dampening spending inequalities by elevating low spending districts rather than depressing their high spending counterparts. The result has been a period in which many individual states have substantially revised their taxing structures.

Generally, state and local tax structures have been strengthened and diversified. In particular there has come about a decreased reliance upon property taxation for school revenues. For example, a 1980 report of the Advisory Commission on Intergovernmental Relations (ACIR) describes property tax revenues as constituting 44.6 percent of total state and local revenues in 1957 (Myers 1980). However, as a consequence of added reliance upon other revenue sources, by 1979 property tax proceeds accounted for only 32.6 percent of state and local income. During the same period, sales tax proceeds rose only slightly, whereas income tax revenues as a percent of state and local total revenue moved from 9.5 percent in 1957 to 23.8 percent in 1979 (Myers 1980). These shifts render state and local tax structures more responsive to economic growth than was previously the case. Also, regressive features of tax patterns have been reduced. Thirty-one states, as of 1980, had circuit breaker or exemption arrangements to dampen property tax burdens upon low income and senior citizen households. In fact, by 1980 the taxation picture had been altered sufficiently to move the ACIR to state:

> In all but a few states, the major challenge ahead for financing education is not the adequacy or equity of the state tax structure, but rather the level of educational costs and the degree to which local schools must raise their own revenues to retain local control. (Myers 1980: 3)

The Judicial Reform Strategy

As stated near the beginning of this chapter, the historic ability of high wealth, high spending school districts to impede legislative reforms inspired a judicial strategy. The nation's highest court failed to honor this strategy. Nevertheless, courts in thirty-six states have. Moreover, even in instances in which no favorable court decision has been forthcoming, legislatures have sometimes been persuaded to act positively for fear of the consequence should a court ruling develop. Thus, at least on the surface, the judicial strategy would appear to have been successful. However, proof of this thesis hinges more upon remedies than upon court decisions themselves. The gap between a favorable judicial decision and a favorable remedy can be a wide one.

In examining remedies, it appears that two major scenarios have developed. One involves a court decision regarding the evil of a state school finance arrangement and a subsequent mandate for legislative action. This has been the nature of decisions in cases such as *Robinson v. Cahill, Serrano v. Priest*, and *Seattle v. Washington.* The other scenario involves the court itself defining an evil and fashioning a remedy. The first mode has come to be described as "agenda setting," with the court setting a topic before a legislative body that the latter otherwise was reluctant to deal on its own initiative. The second mode is labeled "adjudicatory."

The evidence is yet in preliminary form, but the agenda-setting mode would appear to lead to more effective remedies. Whatever their failings, legislative bodies typically have greater information-gathering and policy-setting flexibility than do courts. This reveals itself in the creativity and complexity of legislatively fashioned remedies such as have developed in California, Connecticut, and Washington. These new school finance plans appear far from perfect; indeed, they have not achieved a degree of equalization sufficient to satisfy equal protection idealists. Nevertheless, they have moved toward eliminating disparities and have done so in a fashion that permitted schools to continue operating in a mode acceptable to the public and, if not beneficial, at least not harmful to students.

Agenda setting can have its weaknesses. The New Jersey Supreme Court in *Robinson* found itself in the awkward situation of having to enjoin further operation of New Jersey schools until the legislature finally acted upon a remedy. Even then, a number of districts failed to obey the court's mandate and kept schools in operation. Also, the complexity of the New Jersey solution, with its multifaceted accountability measures, suggests that even legislative solutions can go far afield. Nevertheless, by comparison with the court-designed solution in *Hobson v. Hansen*, most agenda-setting scenarios appear substantially effective. *Hobson* resulted in schools that may well have served student plaintiffs less well than the predecision condition.[21] By contrast, the ESEA Title I spending comparability requirements, in part triggered by *Hobson*, illustrate well the potentially greater effectiveness of legislative solutions to judicially defined problems.

Interaction between Value Streams

Almost every reform state has demonstrated that isolated pursuit of one value is virtually impossible. The coalition building necessary to define, fashion, and implement a widespread reform almost always necessitates concessions to proponents of yet another value stream. Successful school finance reform coalitions, to 1980, were most often formed by proponents of equality and efficiency. Hence, in state after state, redistribution of spending and taxing authority has been accompanied by productivity reforms such as statewide achievement testing, spending limits, state-prescribed teacher-training procedures, state-mandated teacher–pupil ratios, and additional reporting requirements. The outcome in almost every instance has been reduced decisionmaking discretion for local school authorities. Whether or not this consequence will in time foster counterpressures for reforms on the dimension of liberty remains to be seen. Indeed, regarding future interaction between all three values, the extent to which the 1980s will be characterized by conflict or cooperation is the subject for the remaining chapters in this volume.

NOTES TO CHAPTER 1

1. *Serrano v. Priest* originated in the Los Angeles County Superior court. Defendants sought and were granted a demurrer CL.D.298207. Plaintiffs appealed. The California Supreme court ruled in favor of plaintiffs and remanded the case to the court of original jurisdiction to assess whether or not unequal school financing was associated with unequal opportunity (5 Cal. 3d. 584, 487 P. 2d 1241, 96 Cal. Reptr. 601, 1971). The trial court found favorably for plaintiffs (Memorandum Opinion re Intended Decision Serrano v. Priest Civil No. 938,254 Cal. Super. CT. April 10, 1974, 18 Cal. 3d 728, 20 Cal. 3d. 25 1974). This trial court decision was itself appealed by defendants. However, subsequent decisions by the California Court of Appeals (10 Cal. App. 3d. 1110, 89 Cal. Rptr. 345, 1975) and California Supreme Court (18 Cal. 3d. 729 Dec. 30, 1976) sustained the lower court.

2. Jarvis and Gann sponsored a California property tax constitutional initiative in 1978, Proposition 13; a statewide spending limitation in 1979, Proposition 4; and an income tax reduction proposal in 1980, Proposition 9. The latter was rejected by the electorate.

3. A finding reported earlier in Morgan (1962: 306).

4.   For a summary of Coleman report criticisms, see Guthrie et al. (1971); see also, Cain and Watts (1970); Coleman (1970); and Hanushek and Kain (1972).

5.   For an understanding of the role of this network in influencing school finance reform see Fuhrman et al. (1979).

6.   The turmoil associated both with the case and with fashioning a remedy in Robinson v. Cahill is fully described by Lehne (1978).

7.   A description and analysis of the technocratic efforts to achieve accountability are provided by Martin, Overholt, and Urban (1976).

8.   Executive Order 11353, establishing the President's Advisory Council on Cost Reduction.

9.   Beginning in May of 1980, the Department of Health, Education, and Welfare officially changed its name to the Department of Health and Human Services. This alteration reflects the 1980 formation of the federal Department of Education.

10. The 1971 issue of *Current Index to Journals in Education* lists fifty articles referring to performance contracting alone.

11. Two years later the California legislature quietly rescinded the mandate.

12. See James Cooper and Wilford Webber, "Competency-Based Teacher Education: A Scenario" and "Performance Based Teacher Education: An Annotated Bibliography" both published by the American Association of Colleges of Teacher Education and available through the ERIC Clearinghouse on teacher education.

13. An excellent description of NAEP and a history of its early political difficulties is provided by Tyler (1971).

14. See publications of The Clearinghouse for Applied Performance Testing.

15. According to the Spring 1980 issue of the *Testing Digest*, a publication of the Committee for Fair and Open Testing, New York state's landmark law took effect on January 1, 1980. The statute requires sponsors of higher education admissions tests to submit copies of tests and correct answers to students upon request. This law has spurred introduction of similar initiatives in sixteen other states in the United States.

16. Spring 1980 Gallop poll on public acceptance of testing reported in the February 1980 issue of *School and Community*.

17. The *1978 Congressional Quarterly Almanac* covering the second session of the 95th Congress (Congressional Quarterly 1979) contains an extensive description and analysis of these spending limitation proposals at the federal level. Similarly, John Augenblick has summarized state legislative actions in 1978−1979 in an Education Commission of the States Report F 79−4, July 1979.

18. The linkage between responsiveness and the value of liberty is explained thoroughly in Tucker and Zeigler (1980: ch. 1).

19. The 1978 congressional debate regarding tuition tax credit plans is described in detail in the *1978 Congressional Quarterly Almanac*, (Congressional Quarterly 1979). See also Jacobs (1980).
20. The G.I. Bill is known officially as the Service Men's Readjustment Act of 1954, Public Law 78–346.
21. For a description of these experiments see the Winter 1975 issue of *Information*, the quarterly newsletter of the National Institute of Education. Also, see Stoll (1978).
22. This is a point described in detail in Horowitz (1977). Horowitz also explains why the constitutional underpinnings of the *Hobson* decisions were eroded two years later by the court majority's reasoning in Rodriguez v. San Antonio.

REFERENCES

Aaron, Henry J. 1978. *Politics and the Professors, The Great Society in Perspective*. Washington, D.C.: The Brookings Institution.

Agee, Robert. In progress. "School District Budgeting: An Analysis of its Processes and Outcomes in a Period of Decreasing Real Resources. Ph.D. dissertation, Graduate School of Education, University of California, Berkeley.

Allan Nairn and Associates. 1980. *The Reign of ETS: The Corporation that Makes up Minds*. Washington, D.C.: Learning Research Center.

Benson, Charles S., et al. 1972. *Final Report of the Senate Select Committee on School District Finance*. Vols. I and II. Sacramento: Senate of the State of California.

Berke, Joel S. 1974. *Answers to Inequity: An Analysis of The New School Finance*. Berkeley, California: McCutchan Publishing Company.

Berube, Maurice R., and Marilyn Gittell, eds. 1969. *Confrontation at Ocean Hill-Brownsville: The New York School Strike of 1968*. New York: Praeger.

Bowles, Samuel S. and Henry M. Levin "More on Multicollinearity and the Effectiveness of Schools," *Journal of Human Resources* 3 (Summer 1968).

Brazer, Harvey, et al. 1971. "Fiscal Needs and Resources." Consultant's report to the New York State Commission on the Cost, Quality and Financing of Elementary and Secondary Education.

Brown v. Board of Education, 347 U.S. 483, 495 (1954).

Brown v. Board of Education 349 U.S. 294 (1955).

Robinson v. Cahill, 62 N.J. 473, 303A.2d. 273 (1973).

Cain, Glen G., and Harold W. Watts. 1970. "Problems in Making Policy Inferences from the Coleman Report." *American Sociological Review* 35, no. 2 (April): 228–42.

Callahan, Raymond E. 1962. *Education and the Cult of Efficiency*. Chicago: University of Chicago Press.

Civil Rights Act. 1964. Public Law 88-352.

Cohen, David H., and Eleanor Farrar. 1977. "Power to the Parent? The Story of Education Vouchers." *The Public Interest* 48 (Summer): 72-97.

Coleman, James S. 1970. "Reply to Cain and Watts." *American Sociological Review* 35, no. 2 (April): 242-49.

Coleman, James S., et al. 1966. *Equality of Educational Opportunity.* Washington, D.C.: U.S. Government Printing Office.

Conant, James Bryant. 1961. *Slums and Suburbs.* New York: McGraw-Hill.

Congressional Quarterly. 1979. *1978 Congressional Quarterly Almanac.* Vol. XXXIV. 95th Cong., 2nd sess. Washington, D.C.

Coons, John E.; William H. Clune; and Stephen D. Sugarman. 1970. *Private Wealth and Public Education.* Cambridge, Massachusetts: Harvard University Press.

Cox, Donald W. 1969. "A School Without Walls: City for a Classroom." *Nation's Schools* 34, no. 3 (September): 51-54.

Duffy, Patrick S. 1972. "A Review of Supreme Court Decisions on Aid to Non-Public Elementary and Secondary Education." *The Hastings Law Journal* 23, no. 3 (March): 966-89.

Elementary and Secondary Education Act. 1965. Public Law 89-10.

Education Commission of the States. 1979a. *State Education Politics: The Case of School Finance Reform.* (Denver)

_____ . 1979b. "School Finance at a Glance, 1979." School Finance Project, Lawyers Committee for Civil Rights Under Law. 1980. "Update on statewide school finance cases."

Friedman, Milton. 1962. *Capitalism and Freedom.* Chicago: University of Chicago Press.

Fuhrman, Susan, et al. 1979. "The Politics and Process of School Finance Reform: a Review of the Literature," *Journal of Education Finance* (Winter).

Garms, Walter I.; James W. Guthrie; and Lawrence C. Pierce. 1978. *School Finance: The Economics and Politics of Public Education.* Englewood Cliffs, N.J.: Prentice Hall.

Gittell, Marilyn. 1967. *Participants and Participation: A Study of School Policy in New York City.* New York: Center for Urban Education.

Gittell, Marilyn, et al. 1971. *Demonstration for Social Change: An Experiment in Local Control.* New York: Institute for Community Studies, Queens College of the City University of New York.

Goertz, Margaret E. 1978. *Where Did The 400 Million Dollars Go? The Impact of the New Jersey Public School Education Act of 1975.* Princeton: Educational Testing Service.

Goertz, Margaret E., and Janet Hannigan. 1978. "Delivering A Thorough and Efficient Education in New Jersey: The Impact of an Expanded Arena of Policy Making." *Journal of Education Finance* 4 (Summer): 46-64.

Governor's Citizens Committee on Education. 1973. *Improving Education in Florida.* Tallahassee: State of Florida.

Griffin v. County School Board, 377 U.S. 218 (1964).

Guthrie, James W. 1968a. "A Political Case History: Passage of the ESEA." *Phi Delta Kappan* XLIV, no. 6 (February): 302–306.

_____. 1968b. "The 1965 ESEA: The National Politics of Educational Reform." Ph.D. dissertation, Stanford University.

_____. 1976. "Social Science, Accountability, and the Political Economy of School Productivity." In John E. MacDermott, ed., *Indeterminancy in Education.* Berkeley: McCutchan Publishing Corporation.

_____. 1979. "Another Decade of School Finance, Chaos." *California School Boards* (December): 8–10.

Guthrie, James W., et al. 1971. *Schools and Inequality.* Cambridge, Massachusetts: MIT Press.

Hanushek, Eric A., and John F. Kain. 1972. "On the Value of Equality of Educational Opportunity as a Guide to Public Policy. In Frederick Mosteller and Daniel P. Moynihan, eds., *On Equality of Educational Opportunity.*

Hargrave v. Kirk, 313 F. Supp. 944 (M.D. Fla. 1970).

Heath, Robert W., and Mark A. Nielson. 1974. "The Research Basis For Performance Based Teacher Education." *Review of Educational Research* 44, no. 4 (Fall): 463–84.

Hobson v. Hansen, 265 F. Supp 902 (DDC 1967).

Hobson v. Hansen, 327 F. Supp 844 (DDC 1971).

Horowitz, Donald L. 1977. "Hobson v. Hansen: The Calculus of Equality and School Resources." In Donald L. Horowitz, *The Courts and Social Policy.* Washington, D.C.: The Brookings Institution.

Improving Education in Florida: A Reassessment. 1967. Prepared for the Select Joint Committee on Public Schools for the Florida legislature. Tallahassee.

Jacobs, Martha J. 1980. "An Update: Who Would Benefit From Tuition Tax Credits?" *Phi Delta Kappan* 61, no. 10 (June): 679–81.

James, H. Thomas. 1975. "Declining Test Scores: The State's Reaction," *Compact* 9, no. 6 (December): 9–12.

_____. 1976. "National Decline in Test Scores of the College Bound," *Intellect* 105, no. 2378 (November): 130–131.

_____. 1978. and David G. Savage, "The Long Decline in SAT Scores," *Educational Leadership* 35, no. 4 (January): 290–93.

Kelly, James A. 1980. Remarks while addressing school finance reform participants at a Ford Foundation–sponsored conference in San Antonio on May 12.

Kirst, Michael W. 1979. "The New Politics of State Education Finance." *Phi Delta Kappan* 60, no. 6 (February).

Kohl, Herbert. 1967. *36 Children.* New York: New American Library.

Kozol, Jonathan. 1967. *Death At An Early Age.* Boston: Houghton Mifflin.

_____. 1978. *Children of the Revolution.* New York: Delacorte.

LaNoue, George R., and Bruce L.R. Smith. 1973. *The Politics of School Decentralization.* Lexington, Massachusetts: Lexington Books.

Lehne, Richard. 1978. *The Quest for Justice: The Politics of School Reform.* New York: Longman.

Lessinger, Leon M. 1969. "After Texarkana, What?" *Nation's Schools* 84, no. 6 (December): 37—40.

Levin, Henry M. ed. 1970. *Community Control of Schools.* Washington, D.C.: The Brookings Institution.

Levittown v. Nyquist, 94 Misc. 2d 466 (June 23, 1978).

Martin, R., and P. McClure. 1969. *ESEA Title I: Is It Helping Poor Children?* Washington, D.C.: Washington Research Project, NAACP Legal Defense and Education Fund.

Martin, Donald; George E. Overholt; and Wayne J. Urban. 1976. *Accountability in American Education: A Critique.* Princeton, N.J.: Princeton Book Company.

McInnis v. Shapiro, 293 F. Supp. 327 (N.D. Illinois, 1968).

Meranto, Philip. 1967. *The Politics of Federal Aid to Education in 1965: A Study in Political Innovation.* Syracuse: Syracuse University Press.

Morgan, James N. 1962. *Income and Welfare in the United States.* New York: McGraw Hill.

Moskowitz, Jay, and Joel D. Sherman. 1979. "School Finance Litigation: The Use of Data Analysis." *Journal of Education Finance* 4 (Summer): 322—32.

Myers, Will. 1980. "Long Term Trends in State Local Taxes." Washington, D.C.: Advisory Committee on Intergovernmental Relations.

National Center for Educational Statistics. 1976. *The Conditions of Education* Washington, D.C.: U.S. Government Printing Office. 1976.

National Defense Education Act. 1958. Public Law 85—864.

National Journal. 1970. "School Comparability Guidelines." June 13, 1233—34.

New York City Mayor's Advisory Panel on the Decentralization of New York City Schools. 1967. *Reconnection for Learning; A Community School System for New York City.* New York.

New York State Commission on the Quality, Cost, and Financing of Elementary and Secondary Education. 1973. *The Fleischmann Report.* Vols. I, II, and III. New York: Viking Press.

Pascal, Anthony H., and Mark David Menchik. 1979. *Fiscal Containment: Who Gains, Who Loses.* Santa Monica: Rand Corporation, September.

Pierce v. Society of Sisters, 268 U.S. 510 (1925).

Pierce, Lawrence C. et al. 1975. *State School Finance Alternatives.* Eugene: Center for Educational Policy and Management, University of Oregon.

Resnik, Henry S. 1970. "High Schools With No Walls," *Education Digest* 35, no. 7 (March): 16—19.

Rhoads, Stephen; Ann Sutherland Frentz; and Rudolph F. Marshall, Jr. 1978. "AB 65, California's Reply to Serrano." Paper delivered at American Education Finance Association Annual Conference, March 14.

Rodriguez v. San Antonio Independent School District, 337 F. Supp. 380 (W.D. Tex, 1971), 411 U.S. 1, 58 (1973).

Rogers, David. 1968. *110 Livingston Street*. New York: Random House.

School Finance Project, Lawyers Committee for Civil Rights Under Law. 1980. "Update on statewide school finance cases." January.

Serrano v. Priest, 10 Cal. App. 3d. 1110, 89 Cal. Rptr. 345 (1975).

Serrano v. Priest, 18 Cal. 3d 729 (1976).

Serrano v. Priest, 5 Cal. 3d 584, 487 P. 2d 1241, 96 Cal. Rptr. 601 (1971).

Serrano v. Priest, Cal. 3d (1974).

Sexton, Patricia Cayo. 1964. *Education and Income*. New York: Viking.

Shalala, Donna, and Mary Frase Williams. 1974. "State Politics, The Voters and School Finance Reform." *Phi Delta Kappan* 66, no. 1 (September).

Silberman, Charles E. 1970. *Crisis in the Classroom*. New York: Random House.

Stoll, Louise F. 1978. "The Price of a Gift: The Impact of Federal Funds on the Political and Economic Life of School Districts." Ph. D. dissertation, University of California, Berkeley.

Thomas, J. Alan. 1968. *School Finance and Educational Opportunity in Michigan*. (Lansing: Michigan Department of Education, 1968).

Tucker, Harvey J. and L. Harmon Zeigler. 1980. *Professionals Versus the Public: Attitudes, Communication, and Response in School Districts*. New York: Longman.

Tyack, David B. 1974. *The One Best System*. Cambridge, Massachusetts: Harvard University Press.

Tyler, Ralph W. 1971. "National Assessment: A History and Sociology." In James W. Guthrie and Edward Wynne. *New Models for American Education*. Englewood Cliffs, N. J.: Prentice Hall.

U.S. Commission on Civil Rights. 1967. *Racial Isolation in the Public Schools*. Washington, D. C.: U. S. Government Printing Office.

U.S. Department of Health, Education, and Welfare. 1974. *A Century of U.S. School Statistics*. Washington, D. C.

Weiler, Daniel. 1974. *The Public School Voucher Demonstration: The First Year at Alum Rock*. Santa Monica: Rand Corporation, June 19.

Wirt, Frederick M. 1971. *Politics of Southern Equality*. Chicago: Aldine Publishing Company.

Wise, Arthur E. 1968. *Rich Schools, Poor Schools: A Promise of Equal Educational Opportunity*. Chicago: University of Chicago Press.

2 THE POLITICAL ENVIRONMENT OF SCHOOL FINANCE POLICY IN THE 1980s

Michael W. Kirst*
Walter I. Garms**

Financing of public schools is embedded in a societal matrix. It is not possible to consider the future of school finance without examining the size and distribution of future populations, the future of the economy and its effect on money available for schools, and the political context within which decisions will be made. This chapter attempts to state what is known now about these forces and to project them over the decade·of the 1980s.

The public school system is a dependent variable of larger social and economic forces. These forces are sometimes cyclical in nature. For example, in the late 1950s, the Sputnik launching triggered a series of policies that directed resources toward the training of gifted students, especially in science. In the mid–1960s, President Johnson's War on Poverty produced countertrend policies through redirection of resources to the disadvantaged and the handicapped. In the 1980s, the search for alternative energy forms may once again redirect resources toward science and math.

Educational policies are also often determined by actions of special interest groups external to the system. California's Proposition 13 and spending caps, which have substantial impact on the

*Michael W. Kirst, Professor, Stanford University and President, California State Board of Education.

**Walter I. Garms, Professor and Dean, School of Education, University of Rochester.

state's education finance structure, resulted from taxpayers' resentment over property taxes and inflation. Schools were directly affected by an issue in which they were only an indirect target. Special interest groups directly related to education have had a much less powerful effect. These groups include professionals, school boards, and PTAs. Their policy inputs have been muffled not only by social forces and taxpayer groups, but also by external authorities who are more distantly connected with education. For example, the courts have made substantial policy inroads in the areas of desegregation and school finance.

The decade of the 1970s produced for the entire nation a $23 billion growth (after inflation) in education expenditures, despite a downturn in enrollment. While education's share of GNP slipped slightly, there was no dramatic turnaround. Can this impressive fiscal growth be continued in the 1980s? Shifting social and demographic patterns will place education in a weakened political bargaining position for funding increases. A trend toward more intense competition for funds is likely because of threats to local and federal revenue bases. First, for a variety of reasons, voter support of local school finance elections will continue to decline or remain at the current depressed level. The number of people with a direct stake in education (e.g., parents) and those who are not alienated from schools is declining. The only population sectors in which enrollments are increasing, such as Hispanics and low income citizens, have little political influence over budgets. Special programs for these pupils, including bilingual education and desegregation, will further depress voter support.

Second, the number of people with no direct interest in education and who, for a variety of reasons, are probable "no" voters in local school finance elections is increasing (Piele 1980; see also Abramowitz and Rosenfeld 1978; Hall and Piele 1976). There will be a dramatic increase in the total number of senior citizens, who also have the highest tendency to vote. Inflation psychology will depress willingness to increase local taxes. Third, education is expected to face increased competition for funding at the federal level from defense, energy, and senior citizens.

Given the probable erosion of political support at the local and federal levels, increased political cohesion and action among education groups at the state level is crucial. During the 1970s this shift to reliance on state revenues began. Maintaining the impressive growth in state education support will be difficult given the history of state political factionalism. The state revenue base will be the key to future fiscal support. From 1969 to 1979, state education spending increased from $16 billion to $35.7—up 35 percent in real terms. (See Table 2—1.) In an era of tax limits, public education groups may have to use their political muscle to redistribute scarce state dollars from other public services to education.

Demographic prediction is an inherently risky business, but the evidence signals a decline in these pro-education-spending groups. An increase in private school enrollment could even worsen this outlook. The U.S. Bureau of the Census uses four series to project total population. In 1967 it predicted that the 1980 U.S. population would be between 227 and 250 million (U.S. Bureau of the Census 1967: 8, Table 6). In 1971 the prediction was revised to be between 225 and 236 million (U.S. Bureau of the Census 1971: 8, Table 6). The population in 1980 will actually be about 221 million, well below the lowest of the four prediction series used.

Needless to say, predictions of population by geographical area or of components of the population such as number of minorities are bound to be even more in error. Yet population data are the most solid figures we have. Most of those who will be alive in 1990 are already born. Predictions of future economic trends are even more risky, however, for there is much less that is certain. Finally, future political trends may be the most risky of all to predict, for these can shift rapidly and markedly in response to things that we cannot now foresee. With these chastening thoughts in mind, we begin with the least speculative area of short-term demography and end with the most hazy, political predictions.

PROJECTIONS OF ELEMENTARY-
SECONDARY ENROLLMENTS

Most of the projections of population and of school enrollment have been too high and, consequently, overstated related increases in school funding. In order to understand this, it is necessary to analyze projection methods. The birth rate in a given year is the number of children born per 1000 population. This is interesting information, but is not so useful for prediction because the number born depends not only on the rate at which women are having children

Table 2−1.   Revenue receipts of public elementary and secondary schools, by source, 1942−1978.

School Year Ending	Total	Federal	State	Local[a]
	Current Dollars (in millions)			
1942	$ 2,417	$ 34	$ 760	$ 1,622
1946	3,060	41	1,062	1,956
1950	5,437	156	2,166	3,116
1954	7,867	355	2,944	4,568
1958	12,182	486	4,800	6,895
1962	17,528	761	6,789	9,978
1966	25,357	1,997	9,920	13,440
1970	40,267	3,220	16,063	20,985
1974	58,231	4,930	24,281	29,020
1978[b]	80,925	6,575	35,692	38,658
	Constant 1977−1978 Dollars (in millions)			
1942	9,717	137	3,055	6,521
1946	10,513	141	3,649	6,720
1950	14,379	413	5,728	8,241
1954	18,314	826	6,853	10,634
1958	26,693	1,065	10,518	15,108
1962	36,509	1,585	14,141	20,783
1966	49,733	3,917	19,456	26,360
1970	66,771	5,339	26,636	34,797
1974	78,193	6,620	32,605	38,968
1978[b]	80,925	6,575	35,692	38,658
	Percentage Distribution			
1942	100.0	1.4	31.5	67.1
1946	100.0	1.4	34.7	63.8
1950	100.0	2.9	39.8	57.3
1954	100.0	4.5	37.4	58.1
1958	100.0	4.0	39.4	56.6
1962	100.0	4.3	38.7	56.9
1966	100.0	7.9	39.1	53.0
1970	100.0	8.0	39.9	52.1
1974	100.0	8.5	41.7	49.8
1978[b]	100.0	8.1	44.1	47.8

Notes to Table 2-1

a. Includes intermediate.

b. Estimated. For 1979, NEA estimates the state government provided 53 percent of funds, federal 9 percent, and local 38 percent.

Note: Details may not add to totals because of rounding.

Source: U.S. Department of Health, Education, and Welfare (Washington, D.C.: U.S. Government Printing Office, 1979), and preliminary data.

but also on the relative percentage of the population who are women of child-bearing age. In 1980, for example, baby boom World War II children are entering their prime child-bearing years, and this in itself would increase the birth rate even if each woman had the same number of children as was the case in some earlier era.

A better indicator, and one on which we have long-term data, is the birth rate, calculated by dividing births by the number of women aged fifteen to forty-four. The interesting thing, as shown by Figure 2-1, is that this rate has demonstrated a long-term downward trend, with only a single bulge after World War II. Note that the recent decrease has been sharper for black women than for white. Perhaps a better indicator yet is the "total fertility rate." This is the number of births that 1000 women would have in their lifetime if, at each year of age, they experienced the birth rates occurring in the specified year. A total fertility rate of 2110 represents "replacement level" fertility for the total population under current mortality conditions (assuming no net immigration). Another way of expressing this is to say that for the population to be stable in the long term, the average woman must have 2.11 children. The total fertility rate was 2928 in 1965; 2480 in 1970; dipped below replacement level at 2022 in 1972; and was 1768 in 1976 (U.S. Bureau of the Census 1978c: 60, Table 80). Recent surveys indicate that lifetime birth expectations among women eighteen to twenty-four years old have remained virtually unchanged since 1976 (U.S. Bureau of the Census 1978a). Both black and white women report expecting the same number of children, although black age-specific birth rates are still higher than those of whites (U.S. Bureau of the Census 1977a).[1]

There are many reasons for this substantial decrease in fertility of American women. Part of it is undoubtedly the availability of effective means of contraception. Part is a change in lifestyles, with a much larger percentage of the female population working. Part may be the result of the fact that the present cohort of women of child-

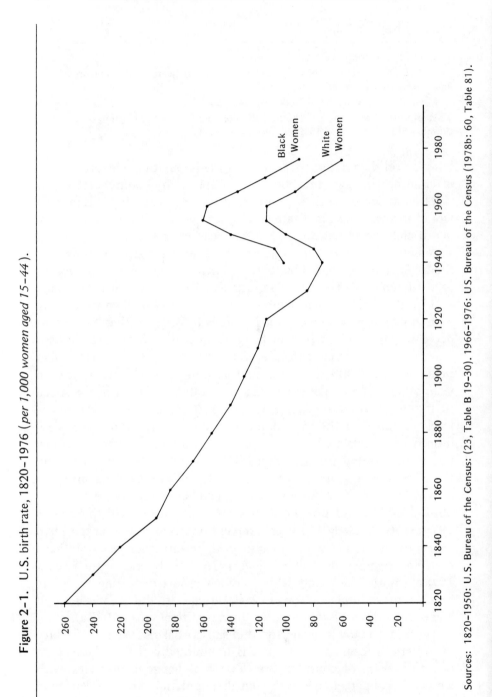

Figure 2-1. U.S. birth rate, 1820–1976 (*per 1,000 women aged 15–44*).

Sources: 1820–1950: U.S. Bureau of the Census: (23, Table B 19–30). 1966–1976: U.S. Bureau of the Census (1978b: 60, Table 81).

bearing age is a large one, composed of the children of the baby boom after World War II. Because the cohort is large, it finds the competition for jobs to be more difficult. This leads to unemployment or to lower incomes than had otherwise been expected, and this could lead to a depression in the fertility rate. Finally, economic conditions in general have an influence on the birth rate, as the low rate in the Depression years of the 1930s indicates. Whatever the causes, it seems likely that the present low rate of fertility will continue without major change for at least the next half-decade. Children born in 1985 will enter kindergarten in 1990, and thus we should be using a fertility rate substantially below the replacement rate to make enrollment projections for the next decade.

It is worth noting that the decline in fertility is not solely an American trend nor even a "developed world" trend. A dramatic decline in fertility is under way in many parts of the underdeveloped world. The downturn has been suggested for several years by U.N. estimates based on vital statistics, but for many countries such data are considered unreliable. Now a series of fifteen single country reports on carefully designed household surveys conducted by the World Fertility Survey has documented the trend. To some extent the decreased fertility is the result of later marriage, but the major reason is that people want to have smaller families (*Scientific American* 1979: 72).

The National Center for Educational Statistics publishes projections of Educational Statistics for a ten year period. The most recent carries the projections to 1986–1987. (Frankel 1978). The projections show a high alternative, a low alternative, and an intermediate alternative, based on assumed fertility rates of 2700, 1700, and 2100. The assumption is that the intermediate alternative is the most likely. Based on the fact that the low level of fertility has now persisted for more years than most experts had believed it would, we feel that the low alternative is considerably more likely.

This assumption on our part makes a difference primarily in projections of elementary school enrollment. Children born in 1979 will only be in fifth grade by 1990. However, these enrollment projections are central, for they determine many other things related to the size of the educational enterprise—teacher demand and its relationship to supply, impact of education on the tax structure, need for school construction or renovation, and many others. Enrollment also has a major impact on political support for increases in school spending.

Let us proceed to make predictions about the demographic future of education in the 1980s. Figure 2−2 contains predictions of enrollment in grades K−12 of regular days schools in the United States. The alternative projections to 1986 shown are those from *Projections of Educational Statistics* (Frankel 1978: 16, Table 3). We believe the low alternative to be the most correct, as explained above, and we have continued that projection to 1990. In doing so, we have used Census Bureau population projections (U.S. Bureau of the Census 1977b: 10, Table 4), the data in *Projections of Educational Statistics* Frankel 1978: 119, Table A−1, and 156, Table B−1), and the cohort survival method used by NCES to extend the lines. The indication is that K−8 enrollment will continue to decline until about 1987 and then show a slight upturn, with about a 4 percent increase between then and 1990.

There are no alternative projections for 9−12 enrollment, since all of the students who will be in those grades in the 1980s have already been born. The line has been extended to 1990 and shows a continued decline throughout the 1980s, although with a plateau from 1983 through 1986. The combination of the two gives a K−12 enrollment that will decline until 1988 and then remain at about the same level for the next two years. Any upturn in overall K−12 enrollment, if it occurs at all, is likely to come in the 1980s. Data for selected years are given in Table 2−2. They show that total K−12 enrollment, which peaked at 51.3 million in 1971, will be less than 43 million by 1990. This is a 17 percent decrease in enrollment in a twenty year period. Kindergarten through eighth grade enrollment peaked in 1969 and by 1990 will have decreased 17 percent; 9−12 enrollment peaked in 1976 and will have decreased 24 percent by 1990. During the 1980s the elementary schools will decrease in enrollment by one million students, a decrease of 3 percent, while the high schools will decrease by 2.6 million or 18 percent of 1980 enrollment. Proportionately, the high school loss of enrollment during the decade will be six times as great as the loss at the elementary level.

Figure 2–2. Actual and projected enrollments, total United States, 1954–1990.

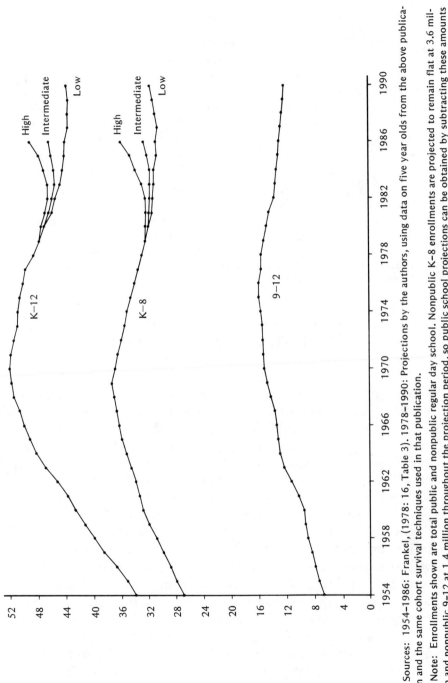

Sources: 1954–1986: Frankel, (1978: 16, Table 3). 1978–1990: Projections by the authors, using data on five year olds from the above publication and the same cohort survival techniques used in that publication.

Note: Enrollments shown are total public and nonpublic regular day school. Nonpublic K–8 enrollments are projected to remain flat at 3.6 million and nonpublic 9–12 at 1.4 million throughout the projection period, so public school projections can be obtained by subtracting these amounts from those shown.

Table 2–2.   Actual and projected enrollment in regular day schools, 1955–1990.

Year	Enrollment (thousands)		
	K–12	K–8	9–12
1955	35,280	27,717	7,563
1960	42,181	32,492	9,689
1965	48,473	35,463	13,010
1970	51,309	36,677	14,632
1975	49,791	34,087	15,704
1980	46,076	31,473	14,603
1985	43,231	29,868	13,363
1990	42,680	30,714	11,966

Sources: 1955–1985: Frankel (Washington, D.C.: U.S. Government Printing Office, (1978: 16, Table 3). 1990: Authors' projections.

IMPACT OF DEMOGRAPHIC CHANGES ON SPECIFIC STATES AND SCHOOL DISTRICTS

Unfortunately, overall statistics do not tell much about how the enrollment declines will affect different school districts. Trying to predict these is more difficult. First, we assume that the patterns of migration that have seen the industrial Northeast (excluding northern New England) and North Central states lose population to the South and West will continue. Figure 2–3 shows the pattern of regional growth from 1920 to 1978 and projected to 1990. The pattern is striking: rapid growth continues in the South and West, with slow growth in the North Central states and the beginning of a decline in the Northeast. By 1990 the Northeast will be the least populous region. It is difficult to say whether these regional population shifts will overbalance general declines in the school age population in the West and the South. We can say with confidence that the declines will be less precipitous than the average in the sun belt regions and faster than the average in the Northeast and North Central states.

The rapid growth of the sun belt states must be understood as only relative to the stagnation and decline of the Midwest–Northeast industrial belt. The rate of enrollment growth of most sun belt states and their metropolitan areas is no faster, and in some cases slower,

Figure 2–3.   Population of the U.S. by region, 1920–1978 and projected to 1990.

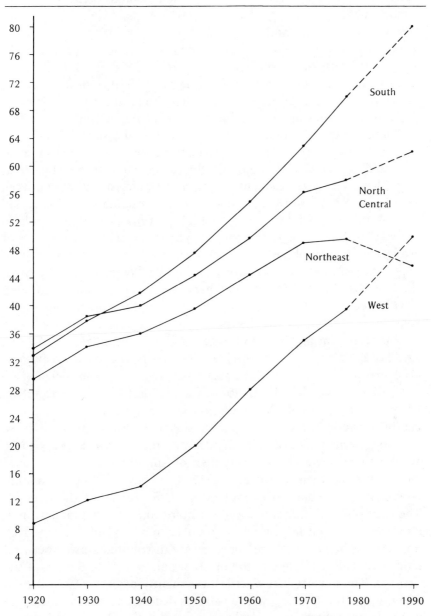

Sources: 1920–1970: U.S. Bureau of the Census (1971: 12, Table 11). 1977–1978: U.S. Bureau of the Census (1979b). 1990: Projection by the authors based on the 1977–1978 rate of change.

than in the 1960s. If the trend toward decreasing fertility and births persists, then population and employment cannot increase in some regions without causing a loss somewhere else. The state revenue systems of the South and West should benefit enough from economic growth to provide ample resources for public services. For example, growth in Texas has permitted a jump from $1.2 billion to $5.1 billion in annual public education funding since 1969 (*Education Daily*, January 21, 1980). An automobile sales plunge caused a 13 percent decrease in Michigan State Education Department funds for 1980.

Another facet of population movement is the shift from metropolitan to nonmetropolitan areas. In the 1960s, metropolitan areas increased in population 16.6 percent, while nonmetropolitan areas only increased by 6.6 percent (Berry and Dahmann 1977). Between 1970 and 1977, however, population in metropolitan areas increased only 4 percent, while it increased 11 percent in nonmetropolitan areas (U.S. Bureau of the Census; 1978b). The current lower rate of growth in metropolitan areas has resulted from a combination of depopulation of the central cities and the slackening growth boom in the suburbs. Since 1970, central cities have lost over two million persons, a decline of 5 percent. Suburbs increased in population 12 percent (U.S. Bureau of the Census), but this is small compared with 26.7 percent during the 1960s and 45.9 percent during the 1950s. The fastest growth in suburbs is in the South; the fastest growth in nonmetropolitan areas is in the West (Berry and Dahmann 1977).

Urban-suburban-rural migration was not uniform among elements of the population. Black population in cities did not grow significantly between 1974 and 1977, marking at least a temporary pause in a long-term trend. Black migration to the suburbs appears to be accelerating, however. The number of suburban blacks increased 34 percent between 1970 and 1977, but they still represent only 6 percent of the suburban population (U.S. Bureau of the Census). The nation's Spanish population was more concentrated in metropolitan areas than either the white population as a whole or the black population; however, it was more evenly distributed between central cities and suburbs than was the black population (U.S. Bureau of the Census). The poverty rate in cities was slightly higher in 1976 than in 1969, while the poverty rate in suburbs declined a little, and the rate in nonmetropolitan areas declined substantially. Forty-two percent of the metropolitan population lives in cities, but 62 percent of the metropolitan poor are city dwellers (U.S. Bureau of the Census; see also Abramowitz and Rosenfeld 1978: Chs IV and VIII). The Council of Great City Schools reported to a congressional committee that its twenty-seven member districts lost 847,000 students between 1970 and 1977. Although minority students made up 46 percent of the enrollment in these districts in 1970, four years later they made up 67 percent (Niell 1979). This demographic change accounts for some of the fiscal stress in such city schools as Chicago, Cincinnati, and Cleveland. Again, the central city fiscal problem will be concentrated in the Northeast and Midwest.

THE LOCAL TAX BASE AND THE VOTERS: EROSION OF SUPPORT FOR EDUCATION

Overall school enrollment declines lead to less direct stakes in education for the voting population, as listed below:

Percent of U.S. Population Ages 15−24
1950 − 15 percent
1965 − 16 percent
1977 − 19 percent
1985 − 17 percent
1990 − 14 percent

The snow belt states will suffer more than the sun belt states, with northeastern metropolitan areas being hit the hardest. This may imply a decrease in "yes" voters for local property tax school financing. A relative increase in the share of households without children may not result in a reduction in electoral support for public education or in reduced total or per pupil expenditure. The tax rate to raise a given level of spending per pupil may fall because there is a higher ratio of taxpayers to students. Many school districts in the East have increased per pupil spending dramatically because budgets have not been cut back commensurate with enrollment declines. Only if state and local finance formulae are precisely linked to commensurate amounts of enrollment decline will per pupil expenditure drop. Nationally, class sizes have declined consistently for the past five years to hit a low of 19.4 pupils per teacher in 1979 (*Phi Delta Kappan* 1979: 8; see also NCES 1979: 81).

Immigration will have a major effect in only a few states. Legal immigration is about 400,000 persons, and these tend to scatter among all regions. But illegal immigration of Mexicans into the border states of California, New Mexico, Arizona, and Texas is a major issue. Unofficial estimates of the number of immigrants in the United States range from two to twelve million. These illegal immigrants create demands for high cost bilingual programs, but the parents cannot vote in U.S. elections to increase state or local school revenue. Any immigration settlement with Mexico in return for Mexican oil is certain to result in a sudden influx into the public schools in the border states. California's Hispanic school enrollment grew from 11 percent of total in 1970 to 23 percent by 1979, along with rising public resentment against state-mandated bilingual education.[2]

While the empirical evidence is that age composition of a community affects support for public schools, we view the overall characteristics of U.S. senior citizens as an ominous sign for school voting. Recall that voters with less education tend to vote no. Nearly half of the population over sixty-five never attended high school. Only 16 percent have one year of college (Katz 1976). The population over sixty-five doubled, from twelve to twenty-four million, between 1950 and 1978 (U.S. Bureau of the Census 1979a). As a percent of the population, those over sixty-five increased from eight to eleven percent. It is estimated that by the year 2030 that proportion will have increased to 22 percent. Moreover, U.S. senior citizens are more likely to own homes than child-bearing age groups. Consequently, they perceive a direct impact of local school expenditures on their property tax. The elderly now account for 25 percent of the federal budget. The U.S. House of Representatives' report on aging projects that, without any additional increases in programs, the elderly will account for roughly 40 percent of the budget by 2050. Citizens over sixty-five turn out to vote at a 62 percent rate compared to 49 percent for the child-bearing years of ages eighteen through thirty-four (Halperin 1979; NCES: 35).

As our initial analysis of demographic trends indicates, however, that growing areas such as rural areas and some of the sun belt areas will continue to experience an inflow of younger residents. They might do better in the voting sweepstakes than older communities in states like Ohio. A crucial determinant will be the turnout of the Hispanic voters and other new immigrants. If they continue to display the low turnouts of the past, public voting support for local education expenditures could drop. Those segments of the population that are increasing their proportionate participation in education may prove to be a mixed blessing. The United States contains an increasing proportion of those children who are nonwhite, poor, and born to teenage mothers. Almost half of the children born in 1976 are expected to live in single parent households at some point before they are eighteen. Families headed by females generally have to subsist on incomes 50 percent lower than those headed by males. The number of such families increased by over 250 percent between 1950 and the mid-1970s (Neill 1979: 7). Thus, while those with no direct interest in public education are increasing in numbers, an increasing proportion of those who have a direct interest will be those who tend to be politically powerless—those among whom voter turnout is lower and who have both less means and less ability to provide campaign resources.

In addition to being politically powerless, many will also require expensive, special programs for the disadvantaged. This will increase the per capita expenditure while eroding the community's political base. Additionally, these students tend to be located in center city districts, some of which will be the least able to finance this "educational overburden." The fiscally distressed eastern and midwestern cities contain disproportionate numbers of Hispanics, blacks, and immigrants. Among the poor, teenage pregnancy rates are not falling. Young mothers tend to have a higher proportion of handicapped children, further increasing the urban school districts per capita expenditures.

COMPETITION BETWEEN PUBLIC SCHOOLS, DAY CARE, AND MANPOWER TRAINING

There are other trends that will have implications for elementary and secondary education financing. One is the increase in labor force participation of American women. In 1960, 25 percent of the women were in the labor force (Niell 1979: 7). By 1978 this proportion had doubled to 50 percent. The labor force participation of young women twenty-five to thirty-four years old increased from 36 percent in 1960 to 62 percent in 1979. During this same period the labor force participation rate for mothers of children under six rose even more dramatically, from 19 to 42 percent (U.S. Bureau of the

Census 1979c). It is estimated that by 1990, 70 to 80 percent of women will be in the labor force (Niell 1979: 7). This has important implications for day care and similar custodial programs for children. For example, the only school level showing an increase in enrollment between 1977 and 1978 was nursery school. There were two-thirds more children in nursery school in 1978 than in 1970 (U.S. Bureau of the Census 1979b).

Moreover, women will increasingly enter the work force as our inflationary society requires more income merely to support a basic standard of living. If current child care arrangements are projected into the future, the number of children of working mothers served by day care centers and nursery schools could increase dramatically. Will this begin to shift public pressure and financing toward pre-school programs and away from kindergarten through twelfth grade?

In the 1960s many school districts wanted little to do with day care programs. As K–12 enrollments decrease, a reversal in attitude seems likely. School lobbies may push to include day care programs under the district's umbrella, but during the 1970s public schools made no significant inroads on the nonschool growth of child care. As the political struggle grows at the state and federal levels, one might expect to find education departments seeking more control over day and education-related programs offered through other governmental departments. After Proposition 13 passed in California, local public school systems wanted to drop their child care programs and put the savings into the K–12 structure. However, child care lobbyists successfully included a prohibition in the Proposition 13 state bailout against any cuts in child care.

From 1969 to 1979, Department of Labor expenditures for out of school manpower programs for youth and adults grew from $2 billion annually to about $12 billion. This prodigious growth was a stark contrast to the $800 million the federal government has provided for high school vocational education. Indeed, the Carter administration tried to reduce vocational education, but was overridden by Congress. Public schools have failed to extend their boundaries to include large numbers of preschool and out of school students. This has cost them dearly in terms of total expenditures. Some of the negative expenditure trends presented in this study could be offset by a larger public school role in these related growth sectors of preschool and out of school education.

A SHORTAGE OF ABLE TEACHERS BY THE LATE 1980s: IMPACT ON PUBLIC SUPPORT OF EDUCATIONAL FUNDING

There is some relationship between the public's perception of teaching effectiveness and a willingness to support increased taxes. In real income, today's teachers earn only 2 percent more than they did in 1965. Since 1974, wage settlements have lagged inflation.[3] In the long run this means that high quality staff will be bid away to other occupations. The teaching market is currently in surplus as education majors face a relatively low probability of being hired. Additionally, relatively few middle and upper middle class women are entering teaching as the number of alternative opportunities has increased in the past few years. Education degrees granted at a bachelor's level are expected to fall off precipitously, from 194,210 in 1972–1973 to 116,340 in 1986–1987, a decline of 40 percent. If teacher demand continues to decline, new entrants may be even lower. This will cause higher per pupil costs for current operations because of the minimal opportunity to replace expensive senior teachers with beginners at lower salary levels.

New teachers will be more likely to come from minority and disadvantaged backgrounds. With adequate training, this could prove to be advantageous to urban districts with increasing numbers of students from similar backgrounds. Without adequate training, districts could find themselves perpetuating old, unsuccessful patterns of behavior rather than developing new, more successful patterns of behavior in students.

The NCES projects an increasing glut in the supply of teachers, despite the decrease in the number of new graduates. A low alternative estimates that the total stock of teachers will decline 8 percent between 1976 and 1986. An increased reserve pool of teachers looking for jobs will reduce the expected value of their individual jobs as each one faces a lower probability of being hired. This will continue to encourage exits from the reserve pool and discourage new entrants. Recently, there has been an alarming drop in the college entrance scores of prospective teachers. According to the American College Board, teachers now rank second to the last in scholastic aptitude test scores among types of college major subjects. Only ethnic studies ranked lower. If the public perceives that the quality of teachers has dropped, it may be more reluctant to support spending increases. The College Board (1979) stresses that 1979 education majors have only a 392 average verbal score and have declined as a percentage of total majors for the past five years.

NEW SOCIETAL FORCES COMPETING WITH EDUCATION FOR FUNDS

A variety of other social factors are likely to interact with demographic trends to influence future school politics and expenditures. For example, energy costs will have many impacts on education. Direct effects include rising fuel costs for heating, transport, and racial integration. The indirect political effect could stem from a reduction in discretionary income of families to pay higher energy costs, which will affect the amount of expenditures taxpayers will allocate for schools. Moreover, high-priced energy may change political demography by encouraging people to live closer to the city.

After the Dayton and Columbus, Ohio, Supreme Court cases, it is apparent that civil rights movements will continue to increase the percentage of children attending integrated schools. Increased transport costs may cause curtailment of other school costs at a time of shrinking budgets and inflation. Moreover, "busing" may have some negative effect on the public's willingness to vote more public school expenditures. Proponents of California's Proposition 13 cited desegregation costs ordered by the California Supreme Court as one of their prime targets.

The 1980s could bring a virtual explosion of centralizing telecommunications such as television, central computer banks, instantaneous video communication, and home-based computer and television systems. These systems may have centralized distribution, but they will be a very individualized home-based education delivery system. One thesis is that the ability to get education in the home through such things as two-way cable television, video cassettes, and so on will lead to a privatization of education. Will consumer spending for education in the home cause less public support of institution-based education outside the home? While the impact of technology on teaching in public schools has been minimal, the technological impact and expenditures for private home-based education systems could be much more significant by 1990. We can only guess at its impact on the public's willingness to fund public schooling. By 1990, computer literacy and technological sophistication will become essential, not merely nice to have. As home computer terminals, two-way cable TV, home video consuls, and laser and satellite communication become within the economic reach of many Americans, the politics of education may change significantly. If skills to handle these computer and technological devices are not taught in the kindergarten through twelfth grade schools, we could see an increase in expenditures for other satellite systems of education, including private technical schools and adult courses.

SUMMARY OF FINANCIAL OUTLOOK: 1980–1990

Projections for educational expenditures look fairly dismal, especially relative to the recent past. There is an increasing national debate about the overall growth of the public sector from 25 percent of the gross national product in 1945 to 33 percent today. Expenditures probably cannot increase at the impressive 1970–1980 rate. Even accounting for constant dollars, per capita education expenditures rose from $875 in 1963 to $1575 in 1976, an 80 percent increase (NCES: 90, Table 28). We doubt that teacher–pupil ratios will continue to decrease as they have in the past. Local school boards are learning the politics of school closing. Moreover, as indicated above, a declining political base of public education is likely. There will be increased competition with social services (e.g., child care and health) that are related but not identical to institutionalized schooling. We suspect 1986 expenditures will be lower than the NCES low alternative, perhaps in the range of $70 to $75 billion (in 1975–1976 dollars). However, there will be large variations by region, with more rapid expenditure growth in Texas and some other sun belt states.

The National Center for Education Statistics also projects public school expenditures for capital outlay and debt service. However, we feel that these are seriously flawed because they merely assume that the 1963–1964 through 1975–1976 trend will continue through 1985–1986. They have fitted linear regression lines to unknown prior trends. Data for capital outlay show an average expenditure of $8.6 billion a year from 1966 through 1970 and then a sharp drop in 1971 to a new average during the next five years of $6.2 billion

(NCES 1979: 94, Table 30; see also ibid., p 153; Hall and Piele 1976). There is no clear trend within either of the five year periods. As a result, we think that the projection of a decline to an average yearly expenditure of $4.5 billion by 1986 may be low. We suspect that something like $5.5 billion a year (in constant 1975–1976 dollars) by 1986 is more realistic. Similarly, a regression line fitted to expenditures for interest is inappropriate when the data series climbed rapidly from 1963 to 1970 (from $1.3 billion to about $2 billion) and since then has remained essentially constant. It certainly is not consistent to project interest costs to increase to $2.6 billion by 1986 when capital expenditures are projected to fall (NCES 1979: 95, Table 31). We suspect interest costs may remain at about the $2 billion level.

Combining these estimates, we believe that public school expenditures by 1986 will be in the range of $78 billion to $83 billion in 1975–1976 dollars by 1985–1986 as against about $75 billion in 1975–1976. This is substantially lower than the $93.5 billion projected as its best estimate by NCES. For several years, education has been losing ground relative to other social services, and we project this trend to continue (see Table 2–3).

Since 1965 the average proportion of all public expenditures spent on welfare has doubled, and health expenditures have increased by nearly a third, whereas education expenditures have decreased by over 20 percent. This may prove not only a difficult trend to reverse, but also one that may feed on itself. The political power of organized teachers, however, might offset some of the causes of our pessimism. Elementary pupil–teacher ratios declined from 28.7 in 1958 to 20.9 in 1978. A continuation of this trend could keep education expendi-

Table 2–3.   Government spending patterns 1965–1975.

	1965	1970	1975	Net Change 1965–75
Income maintenance	47.4	41.7	46.1	−1.3
Health	12.4	17.3	17.4	+5.0
Welfare	3.8	5.3	7.6	+3.8
Education	36.5	35.6	28.9	−7.6
Total	100.0	100.0	100.0	

Source: NCES (1979: 144).

tures rising at the rate of prior decades. Our estimate is that a combination of forces listed in Table 2−3 will prevent a pupil−teacher ratio of 12.1 in 2000. Such a low pupil−teacher ratio would be required to preserve the expenditure growth rate of 1958−1978 (see Table 2−4).

POLITICAL STRATEGIES TO INCREASE EDUCATION'S SHARE OF PUBLIC EXPENDITURES

Many observers who have examined trends discussed in this chapter have developed a pessimistic view. For example, Samuel Halperin of the Washington-based Institute of Educational Leadership stated:

> As education's traditional student body diminishes in number, and as the politically powerful demands of the aging mount (national health insurance, old age assistance and welfare reform) − along with other high social priorities (energy, R & D, crime control, rebuilding our cities, and upgrading transportation systems) − will education's share of the GNP be politically able to keep pace? Not without a thorough restructuring of education's tattered alliances and a radicalization of the teaching profession. (1979: 10; see also Kirst 1980; Hamilton and Cohen 1975)

The big gainer at the federal level is the defense budget, which is increasing much faster than inflation (to keep commitments to NATO and to counter Soviet initiatives). Moreover, most social security benefits and other payments for individuals (federal retirement, veterans' payments, food stamps, public assistance, and medicare) continue to rise as the number of beneficiaries increases and as medical prices rise. To keep the nondefense totals the same in real terms, President Carter's 1981 budget cut grants in aid to state and local governments, including some education programs. The oil windfall profits tax might radically alter this pessimism if it frees general federal revenue that would have been used for welfare and mass transit. Since the oil companies will shift it, the windfall profits tax is actually a large consumer tax increase that might have some spillover effect on the rest of the federal budget. Other forces, such as state legal mandates for school finance reform, inflation, and elastic state tax structure, may offset our pessimistic projections.

A threatening and more competitive social and economic context, however, requires that educational leadership exercise tremendous

Table 2–4. Classroom teachers in regular elementary and secondary day schools, by control of school, fall, 1958–1986.

Year	All School Teachers			Public School Teachers			Nonpublic School Teachers[a]		
	K–12	Elementary	Secondary	K–12	Elementary	Secondary	K–12	Elementary	Secondary
				(In thousands)					
1958	1,475	931	544	1,306	815	491	169	116	53
1960	1,600	991	609	1,408	858	550	192	133	59
1962	1,708	1,021	686	1,508	886	621	200	135	65
1964	1,865	1,086	779	1,648	940	708	217	146	71
1966	2,012	1,153	859	1,789	1,006	783	223	147	76
1968	2,161	1,223	938	1,936	1,076	860	225	147	78
1970	2,288	1,281	1,007	2,055	1,128	927	233	153	80
1972	2,388	1,292	1,046	2,103	1,140	963	235	152	83
1974	2,404	1,302	1,084	2,165	1,167	998	239	153	86
1976	2,440	1,328	1,112	2,193	1,170	1,023	247	158	89
1978[b]	2,446	1,336	1,110	2,196	1,176	1,020	250	160	90
				Projected[c]					
1980	2,360	1,327	1,033	2,104	1,160	944	256	167	89
1982	2,342	1,351	991	2,080	1,178	902	262	173	89
1984	2,371	1,393	978	2,103	1,214	889	268	179	89
1986	2,454	1,490	964	2,180	1,305	875	274	185	89

	Public School Pupil–Teacher Ratios		Nonpublic School Pupil–Teacher Ratios	
	Elementary	Secondary	Elementary	Secondary
1958	28.7	21.7	38.7	18.2
1960	28.4	21.7	36.0	18.3
1962	28.5	21.7	36.3	18.5
1964	27.9	21.5	34.3	18.3
1966	26.9	20.3	32.3	18.1
1968	25.4	20.4	29.8	17.3
1970	24.4	19.8	26.5	16.4
1972	24.0	19.1	24.5	15.7
1974	22.6	18.7	23.5	15.9
1976	21.7	18.5	22.8	15.7
1978[b]	20.9	18.1	22.5	15.6
Projected[c]				
1980	20.7	18.1	21.5	15.7
1982	20.1	17.9	20.8	15.7
1984	19.6	17.7	20.1	15.7
1986	19.1	17.5	19.5	15.7

a. Instructional staff and classroom teachers are not reported separately. All data estimated except for secondary in 1960 and elementary and secondary in 1968 and 1970.

b. Estimated.

c. Projections are based on data through 1976.

Source: Frankel (1978) and unpublished tabulations.

understanding and insight. It also suggests that education will have to compete through an even greater effort in the traditional political mechanisms of pressure groups and participation in elections. Campaign contributions and campaign work for political candidates will be increasingly important. As indicated above, we see little hope for large-scale federal increases; therefore, this elite political activity will have to focus its pressure on state government and sun belt localities. If public school finance continues to increase in terms of the percentage of state support, then local tax elections may become less important. The future may look more like Florida, where older people predominate and contend that they already paid for education once in the Midwest. Consequently, most local Florida educators realized that the state level was their only hope and reluctantly supported de facto full state assumption.

Local voter turnout and referenda analysis will become less important than elite interest group activity at the state level. A great deal will depend on the willingness of educators to coalesce among themselves and include allies such as child care and child health advocates. Fiscal outcomes will depend on state-by-state developments and on the effectiveness of political leadership by state level interest groups. The political split between parents and teachers in many states needs to be bridged. The foregoing demographic and social analysis suggests that a state policy pattern of splintered schoolmen, unable to coalesce and engaging in internecine warfare, will lead to a much lower rate of school expenditure increases than in 1970–1980. Moreover, education is about 40–70 percent of the state budgets and will be vulnerable to initiatives like Proposition 13 in twelve states that have direct democracy. Education's best fiscal strategy is militant state electoral politics with heavy emphasis on campaign contributions and grassroots workers. For example, much of the effort expended at the national level by organized teachers should be redirected to state political campaigns and lobbying.

SCHOOL GOVERNANCE IN THE 1980s— EVERYBODY AND NOBODY IN CHARGE

Along with this changed fiscal context, local school district discretion will continue to shrink. The increased reliance on nonlocal funding forces will be part of this. Specifically, the local superintendent of instruction will continue to lose his once preeminent position in setting an agenda and controlling decision outcomes (Boyd 1976). The local superintendent and administrative staff are now a reactive force trying to juggle diverse and changing coalitions across different issues and levels of government. Many school reforms disappeared, but those that left a deposit generated structural organizational additions that could be easily monitored and created a constituency. Part of the legacy of the prior era was a tremendous growth in specialized functions of the school, including administrative specialists in vocational education, driver education, nutrition, health, and remedial reading. Many of these new structural layers diluted the influence of the superintendent and local board. These specialists were paid by federal or state categorical programs and were insulated from the superintendent's influence by the requirements of higher levels of government. Their allegiance was often to the higher levels of education governance rather than the local community.

Our basic thesis is that the discretionary decision zone of local superintendents and boards became squeezed progressively into a smaller and smaller area during the last decade. We see nothing to reverse these trends in the 1980s. From the top, local discretion was squeezed by the growth of federal government, state governments, and the courts. Moreover, there was an expansionary influence of private interest groups and professional "reformers" such as the Ford Foundation and the Council for Basic Education. Interstate organizations such as the Education Commission of the States and nationally

Table 2–5. Trends in educational governance, 1980–1990.

− School board	+ Federal
− Local superintendent	+ State
− Local central administration	+ Courts
	+ Interstate organizations (school finance reform, competency education, tax limits)
	+ Private business, etc.
	+ Teacher collective bargaining
	+ Administrators bargain?
	+ Community-based interest groups (nonprofessionals)

Key: + increasing influence;
      − decreasing influence.

oriented organizations like the Council for Exceptional Children increased their role. Superintendents and local boards found themselves squeezed in terms of their decision space from the bottom by such forces as the growth of local collective bargaining contracts reinforced by national teacher organizations. A recent study by the Rand Corporation documents the incursion of teacher organizations into education policy (McDonnell and Pascal 1979; see also van Geel 1976).

The 1960s was a period of growing local interest groups, often resulting from nationwide social movements. These national social movements that penetrated the local system included such topics as civil rights, women's roles, students' rights, ethnic self-determination, and bilingual education. These nonlocal social movements spawned local interest groups that began agitating for various changes in local standard operating procedures. They advocated such changes as suspension of students, curriculum differentiation, and so on. Traditional parent groups such as PTA and AAUW that provide diffuse support of local school authorities became less influential.

Beleaguered local policymakers found that during the 1970s their decision discretion decreased due to such outside forces as economics and demography. The declining population of students and spreading resistance to increased school taxes further constrained local initiative and options. The end of the 1970s has seen a period in many states of disillusionment with professionals in general and educators in particular. Distrust has grown, and more actors squabble over a decreasing resource base at the local level for supporting public schools.

All of this is exemplified by the spreading movement of accountability, coming largely from federal, state, and court sources. Such diverse things as due process and competency-based graduation are good examples of this accountability era. Moreover, social movements in the 1970s differed from the nineteenth century. In the nineteenth century, social movements, exemplified by Horace Mann, were interested in building institutions like the schools; now, many social movements are interested in questioning these public institutions and trying to make them more responsive to forces outside the local administrative structure. Some would even assert that these social movements are fragmenting school decisionmaking in such a way that local citizens cannot influence local school policy. The litany of the newspapers reflects violence, vandalism, and declining test scores as the predominant state of public education and further encourages federal and state interventions.

In California, this situation has become so serious that schools suffer increasingly from shock and overload. The issue becomes, How much change and agitation can an institution take and continue to respond to its local clients and voters? Moreover, Californians are confronted with numerous initiatives, such as Proposition 13, vouchers, spending limits, and a 1980 proposal to cut the state income tax in half. Local citizens go to the local school board and superintendent expecting redress of their problems and find that the decision-making power is not there. The impression grows that no one is "in charge" of public education.

All of this does not mean that local authorities are helpless; rather, it means that they cannot control their agenda or structure most of the decision outcomes as they could in the past. The local superintendent must deal with shifting and ephemeral coalitions at various government levels that provide marginal advantage for a brief period. Increasingly, policy items on the local board agenda will be generated by external forces (federal, state, courts) or are reactions to proposals from the local interest group structures, including teachers. The era of the local administrative chief (e.g., superintendent) has passed with profound consequences. The state-based finance strategy outlined above will probably intensify these trends favoring nonlocal influences on education policy.

It is overly simple to characterize this changing governance structure as "centralization." There is no single central control point, but rather a fragmented "elevated oligopoly." From the local school board perspective, this latter term refers to higher authorities (federal, state, courts), outside interests (ETS and Council for Exceptional Children), local internal interests (vocational education coordinator), and other local agencies such as police and health with an impact on education. Moreover, the shift of influence to higher levels has not resulted in a commensurate loss of local influence. Parents of handicapped and bilingual students have considerably more impact in local settings than they did twenty-five years ago. Indeed, as the number of actors surrounding education policymaking increases, discretion at the school level may also increase. One outside force can be played off against another.

In sum, governance of education will become more complex and unclear; concepts such as bureaucratization and centralization imply clear hierarchies that do not exist. Changes in finance will have an impact on the 1980s governance pattern but will not be an overwhelming influence.

NOTES TO CHAPTER 2

1. Low income black voters have tended to vote for local school budget increases, but black birth rates have declined as much as whites.
2. A bill to repeal state bilingual programs passed by a two-thirds vote in the California Senate in January 1980.
3. In this section statistics on teachers are derived from NCES (1979: 81–88).

REFERENCES

Abramowitz, Susan, and Stuart Rosenfeld, eds. 1978. *Declining Enrollment.* Washington, D.C.: NIE.

Berry, Brian J.L., and Donald C. Dahmann. 1977. "Population Redistribution in the United States in the 1970's." *Population Development Review* 111, no. 4 (December): 443–71.

Boyd, William. 1976. "The Public, The Professionals, and Education Policymaking: Who Governs?" *Teachers College Record* 77, no. 4 (May).

College Board. 1979. *National Report on College Bound Seniors, 1979.*

Frankel, Martin M., ed. 1978. *Projections of Educational Statistics to 1986–87.* Washington, D.C.: National Center for Education Statistics, U.S. Department of HEW.

Hall, John, and Philip Piele. 1976. "Selected Determinants of Precinct Voting Decisions in School Budget Elections." *Western Political Quarterly* V, XXIX, no. 3 (September): 440–56.

Halperin, Samuel. 1979. "The Future of Educational Governance." Prepared for the Summer Institute of the Council of Chief State School Officers, Jeffersonville, Vermont, July.

Hamilton, Howard, and Sylvan Coehn. 1975. *Policy Making by Plebiscite: School Referenda.* Lexington, Massachusetts: D.C. Heath.

Katz, Martin. 1976. "Demographic Changes and School Finance." Croton, New York: Hudson Institute, H–I–2678–P.

Kirst, Michael. 1980. "A Tale of Two Networks: School Finance versus Tax Limitation." *Taxing and Spending* (Winter).

McDonnell, Lorraine, and Anthony Pascal. 1979. "National Trends in Teacher Collective Bargaining." *Education and Urban Society* II, no. 2 (February): 129–51.

NCES. 1979. *The Condition of Education 1979*. Washington, D.C.: Government Printing Office.

Neill, Shirley Boes. 1979. "The Demographers' Message to Education." *American Education* (January–February).

Phi Delta Kappan. 1979. (November).

Piele, Philip K. 1980. "Voting Behavior in Local School Financial Referenda: An Update of Some Earlier Projections." Address to the American Education Finance Association, San Diego, March.

Scientific American. 1979. "Science and the Citizen." 241, no. 4 (October).

U.S. Bureau of the Census. 1978. *Historical Statistics of the United States, Colonial Times to 1957*. Washington, D.C.: U.S. Government Printing Office.

_____. 1967. *Statistical Abstract of the United States, 1967*.

_____. 1971. *Statistical Abstract of the United States, 1971*.

_____. 1977a. "Fertility of American Women: June 1977." *Current Population Reports* Series P–20, no. 325 (September).

_____. 1977b. "Projections of the Population of the United States: 1977 to 2050." *Current Population Reports* Series P–25, no. 704 (July).

_____. 1978a. "Fertility of American Women: June 1978." *Current Population Reports* Series P–20, no. 330 (September).

_____. 1978b. "Geographical Mobility: March 1975 to March 1978." *Current Population Reports* Series P–20, no. 331 (November).

_____. 1978c. *Statistical Abstract of the United States, 1978*.

_____. 1979a. "Estimates of the Population of the United States by Age, Sex, and Race: 1976 to 1978." *Current Population Reports* Series P–25, no. 800 (April).

_____. 1979b. "Population Estimates and Projections." *Current Population Reports* Series P–25, no. 799 (April).

_____. 1979c. "Population Profile of the United States: 1978." *Current Population Reports* Series P–20, no. 336 (April).

_____. 1978d. "Social and Economic Characteristics of the Metropolitan and Nonmetropolitan Populations: 1977 and 1970." *Current Population Reports* (Special Studies) Series P–23, no. 75 (November).

U.S. Department of Health, Education, and Welfare, National Center for Education Statistics. 1979. *Digest of Education Statistics, 1977–78*. Washington, D.C.: U.S. Government Printing Office.

Van Geel, Tyl. 1976. *Authority to Control the School Program*. Lexington, Massachusetts: D.C. Heath.

THE PURSUIT
OF EQUALITY

3 EQUITY IN FINANCING PUBLIC ELEMENTARY AND SECONDARY SCHOOLS

K. Forbis Jordan*
Mary P. McKeown**

INTRODUCTION

Responsibility for governance and support of public elementary and secondary schools in America has shifted from a tradition of the local district having considerable discretion in finance and control of schools to current conditions under which the state assumes an increasingly active role. During the 1920s, school finance theorists drew attention to inequities that had developed within states as a result of heavy reliance upon local wealth and local decisionmaking. Concepts such as a "foundation program" under which all pupils would have access to an adequately funded educational program, a "percentage equalizing" approach under which local school officials would determine level of funding, and "full state support" of local education programs were among the proposals that offered to assure more equity in the funding of education and in the provision of local educational services. The intent of these early efforts was to provide state funds in an inverse relationship to local district wealth so that "poor" districts would be compensated by the state for their relative lack of property wealth and would have more fiscal resources for

*K. Forbis Jordan, Senior Specialist in Education, Congressional Research Service, United States Library of Congress, Washington, D.C.
** Mary P. Mc Keown, Finance Analyst, Maryland State Board of Higher Education.

their schools. The dominant approach was the foundation program, but local districts were normally permitted to supplement the foundation minimum-spending level through additional local tax efforts. This local leeway permitted a degree of inequity, as districts with higher levels of local wealth or aspirations provided funds beyond those available from the foundation programs supported from state and local sources.

This traditional pattern of school support continued until the school finance reform efforts of the mid–1960s and 1970s, when legal challenges were made to the existing state school support programs, contending that pupils were receiving unequal treatment under the current systems. Legal decisions established that education was a state rather than a local function. Thus, the state had a responsibility to provide an equitable system of school funding.

The result has been that two traditional American values have come into conflict in the financing of public education in the various states. The egalitarian position of equal treatment irrespective of circumstances has come into direct conflict with the libertarian position of freedom to choose. Governance systems for American public education have been formulated on the assumption that local school officials would have freedom to choose the level of funding for their schools, irrespective of the quantity of funds to be provided by the state. This tradition of local choice has contributed to wide diversity in expenditures per pupil among school districts within states; the result has been unequal treatment of pupils among school districts within a state. Consequently, legal theorists, political scientists, and school finance researchers have become immersed in a continuing quest for resolution of the conflict of values in the financing of the public schools. Through litigation, equal protection clauses and other articles related to education in state constitutions have become more than ideals and goals. Equity has become the focal point of inquiry and reform.

The concept of equity in the financing of state school finance programs might be described as an admirable but possibly unachievable goal, given the current state of school finance research. To achieve this goal, the assumption is made that a state school finance program can be formulated that will provide equal treatment of pupils in equal circumstances; however, efforts to achieve this goal have not been completely successful.

Researchers appear to be in general agreement that pupils do not have equal educational needs in terms of either their physical and mental conditions or their career aspirations. For example, a blind child will require services beyond those needed by a normal sighted child with equivalent intellectual ability and aspirations. In the same manner, a child gifted in music or with certain specific career aspirations may desire supplementary services and programs to assure optimal development. The combination of these examples illustrates the complexities involved in assuring equity for all pupils.

To add to problems of defining equity, common agreement has not been reached concerning elements that should be considered in the calculation of fiscal ability. Even though property wealth per pupil or some modification thereof has been a traditional measure of local school district ability to pay, questions are raised concerning this measure's appropriateness. Administration of property taxes leaves something to be desired. In addition, questions are being asked concerning the appropriateness of incorporating income, or another expression of economic activity, into the measure of a local district's capacity to support schools.

During the period between the 1920s and the late 1940s, the goal of school finance reform was to raise the level of educational opportunity in rural and burgeoning suburban school districts. Large city districts, with their more comprehensive and better financed schools, served as "lighthouses" for American education (Johns 1972). This pattern shifted as the cities lost their relative fiscal advantage and were confronted with requirements for a more extensive range of governmental services. Large cities also underwent a change in the composition of their pupil populations, requiring introduction of compensatory and remedial education programs. These developments contributed to educational finance theorists drawing attention to concepts of educational and municipal overburden. Educational overburden refers to the greater incidence of pupils with needs for high cost programs. Municipal overburden is related to the broader range of governmental services being provided in urban areas. However, these latter contentions were more a topic for theoretical discussion than political action. Only limited attention was given to them in revisions of state school finance programs in the 1960s.

Dorfman contends that the concept of equity exists at three separate levels: (1) a vaguely defined, but timeless concept that guides evolution of a popular ideal; (2) a popular ideal, but a somewhat ambiguous and changing concept that provides a practical standard against which existing laws and programs are judged; and (3) existing laws and programs that provide concrete standards against which actual administrative practice is judged (NCES 1978: 9). These three levels of definition for the concept of equity provide further evidence of the operational dilemmas involved in the quest for equity.

The concept of equity is not unique to the financing of schools; it is also a challenge in allocating funds for a variety of social welfare programs provided under governmental auspices. Perhaps the significant difference is that education has been judicially determined to be a function of state level government but is a service with a long tradition of local decisionmaking. In view of the absence of a demonstration of equity in the operation of a system for financing schools, the following discussion focuses on the concept of equity as it has been discussed relative to other social welfare programs.

DECISION ECONOMICS

In addition to being a major concern for the funding of public elementary and secondary education, the quest for equity also has been an illusive goal in other social sciences. For example, in the field of economics, there has been an interest in the collection and redistribution of income as a means of financing the welfare system. Economists have defined a welfare system as a collection of institutions that effect transfers of income from one set of individuals to another set of individuals whose members are less fortunate by some measure of "fortune" (Daly and Giertz 1972). In essence, this is the system used for financing education—taxpayers provide funds that are then distributed for the purpose of providing an education based on the need for funds, as opposed to centrally collecting and rebating funds in the proportion reflected in the collection. Some contend that one purpose of educational institutions in America is to equip students so that upward economic mobility is possible, resulting in a redistribution of income among classes of individuals over generations. If this should be true, education in the United States is a welfare system or a collection of welfare systems. Using this logic, economists have supported the outlay of public funds for education (Due 1968: 3).

Decision Theory

The philosophical underpinnings of welfare theory are found in decision theory (Kassouf 1970: 7), and the principles have direct relevance to problems associated with the quest for equity in funding education. The premise is that a decision situation exists if there is a choice among alternate courses of action; it is this choice among alternatives that has contributed to definitional and operational dilemmas related to equity in educational funding. Decision situations are an integral part of life in a complex society: Should a shopper purchase $3 worth of hamburger or $3 worth of steak? Should the old car be repaired, or should a new one be purchased? Should limited tax funds be used for police protection or recreation? Should a state school support program allocate funds so that all districts have the same amount per pupil or so that local districts may determine their level of spending per pupil? Should a state school support program assume that all pupils have similar educational needs or that pupils have different needs that can be accommodated in the funding formula? Should cost differences among districts be recognized in the allocation of state funds? These questions began with illustrations of individual choices and then move to more complex choices that confront public policy decisionmakers.

In determining which course of action, or strategy, is best, efforts should be made to examine possible outcomes. If all results of a certain strategy are known unequivocably, this is called a state of certainty. (Unfortunately, most educational funding decisions are made under conditions of extreme uncertainty.) Most economic theory is concerned with states of certainty and assumes that the decisionmaker(s) is (are) rational. This means that when faced with two possible outcomes of a strategy, called R_1 and R_2, the decisionmaker will either prefer R_1 as much as R_2 or R_2 as much as R_1. This is expressed as $R_1 \geq R_2$, $R_2 \geq R_1$, or $R_1 = R_2$.

It is also assumed that if at least three possible outcomes exist and if R_1 is preferred as much as $R_2 > (R_1 \geq R_2)$ and R_2 is preferred as much as R_3 $(R_2 \geq R_3)$, then R is preferred as much as R_3 $(R_1 \geq R_3)$. This is called the associative law of preferences.

A basic assumption is that consumers desire more or less of a good and decisionmakers face the challenge of accommodating desires of consumers in the allocation of scarce resources. Some might contend that if consumers preferred less of a commodity to more, the com-

Figure 3−1.   Consumer choice number one (*hypothetical*).

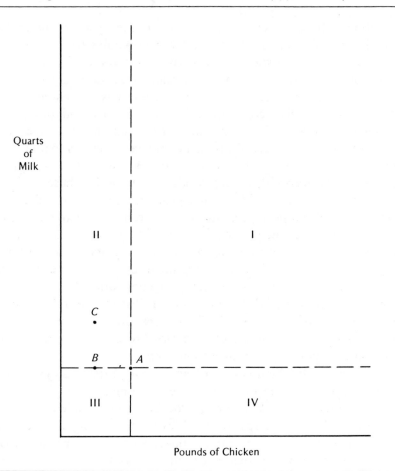

Pounds of Chicken

modity could be called a "bad" rather than a "good." Allocating public funds in a manner so that the societal need is met and the service retains a marginal image of goodness is the ultimate goal of the political process. For illustrative purposes, household shopping decisions in the following examples will be used to show the manner in which preferences dictate decisions in the allocation of resources.

Each person faces a decision situation whenever grocery shopping is done. Consider the consumer who has $10 and wants to purchase only two items, chicken and milk. The situation could be depicted graphically, as is shown in Figure 3-1, to assist the consumer in making a decision on how many of each good to purchase. Quarts of milk are plotted on the vertical axis and pounds of chicken are plotted on the horizontal axis. Every point on this graph represents some combination of milk and chicken. Point A, for example, represents five quarts of milk and five pounds of chicken. If horizontal and vertical lines are drawn through Point A, the graph is divided into four quadrants. Let those quadrants be called I, II, III, and IV. If the consumer wishes to purchase the amounts of chicken depicted by Point A, then every point in Quadrant I would be preferred to A, since all of the "baskets of goods" depicted by all the points in Quadrant I contain more chicken and more milk (and consumers always want, or prefer, more of a good). All of the points representing baskets of goods in Quadrant III would be less preferred than A, since all of the baskets in this region contain less of both goods. If any baskets of goods exist that are as desirable as A, they are in Quadrant II or III. If it is desirable to find all baskets of goods that are as equally acceptable to the consumer as Point A, the consumer might start with five quarts of milk and two pounds of chicken (Point B) and add milk until Point C is reached, which the consumer considers as good as Point A (C = A). If the consumer considers all points that represent the baskets of goods that are as preferable as A and connects these points by a line, as shown in Figure 3-2, the resulting curve would be called an indifference curve. The whole graph can be filled with indifference curves, the complete set of which is called the consumer's indifference map.

An economist might be called upon by the consumer to assist in determining which basket of goods the consumer should buy with $10. If chicken is $1 per pound and if milk is $.50 per quart, the consumer could buy twenty quarts of milk and no chicken or ten pounds of chicken and no milk. If these two points are plotted on Figure 3-2 and connected with a line, this line is called the budget line and represents all available outcomes possible from strategies the consumer could take. The consumer would be advised to choose the strategy that places him or her on the highest possible indifference curve that was drawn to represent the consumer's preferences or indifference map. This strategy would be advised, since higher curves mean greater preference, and the consumer always prefers more of a good. This point occurs where the budget line is tangent to an indif-

Figure 3–2.   Consumer choice number two (*hypothetical*).

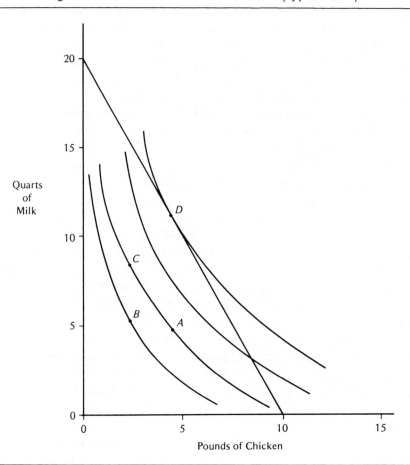

ference curve and occurs at Point D. The consumer would have been advised to maximize his or her utility function, or choice, by choosing the highest point.

Previous examples assume that the consumer is rational and that the decisionmaker can operate under conditions of certainty. However, such conditions are not characteristic of the educational decision process, for most educational decisions related to funding are made when outcomes are uncertain and without assurances that one outcome has a higher probability of yielding productive returns than another or of when such information will be available, if at all.

Moreover, clear-cut preferences among strategies do not always exist. Given the governance structure of education, funds cannot be allocated with assurances that the decrease or increase in amount will be reflected in a change in the quantity of educational programs and services or in the learning outcomes of students. Basically, sufficient information is not available. Through constraints or mandates used as conditions in the allocation of funds, efforts can be made to influence the course of events, but that assumes consensus on constraints or mandates.

To add to the dilemma, many educational decisions, especially funding choices, are made by groups of individuals, not by one person. If all members of a group have the same preferences and possess the same estimates of probability of outcomes, then the situation becomes identical with the individual decisionmaking situation depicted in the consumer's choice of how much milk and chicken to purchase. However, when members of a group have different preferences, the decision situation changes and becomes more like reality. The group may select a strategy because of tradition (schools have always been funded by local property taxes), by allowing one individual, like a dictator, to decide (e.g., the superintendent decides that there shall be no busing to achieve racial balance among the schools in the district). The "equitable" choice in an egalitarian society is to rely upon majority rule to express group preference (as in a referendum on educational vouchers); however, this may impinge upon minority rights, or conflict with broad societal goals. (For a more complete discussion of decision theory see Menges [1973].)

Arrow Paradox

In a situation involving at least three outcomes, such as efficiency, equity, and family choice, majority rule often leads to inconsistent choices. These inconsistencies are called the Arrow Paradox.[1] Arrow has shown that if a group's preferences are to follow certain "reasonable" conditions, then majority rule may not lead to a "reasonable" outcome. Even though Arrow's basic concepts were derived as a part of welfare theory, the following discussion is pertinent to education because majority rule is a part of the conventional decisionmaking process in American education as well as in welfare theory and welfare systems. The problem is that decisions based on majority rule may lead to paradoxical results and may not equally benefit all affected persons.

Arrow contends that decisionmaking can lead to irrational outcomes. Governments, however, still make decisions, which are sometimes called "optimal," so something else must intervene in the decision process. However, only a few alternatives may be available that society would consider "optimal," thus limiting available choices; or the outcome may be based on the strength of individual preferences and the revealing of those preferences to influence others. The 1978 work of Howard Jarvis and Paul Gann to pass Proposition 13 into law in California is an example of these phenomena.

Contemporary society appears to have two primary objectives or welfare functions—maximization of per capita income and equitable distribution of income among members of society. To attain these objectives, rational decisions must be made that require knowledge of individual and societal preferences and efficiency in resource allocation and use. Society appears to have strong preferences regarding equity of income distributions, although the nature of these preferences and the optimal distribution of income is difficult to specify (Due 1968: 5).

In the United States, society appears to prefer use of markets— that is, trading of goods and services in the private sector—over use of governmental activity in achievement of goals. Therefore, governmental economic activity, of which educational funding is an example, reflects societal belief that the private market economy does not attain the goals of per capita income maximization and equitable distribution of income across individuals. Thus, governmental activity in funding public schools reflects societal preferences and the desire for fairness of income patterns and relative "equity" (Due 1968: 7).

In evaluating societal preferences and changes in total satisfaction of individuals, the general consensus appears to be that any change benefiting at least one person without harming others increases total satisfaction. An optimum is attained when no further changes of this type can occur; this is called the "pareto optimal" criterion. Optimal governmental activity is determined when pareto optimality is achieved (Due 1968: 7). Since redistribution of income usually involves benefiting some at the expense of others, pareto optimality rarely occurs in decision situations involving school funding. That is, most of the changes in school finance systems in states could not be classified as pareto optimal, since one class of individuals benefits at the expense of another class. However, politicians seek changes that they perceive to be pareto optimal—that is, changes in funding of schools in which no one loses and at least one district gains. In the case of majority rule, then, the pareto optimality criterion is relaxed to achieve a relative optimality: the decision is reached that benefits those who have the majority of the votes or the political power. Thus government, whether it is state, local, or federal, relies on relative preferences of individuals to make decisions and seeks to bring societal distribution of services, such as education, to the level apparently preferred by society.

Decisionmaking by state, local, and federal governments differs from a consumer's decisionmaking in several important ways: (1) Although a consumer could decide how much milk and chicken to buy at the going price, the student, or consumer of education, cannot directly decide how much education to buy nor how much to pay for it, (2) The consumer knew what benefit(s) could be derived from the milk and chicken, while benefits from education accrue to the community as well as to the individual. The individual student or citizen may not even be aware of potential benefits (Due 1968: 37).

Individual preferences for public goods are influenced by individual tastes and emotions and the amount of information available about a good. If individuals have no knowledge of education benefits, they will not desire this good and, consequently, will be unable to reach an optimal decision or preference related to consumption of educational services and programs.

However, governmental decisionmaking related to education has assumed that it is the individual's, or the school district's, right to choose among available levels of funding or among various programs. The result of this has been that funding, and the provision of educational services, has been inequitable.

The decisionmaking process, relative to continued provision of education by local, state, and federal governments, is influenced by society's attitude toward public and private benefits of education. Theorists tend to view provision of public support for education as an investment in human capital that yields societal benefits. Total societal outputs may increase when different workers have better physical capital or when workers are supplied with more skills through education. Thus, outlays on education enhance capabilities of workers to acquire more skills, and skills enable the workers to be more productive (Benson 1975: 5). In addition, the education of one worker may improve productivity of other workers and enhance the social environment of a community (Garms, Guthrie, and Pierce 1978: 47), contributing to improved citizenship and a more cultivated society. Moreover, education improves social mobility, one of the apparent objectives of contemporary American society. If all families had to pay for education of their children and themselves, poorer families would be able to purchase less education, decreasing opportunities for social mobility (Benson 1975: 8). As society becomes increasingly mobile and interdependent, those who benefit from local governmental programs, especially education, tend to be from nonlocal as well as local populations. These "spillover" benefits may result in underfinancing of the services of education at the local level and justify outside—that is, state and federal—financial support for education (U.S. Advisory Commission 1969: 6). Thus, it becomes especially important that each recipient of the benefits of societal goods has equal access to a fair and equitable share of the benefits of that good.

This philosophical stance of each individual having a fair and equitable share of the benefits has been called "a highly esteemed value in the American culture (R.L. Johns, cited in Indiana School Finance Study 1979: 13). The concept of equality of educational opportunity is a fundamental principle of American education and is based on the value judgment that the egalitarian society is best served by extending to all children equally minimally adequate opportunity for education (Mort and Reusser 1941: 99). But how does society decide what is a "fair and equitable" share of the benefits of education for each individual? It was previously suggested that the societal decision structure, using majority rule or voting, can result in inconsistent or irrational choices (the Arrow Paradox). It was also suggested that governments try to make decisions that result in pareto optimal changes (at least one person gains and no person loses).

Thus, to reach a rational and pareto optimal decision about how best to achieve a "fair and equitable" share of the benefits of education for each individual, alternatives must be evaluated, strategies developed, and decisions made based on some ordering of personal preferences, as expressed in group preferences. In order to do this, individuals and society must be informed about private and public benefits of education. Individuals must also be willing to reveal preferences and to influence others to share preferences. It might be said that the outcome of the egalitarian decisionmaking process to provide benefits of education to all (i.e., to achieve an optimal and equitable distribution of services among members of society) results in libertarian individuals who have sufficient information to make rational choices.

If the premise is accepted that one of the primary goals of education is to bring about equitable redistribution of income, then to reach a rational decision on how best to achieve this goal, individual preferences must be known among strategies for achieving this goal so that societal, or group, preference functions can be determined.[2] Individuals may not reveal their true preferences among alternatives. It has been shown that if voting decisions on educational funding are made, outcomes can be arbitrary (Musgrave 1970), especially since each voter's satisfaction in achieving a specific result from voting (winning) is not equal to every other voter's. Voters with strong preferences usually try to persuade those with weak preferences. Thus, a solution provided by voting, even if "efficient" and pareto optimal, may not be equitable, since it is dependent upon voter preferences. Failure to pass funding referenda for public schools in many districts is an example of this.

However, this lack of revelation of preferences could be overcome. Let a game be devised in which revelation of preferences would be unnecessary, where when "players" act rationally in their own self-interest, the outcome will be "equitable." Let this game be played by a rich person and a poor person who are given a set of incomes to be divided among them. The rich person may elect to split the incomes sixty-forty, giving the larger share to the poorer person, since this distribution would give the rich person greater satisfaction than a fifty-fifty split. If the poor person accepts this, the distribution is "equitable," since it was arrived at in an egalitarian manner and the resulting outcome was pareto optimal. Both individuals, without revealing their true preferences, would be involved in the decision, and both would be better off as a result (since the incomes being split would not have been theirs to begin with).

However, the poor person could decide to split sixty-forty, giving the larger share to the rich person, since this split would bring the poor person greater satisfaction. This decision could still be equitable, egalitarian, and pareto optimal. In determining the pareto optimal outcome, the procedure itself need not be pareto optimal, because both players in the game may prefer an alternative to "fair division." For example, assume that the players toss a coin to determine who will receive the larger share and the winner is unwilling to accept another division. The outcome would be pareto optimal, since both players are better off, even though over time the two players might prefer to share equally (Lua and Raiffa 1958: 363–65). Therefore, "equitable" redistribution of income over time, through education, might be achieved through conditions, and decisions, that are not pareto optimal.

Some group understanding or definition of "fairness" and "equity" is necessary, then, for the group decision situation relative to the redistribution of income or the provision of education to redistribute income. In terms of the provision of educational services to the citizenry of a town, state, or country, what is the "equitable" provision of education, of resources for education, or of access to the education or funding? If one of the primary goals of modern society is fair and equitable redistribution of income among members of society, and if this goal is seen to be approachable through the avenue of education, how does society determine if each individual has fair and equal access to means to achieve this goal?

Despite the attention this concept has received, there seems to be little consistent agreement on the meaning of equality of educational opportunity. Economic decision theory would suggest that this lack of agreement on a definition of equity could exist for several reasons: (1) lack of adequate information; (2) unwillingness or inability of individuals who are involved in the group decision to reveal true preferences among strategies and outcomes. Indeed, if the Arrow paradox is a valid description of reality, then lack of a consensus definition of equity is the expected outcome. Because more than two individuals are involved and their preferences among more than three strategies to achieve equity differ, it would be expected that the group decision process would yield more than one outcome, that these outcomes might be inconsistent, and that results could be viewed by one set of members of the group as "irrational."

Berne (1979: 44) notes that definitions of equity involve value judgments and that rational individuals could have differing answers to value-laden questions about equity. Thus, in the rational decision-making process, relative to provision of equal educational opportunity, it would be expected that differing viewpoints, or definitions, of equity would result. Berne additionally observes (1979: 48) that whatever the individual's definition of equity, there are many ways of measuring societal attainment or nonattainment of the societal value of equal educational opportunity.

Berne's position is consistent with two early writers in the field of the measurement of inequality. Most early work was concerned with differentiating between measures of inequality; but in 1917, Allyn Young noted that any degree or measure of the degree of inequality must in itself be referred to a standard or to a value judgment about a normal or justifiable degree of equality. Young went on to note that "the most serious aspect of the distribution of incomes . . . is the general distortion of the whole income scheme, reflecting as it does presence of a high degree of inequality in distributions of opportunity" (1917: 482–83). Mary Jean Bowman (1945: 626) agreed and added that "any single graphic device is incomplete." She implied that since use of more than one measure of equality can give different results, it is better to examine a range of measures of inequality. Recent researchers appear to have observed this principle in assessing equity of school finance programs.

In 1933, Yntema ranked inequalities in sets of income data by eight statistical measures of inequality and demonstrated that the measures yielded inconsistent results, just as Berne and Stiefel (1979) did in 1979. Yntema concluded that it would be better to use more than one measure of a social welfare system's equality or inequality. Pioneering work in the field of inequality measurement was conducted in the early decades of this century by Pareto (1897), Gini (1921), and Lorenz (1905). In 1930, Dalton pointed out that any measure of inequality or equality is based on some concept of social welfare and that economists should be concerned with the concept of social welfare that underlies the measures of equality.

In determining the measures, or measure, of equality, at least two alternative objectives are available—to obtain a ranking of distributions (for example, to determine if prereform distribution of revenues for schools is more or less equitable than the postreform distribution) or to obtain some quantifiable measure of the degree of inequality between the two distributions. Most measures of equity, however, are concerned with the difference in inequality between two distributions (Atkinson 1970: 245).

Equity Measures

The use of specific measures of equity is not dependent upon the definition of equity, and equity measures discussed here could be used with modifications to assess equity by several definitions. Although a thorough discussion of measures of equity is not possible here, major measurement tools will be noted. The following symbols will be used in describing formulas.

$$M \quad = \text{median level of revenues,}$$

$$N \quad = \text{number of districts,}$$

$$P_i \quad = \text{number of unweighted pupils in district } i,$$

$$R_i \quad = \text{revenues per unweighted pupil in districts } i,$$

$$\overline{x}_p \quad = \text{mean revenues per pupil,}$$

$$\overline{x}_p \quad = \quad \frac{\displaystyle\sum_{i=1}^{N} P_i R_i}{\displaystyle\sum_{i=1}^{N} P_i}$$

$$w_i \quad = \text{wealth per unweighted pupil in district } i,$$

$$\overline{w} \quad = \text{mean wealth per pupil,}$$

$$\text{where} \quad \overline{w} \quad = \quad \frac{\displaystyle\sum_{1}^{N} P_i W_i}{\displaystyle\sum_{1}^{N} P_i}$$

Measures of inequality were first conceptually formulated by Pareto and were defined by the equation

$$\log N = \log A - \alpha \log x$$

where N = the number of individuals having that (income) or larger, x = income size, and A and α are constants. This basic formulation, called Pareto's law, was widely used in the first half of this century to measure inequality in distribution of wealth. The coefficient α, the slope of the straight line, was used as the measure of inequality.

The larger or steeper the slope, the smaller the inequality. However, Pareto himself suggested that the less the slope of the curve, the more equality. The confusion of the meaning of the slope of the Pareto curve was one of the factors that led to the discrediting of this measure as an index of equality (Kuznets 1933).

Corrado Gini's (1921) original work in the measurement of inequality of distributions took account of the aggregate of the variable being measured above or below a certain point in the distribution and took the form of

$$\log N = p + \delta \log A_x$$

where x = size of the variable being measured, usually income; N = number of persons receiving this level of income or less; and A_x = aggregate income above the level x. The slope δ, of the line in the Gini formula was used as an index of degree of inequality in the distribution and was called the "index of concentration." The smaller the slope of the Gini curve, the greater the equality.

When Lorenz developed the "Lorenz curve," the most widely used technique to indicate differences in degree of inequality in different distributions (Bowman 1945: 613), Gini directed his attentions to development of the interpretation of the Lorenz curve and devised the "concentration ratio," which is the Gini measure that will be discussed later. This concentration ratio measures comparative degrees of inequality on the assumption that equal arithmetic differences in a variable are to be regarded as of equal importance.

Atkinson's Index.   This measure has the following form:

When $E > 0$ and $E \neq 1$:

$$1 - \left[\left(\sum_1^N P_i \ (x_i / \overline{x}_p)^{1-E} \right) / \left(\sum_1^N P_i \right) \right]^{\frac{1}{1-E}}$$

where E is the measure of the degree of inequality aversion or relative sensitivity to transfers at different income levels. As E rises, more weight is attached to transfers at the distribution's lower end. This measure has the advantage of being able to weight the bottom of the distribution to reflect value judgments of the evaluators. Atkinson's index may take values between 1 and 0; the smaller the value, the less dispersion there is and thus greater equality.

Coefficient of Variation. This measure is defined as the square root of the variance divided by the mean or as the standard deviation divided by the mean. The coefficient of variation determines equality relative to the mean of the distribution and can assume values greater than zero. As the coefficient of variation decreases (approaches zero) variability decreases; thus equality is greater.

Correlation Coefficients. These measures express degree of relationship between two or more variables and can take any value between −1 and +1. The correlation coefficient for two variables can be defined as the covariance of the two variables. A correlation coefficient not only summarizes strength of association between two variables but also compares the strength of the relationship. The closer to +1 or −1, the stronger the relationship. Spearman's Rho and Kendall's Tau are only two of the many correlation measures.

Elasticity Coefficients. Elasticity coefficients are wealth neutrality measures where the measure is computed by multiplying slope of a regression equation by mean revenues per pupil. Various elasticity coefficients can be used, but all are based on some form of regression equation. Generally, since these measures are based on the slope of a line, the smaller the slope, the greater the equality.

Federal Range Ratio. The federal range ratio is defined as the difference in per pupil expenditures at the fifth and ninety-fifth percentiles and is expressed as a ratio. This ratio can assume any value greater than or equal to 1 and is a measure of the disparity between expenditures for two groups of children. The closer the ratio is to 1, the more even is the distribution of expenditures. This measure is used in federal guidelines as an expenditure equality measure.

Gini Coefficients. The Gini coefficient is a measure that reveals how far the distribution (of revenues or expenditures or some other variable) is from providing a specified percentage of students with the same percentage of the variable being measured and is sensitive to transfers affecting the middle of the distribution. The Gini coefficient is computed as:

$$\frac{\left(\sum\limits_{i=1}^{N} \sum\limits_{j=1}^{N} P_i P_j \mid x_i - x_j \mid \right)}{2 \left(\sum\limits_{i=1}^{N} P_i \right)^2 \ \overline{x}_p}$$

The measure most commonly used in school finance research is called the bivariate Gini index, or a coefficient of concentration, because it is based on the distribution of two variables. The index is computed by ranking school districts from high to low upon some specification of wealth or revenues and calculating a cumulative percentage of students starting from the poorest. A similar ranking is completed for revenues or some other measure, and these two variables are then graphed to form a Lorenz curve. If a specified percentage of students receives the same percentage of funds, the line graphed will be a 45° line; this line is called the Lorenz curve. Any dispersion from the 45° line indicates that fiscal neutrality has not been achieved. The Gini index is usually greater than zero; negative Gini indexes can occur, but their interpretation is ambiguous.

McLoone Index.   The McLoone index is the ratio of the actual total revenues for students below the median to the total revenues, if all students were at the median, and is calculated by the following formula:

$$\frac{\sum\limits_{i=1}^{J} P_i x_i}{M_p \sum\limits_{i=1}^{J} P_i}$$

where districts *l* through *J* are below M_p (the median). This measure is based on the dollars required to raise the lower half of pupils to the state median expenditure. The larger the index, the closer the measurement is to equality.

Permissible Variance.   Like the McLoone Index, permissible variance is based on dollars needed to bring all districts spending below the median level of per pupil expenditure to the median level and is calculated by the following formula:

$$\frac{\sum\limits_{i=1}^{J} P_i x_i}{M \sum\limits_{i=1}^{J} P_i}$$

The larger the ratio obtained, the closer to equality is the measurement.

Range.   Range is defined as the difference between the high and the low observation per pupil. It is always greater than zero; the higher the measure, the greater the disparity that exists.

Restricted Range.   Restricted range is defined as the difference between two specific points in the distribution, usually where specific points are defined as percentiles. It is employed more often than the range because of the sensitivity of the range to extreme values. It is always greater than zero, and the higher the value obtained, the greater the disparity.

Relative Mean Deviation.   This measure is defined as the absolute value of differences between each district's per pupil expenditure and mean per pupil expenditure, divided by total expenditures in the distribution. It is expressed as a percentage and is calculated as:

$$\frac{\sum\limits_{i=1}^{N} P_i \;\; \overline{x}_p - x_i}{\overline{x}_p \sum\limits_{i=1}^{N} p_i} \; .$$

The smaller the value, the closer to equity. This measure is insensitive to transfers on the same side of the mean.

Standard Deviation of Logarithms.   This measure is concerned with transfers from the mean and is calculated as:

$$\sqrt{\left(\sum_{i=1}^{N} P_i \; (\log u - \log x_i)^2 \right) / \sum_{i=1}^{N} P_i}$$

where u = mean per pupil expenditure. This measure weights transfers at the lower end of the distribution more heavily.

Theil Coefficient.   This measure shows how far each student is from receiving an equal share of revenues (or expenditures) and is calculated as follows (Theil 1958: 32):

$$\sqrt{\frac{\sum (x_i - \overline{x}_p)^2}{\sqrt{\sum x_i^{\,2}} + \sqrt{\sum \overline{x}_p^{\,2}}}}$$

The Theil measure has values from zero to one and the larger it gets, the greater is the disparity from each child receiving an equal share. Perfect equality would be indicated by a coefficient of zero.

Variance.   Variance is defined as the average of the squared deviations from the mean and is expressed as:

$$\frac{\sum\limits_{i=1}^{N} P_i \, (\overline{x}_p - x_i)^2}{\sum\limits_{i=1}^{N} P_i}$$

The variance can be greater than or equal to zero. The smaller the variance, the smaller the variation from mean value. Use of this measure implies increasing inequality aversion (Atkinson 1970: 256).

EQUALIZATION OF EDUCATIONAL OPPORTUNITY

To determine which or how many of the various equity measures to apply in any given situation to assess the "equity" of a school finance plan, "equity" must be defined so that what is being measured is known. As suggested earlier, alternate definitions of "equity" have been advanced by persons in diverse professions—for example, educators, jurists, parents, scholars, civil rights workers, and legislators. Each definition of equity depends on available information as well as on value judgments and preferences. Many writers have tried to explain the concept of equality of educational opportunity by confining their attempts to a narrower field, like fiscal equalization.

The first clear expression of the concept of fiscal equalization of educational opportunity was made in 1906 by Cubberley when he suggested that all children in the state are equally important and all are entitled to have the same advantages.

Theoretically, all the children of the state are equally important and are entitled to have the same advantages; practically this can never be quite true. The duty of the state is to secure for all as high a minimum of good instruction as is possible, but not to reduce all to this minimum; to equalize the advantages to all as nearly as can be done with the resources at hand; to place premium on those local efforts which will enable communities to rise above the legal minimum as far as possible; and to encourage communities to extend their educational energies to new and desirable undertakings. (1906: 17)

Updegraff expanded this definition in 1922 by suggesting that state support programs should be variable, depending on the amount of local effort for schools. Updegraff noted that the purpose of state aid for education was to guarantee to each child, regardless of where that child happens to live, opportunity equal to that of any other child for the education that will best fit the child for life (Updegraff and King 1922).

In 1923, Strayer and Haig provided what has been called the "greatest impetus to the concept of fiscal equalization and educational opportunity" (Indiana School Finance Study 1979: 20) by asserting that state programs of school support should furnish each child with a minimum of educational opportunities and that the tax burden for the support of these schools should be borne by individuals in relation to their ability to pay (Strayer and Haig 1923: 173).

The concept of equalization of educational opportunity as it existed in the 1920s was described by Strayer and Haig as follows:

> There exists today and has existed for many years a movement which has come to be known as the "equalization of educational opportunity" or the "equalization of school support." These phrases are interpreted in various ways. In its most extreme form the interpretation is somewhat as follows: The state should insure equal educational facilities to every child within its borders at a uniform effort throughout the state in terms of the burden of taxation; the tax burden of education should throughout the state be uniform in relation to tax-paying ability, and the provision for schools should be uniform in relation to the educable population desiring education. Most of the supporters of this proposition, however, would not preclude any particular community from offering at its own expense a particularly rich and costly educational program. They would insist that there be an adequate minimum offered everywhere, the expense of which should be considered a prior claim on the state's economic resources. (Strayer and Haig 1923: 173)

Paul Mort (1924), a student of Strayer's, advanced these ideas and suggested that a satisfactory equalization program should have objective measures of educational needs as a primary component. Morrison (1930) further expanded the concept of equalization of educational opportunity by noting that the great disparities of wealth among school districts caused great inequities in opportunities for education. He maintained that states would not meet the educational needs of children and simultaneously provide an equitable system of taxation to support schools. Early definitions of equity, then, were primarily related to equalization of educational opportunity.

There are other interpretations of the early interest in "equalization": instead of an interest in equality of educational opportunity, it has been interpreted as interest in the equalization of local tax burden or effort (Superintendent's Advisory Commission 1972: 3). This interpretation appears to be based on the attempts to mandate minimum levels of services by states without regard to differences in local resources available to support services (Burke 1957). The notion of equal effort by taxpayers in support of education seemed to be one of the causes for action in the case of *Serrano v. Priest* (1971).

During the Great Depression and the first half of the 1940s, there was little written on equalization of educational opportunity or any other kind of equalization. Occasionally a volume would appear commenting on disparities in services or expenditures for children in different school districts within a state (see, e.g., Johns and Morphet 1952; Mort and Cornell 1941). The issue of equality of educational opportunity did not receive renewed attention until the case of *Brown v. Board of Education* reaffirmed in 1954 that every child was entitled to an equal opportunity to educational services and that equality could not be provided in racially separate school systems. This finding was in agreement with the Supreme Court ruling of 1890 that "clear and hostile discrimination against particular persons or classes" is a violation of the 14th Amendment (*Bell's Gap* 1890).

Egalitarian goals for school finance systems in the states did not appear to be of high priority in the early 1950s, as evidenced by this statement in a school finance textbook:

> Indeed, equality of educational opportunity is not attainable in a single school system. It is not even desirable in a decentralized school system. What is desirable is a rising standard of educational services, not equality of service. This means that it may be more important to see that the able and willing can move ahead than to concentrate upon correcting the worst conditions (Burke 1957: 561).

This feeling did not persist into the 1960s: much activity in the area of the definition of equality and the measurement of that equality in educational finance took place. Johns and Morphet declared (1960: 138) that "Equality of educational opportunity is an objective to which practically every citizen has subscribed in theory for many years." They went on to add:

> Equality of educational opportunity for all does not mean that every person should have the same program of education. Instead it means that every person should have the opportunity for the kind and quality of education that will best meet his needs as an individual and as a member of the society in which he lives (1960: 138).

James reaffirmed that inequalities of expenditure, tax effort, and fiscal capacity are important focal points for research in the finance of education (James, Thomas, and Dyck 1961), while McLure (1964) and Lane (1964) explored interdistrict inequalities. A procedure for determining the equity of a state's school finance plan was developed in California that revealed that in the most wealthy districts in a state, taxpayers and pupils, or both, had a decided advantage over taxpayers or pupils in a less wealthy district (Morphet 1958).

After the mid decade of the 1960s, social upheavals began to occur in inner cities. Riots protesting inequality of treatment among races were commonplace, and minority group militancy served to bring the subject of inequality in educational opportunity to the front pages. The Coleman report on schools had significant impacts outside educational circles and provided impetus for a movement in the judiciary to examine the concept of equalization of educational opportunity. In all of these movements throughout society, the question of what was to be equalized seemed to be answered by "equalization of educational opportunity" (Superintendent's Advisory Commission 1972: 6).

The question "Equalization of what?" is still being answered differently by different people, depending on the information that these people have and their value judgments. As was suggested earlier, it is to be expected that differing definitions will exist. Different solutions to the problem of providing equity will continue to be formulated because of differing orderings of preferences among solutions in the quest for equity among those involved in the decision-making process.

There have been many formulations or attempts to define "equity." One definition advanced in the economic literature differentiates between horizontal equity and vertical equity. Horizontal equity is the equal treatment of equals, while vertical equity is the unequal treatment of unequals. Horizontal equity could refer to the equal treatment of one class of students as opposed to another class of students or to equal treatment of taxpayers in one community as opposed to another group of taxpayers in a different community. Equal treatment might require equal tax burdens for equal ability to pay, equal revenues per pupil for equal ability to pay, or some other "equalness" among groups of "equals."

On the other hand, vertical equity requires that differences between individuals or groups will be recognized. Advocacy for vertical equity suggests a progressive tax system to bring about taxpayer equity or a system of weightings to recognize special needs of some students to bring about pupil equity. Berne (1979) has noted that value judgments play an important part in these definitions. Value judgments are needed to determine how to measure degree of inequality among equals. Since value judgments are required, it is possible for rational individuals to arrive at different decisions based on different orderings of value preferences. Consequently, different definitions are almost the expected result.

Concepts of horizontal and vertical equity do not identify the group on which equity is to be assessed. Should the unit of analysis be students, taxpayers, the family, or some other "group?" The choice of children as the group upon which to focus the measure of equality is based on the concept of equality of educational opportunity. Since education is a public service, it should be provided equally to all. Assuming that education improves the quantity and quality of the nation's human capital, all children should be treated equally in the process of providing education (Odden, Berne, and Stiefel 1979: 9). If the family or taxpayers are chosen as the target groups for measurement of equity, this gives credence to the contention that taxpayers are the group that pays for education and that resources are used to purchase goods other than education.

If the student is the appropriate unit upon which to base the measure of equity, then the issue to be addressed is whether equity means equal treatment of equals or unequal treatment of unequals. Vertical equity, in the case of students, might demand that special needs of different students be recognized in the measure of equity. It has long been recognized that certain student groups, like the economically disadvantaged, non-English speaking, and handicapped, "need" more resources in order to be provided with an education equivalent to that of other children. Some would content that virtually all children have special needs or talents; each child, then, is "special" in some way and requires "special" treatment to assure maximum development. The concept of need may also apply to the child's age or grade level. School finance programs in several states have weighting factors to provide additional funding for students in grades 9–12 or in kindergarten and prekindergarten programs. Early childhood specialists might also contend that since learning at the kindergarten and primary school level is so important, additional funds should be spent on those pupils. Various educational policy choices are involved in development of pupil-oriented state school finance programs, and the challenge is exacerbated by diversity in educational delivery systems along local school districts within a state. The concept of pareto optimality is extended to educational as well as political decisionmakers.

If the group under consideration is the school district, different needs may be postulated for different school districts. For example, the concept of municipal overburden as a measure of the special needs of urban school districts is often advocated. Support can also be found for recognition of special needs for transportation, geographic size of the district, or other demographic factors in determining the special needs of school districts. Rather than being empirically based, decisions are based on value judgments, with various answers among rational individuals.

If the taxpayer is the unit upon which measures of "equity" are to be based, different positions may be expressed concerning "equal" in relation to taxpayers. Since different school districts have different abilities to pay for educational services provided to students, some would maintain that equality would be achieved when each district provides, or requires, an equal tax burden for equal ability to pay. Issues related to this include whether all taxes should be included in the measure of the tax burden borne by the individual taxpayer or whether only the educational tax burden should be considered. In determining tax burden, some would consider only the burden of local taxes, while others would consider the burden of both local and state taxes. Another related issue is the measure used to compute taxpaying ability. Some would recommend only a property measure of wealth, while others would include income as a measure of ability to pay.

Another issue in the area of the taxpayer's ability to pay is whether the concept of willingness to pay should be considered. The decision of taxpayers of one district to tax themselves above the required level to provide special services to children in that district is a taxpayer value judgment. Some consider that it is a parent's right to spend more on the education of his or her child, while others would consider this inequitable. The question is twofold: Should this inequity be permitted? And if so, should the state consider this additional effort in the allocation of funds?

After determining the unit upon which to focus in the quest for equity and making the decision to address both horizontal and vertical equity, the issue of equity in terms of what is to be equalized becomes the next question. The focus might be on resources available for education, process of education, or outputs of the educational process. These three categories might also be identified as inputs, process, and outputs.

Inputs of or to the educational process include the resources, in terms of dollars, materials, facilities, and teachers, as well as abilities that children bring with them to the classroom. Traditionally, equity has been measured on the basis of dollars—either revenues or expenditures. Revenues are funds that are made available for spending on the educational process, while expenditures are monies that are spent or revenues that are consumed during the process. (Revenues do differ from expenditures, especially in those areas where deficit financing of current operations is permitted. Revenues may also differ from expenditures because of the different times for collection and expenditure of revenues.)

Revenues are used to purchase different inputs to the educational process (books, supplies, teachers, support personnel, etc.). Some view provision of educational inputs in terms of different amounts that can be purchased with the same dollars in separate areas. These persons would argue that dollars must be adjusted to reflect differences in buying power (by cost of education indexes).

Another portion of the inputs to the educational process that could be measured to assess equity are nonmonetary resources, such as quality of teachers, books, and supplies. Measurement problems abound in this area; however, the sophistication of educational research might someday reach a point at which these inputs could be assessed and required to be equal for equals or unequal for unequals.

Some would contend that the educational process itself should be made more equitable or that an equivalent process should be provided for all children. Others would contend that outputs from the educational process, or what individual and societal benefits are accrued from the educational process, should also be equal. If one of the main goals of education is to provide for equitable distribution of incomes across individuals, then the outcome of education in achieving this goal should be measured to determine whether the benefits of education have accrued equally to all. Practically, both individual and societal benefits from education are difficult to measure with accuracy. If output measures of the educational process were threshold performance on an achievement test or passage of a minimal competency test, it would be possible to determine if every child did indeed achieve a prescribed level and thus had gained a level through the access to education.

Recent discussion has emphasized that equity should be viewed on two dimensions, horizontal and vertical. Traditional approaches in school finance have given attention to horizontal equity, with an emphasis on providing equal levels of funding through a state aid program. This equity can even result in different levels of funding per pupil among school districts because of different levels of effort as found through percentage equalizing or district power equalizing approaches; or, it may provide for equal levels of funding through a foundation program. Vertical equity is operationalized by recognition that districts are different in terms of distributions of pupils who require high cost programs to assure equalization of educational opportunity or access to programs that will permit maximum development of potential. Another dimension of the concept of vertical equity relates to differences in expenditures that are required to provide equivalent educational services and programs, referred to as cost of education or, in some cases, as municipal overburden. A basic problem with this latter concept of equity is the lack of agreement or research concerning how school finance programs can address the problem.

Another way to address the definitional problem is to consider ways in which different people view the term. Philosophers and some educators consider the term to be an idealistic goal sought by all, but not achievable in its ultimate sense. In this context, no effort is made to develop a precise definition. Legislators cope with the term through the process of balancing power blocks and forces to bring about slow progress, but within the context of political reality reflected in so-called "hold harmless" clauses. The result may be help for some, but only limited progress in terms of philosophers' idealistic aspirations. The latter position has frustrated school finance reformers as they have sought redress through the judicial system. They have sought an absolute definition of equity that will assure equal treatment for all. A basic problem is reflected in the statement that there is nothing so unequal as the equal treatment of unequals, whether the unequals be pupils or school districts in the funding formula. With pupils, the inequality is recognizable, but with school districts the task may be more difficult, for inequality may be in the economic status of the district and its citizens or in the composition of the wealth of the district. The difficulties associated with acceptable definitions of equity have been reflected in the decisions of the courts for the past several years, starting quite some time before the litigation of the 1970s.

JUDICIAL VIEWS OF EQUITY

The concept of equity has evolved through the judicial system from early decisions that established the power of the state to tax on a statewide basis and return funds on the basis of pupils to more recent decisions addressing intricacies of financing schools such as fiscal neutrality, equal expenditures among school districts within a state, differences in educational needs of pupils, and the impact of other governmental expenditures on availability of funds for education.

In the absence of an empirically based body of knowledge to guide courts in the area of equity in educational programs and services, recent cases initiated by advocates for pupil equity have focused on equal distribution of funds. Since the local property tax has been a major source of revenue for schools and since wide variations exist in the property wealth per pupil among local districts, this equity movement has resulted in a high level of attention being given to use of the property tax as a means of school support. Judicially imposed equity standards have altered the property tax as a primary vehicle to support education. It should not go without notice that a property tax revolt has occurred simultaneously with the school finance equity movement and that expenditure and revenue limitations have been imposed in many states. As a result, there has been considerable misunderstanding concerning the position of the courts relative to reliance upon the property tax as a means of school support, but courts have not prohibited its continued use. Rather, they have found that the current pattern of taxation for schools has resulted in unequal distribution of funds among school districts within states.

Much recent litigation has been based upon the equal protection and due process requirements of the Fifth and Fourteenth Amendments to the U.S. Constitution and individual state constitutional provisions that relate to education or include phrases similar to those found in the Fifth and Fourteenth Amendments. Desegregation cases from the federal courts have provided much of the legal precedent, with the goal of invoking equal protection rights to force equitable distribution of tax funds for education. These cases have a significant legal implication in terms of their impact upon the discretion of the state legislatures to levy taxes, gather revenues, and redistribute those revenues. As with cases concerning reapportionment and desegregation that have imposed judicial requirements upon state legislatures, this legal action has the potential of limiting the power of the state legislatures to regulate, control, and fund education.

In contrast to what might be assumed by some persons, judicial precedents related to funding for education have a long and evolutionary history. In the early years, the aggrieved party was the taxpayer, who challenged the power of the state to impose a tax on the basis of wealth and then distribute proceeds on some basis of need as defined by the state. This pattern of litigation began before the turn of the century and continued through the first half of the 1900s.

In the 1960s, litigation was initiated from the standpoint of pupil rather than taxpayer equity. In these and more recent cases, aggrieved students have contended that funding should not be dependent upon the local school district's fiscal ability. Litigants have challenged the right of the state to establish and maintain systems of taxation for education that resulted in differential treatment of students in similar circumstances.

Another group of cases has focused on the state's duty to provide differential treatment in the allocation of funds to compensate for variations in educational programs that are required for different students. The contention in these cases has been that the state has the responsibility to allocate funds in a manner designed to correct for social, economic, or individual mental or physical deficiencies of students.

Constitutional Authority of the State

The traditional position of the courts toward powers of state legislatures over education and taxation has been that the judiciary would not intervene unless plaintiffs clearly demonstrated that the legislature did not have the power to take particular action or that action had been exercised arbitrarily or capriciously to the prejudice of the rights of some citizens (Johns, Alexander, and Jordan 1972: 474). Legal precedent suggests that legislative acts would be upheld unless an action obviously violated prescribed constitutional standards.

In early cases, courts were asked to determine if the state school support programs or financing arrangements for education created unconstitutional classifications or violated equality and uniformity of taxation requirements. Most state constitutions contain equality and uniformity of taxation clauses. Therefore, litigation was in state court systems. However, in some instances, the equal protection provision of the Fourteenth Amendment to the U.S. Constitution was used as the basis of litigation; then the action was in the federal courts.

The equal protection clause of the Fourteenth Amendment was applied to the area of state taxation by the Supreme Court of the United States in 1890. Among the findings were that equal protection did not require identical treatment, that classifications or differences in treatment must be based on real differences, that differences in treatment must have some relevance to the purpose for which the classification was made, and that differences in treatment must not be so great as to be wholly arbitrary (Johns, Alexander, and Jordan 1972: 474). This basic precedent has contributed to the evolution of the concept of "reasonableness" as a guideline in school finance litigation. Rather than applying the concept of strict scrutiny to the taxation and distribution system for school revenues, courts have left the decisions to the discretion of the state legislatures and have indicated that redress is with the people, not with the courts (Ibid.).

The court went further by stating that, for taxation to be equal and uniform in the constitutional sense, it is not necessary that all persons receive equal benefits or that all persons participate in each particular benefit (*Sawyer* 1912). As this legal precedent guided school finance litigation until the late 1960s and early 1970s, the courts refused to apply equal and uniform taxing provisions to the state school-financing programs. However, in virtually all of the early litigation, plaintiffs were seeking to deter the movement toward more equal treatment in terms of available funds for pupils and school districts. Essentially, courts were ruling that equal protection clauses could not be used by taxpayers to prevent equalization of resources among school districts within a state.

In the 1960s, litigants in South Dakota sought to prevent implementation of an equalized state school support program. A taxpayer in a district with no schools challenged the statute because tax receipts were not uniformly distributed, even though uniformly raised (*Dean* 1964). The courts ruled that constitutional provisions requiring uniformity and equality related to the levy of taxes and not to distribution or application of the revenue derived therefrom.

Quite in contrast to the recent school finance litigation in which plaintiffs have been students, early cases were initiated by taxpayers seeking relief from a taxing system that collected taxes on the basis of ability to pay and redistributed proceeds on the basis of an educational program. The issue was too much equalization or equity in school financing, not too little. Since cases were brought by taxpayers, courts applied the equal protection clause only in terms of taxation. The only test applied to revenue distribution was that the system be rational and reasonable. Several decisions recognized that varying economic conditions existed among school districts and that these conditions provided a logic and rationale for allocation of funds on a basis that otherwise might appear to be somewhat arbitrary. In this series of cases, courts did not determine what degree of equalization in school funding was required, but that the state could take action to bring about greater equity in the allocation of funds for local school districts.

Constitutional Responsibility of the State

Since the decision of the U.S. Supreme Court in *Brown v. Board of Education* (1954), increased attention has been given to rights of an individual under the equal protection clause of the Fourteenth Amendment and similar provisions in constitutions of individual states. In contrast to earlier cases in which the plaintiff was the taxpayer, the plaintiff in this landmark case and in the following series of cases was the student who had received differential treatment because of the manner in which the state school support program had been constructed. Following *Brown*, the landmark decision in this area is considered to be the *Serrano* (1971) decision of the Supreme Court of California.

The current status of education under the Constitution of the United States is somewhat unclear. In *Brown* (1954), the Supreme Court was specific in confirming that education was the most important function of state and local governments and that such education must be available to all on equal terms. However, in *San Antonio Independent School District v. Rodriguez* (1973), the Supreme Court failed to indicate that education was a guaranteed right under the Constitution. The Court heard the contention that the Texas system for financing schools violated the equal protection clause in the manner in which the state's school-financing system relied upon local property taxes as a source of revenue. In *Rodriguez*, the Court ruled that the Texas system was a rational approach to school finance and did not operate to the disadvantage of a suspect class of citizens. Even though the Texas system had recognized deficiencies, the Court found that the school finance plan was a reasonable means of accomplishing the state's interests in local control of educational decisions and did provide a minimum educational program to all districts. The final judicial reasoning in this case is somewhat similar to previous decisions in the above-mentioned taxpayer-initiated cases.

Among possible explanations for confusion between the direction provided by the two decisions are that *Brown* has principally been applied to intradistrict desegregation issues and that a favorable decision for the original plaintiffs in *Rodriguez* would have resulted in a national mandate for states to reform their school-support-financing mechanisms. A decision in this latter direction would have resulted in a dramatic shift in the traditional distribution of powers among the federal and state governments in the field of education. The effect of *Rodriguez* has been to reinforce the traditional position that the state is preeminent in educational matters (Jennings 1979: 398). Thus, redress for inequities in state school-financing systems resides in the state rather than federal courts and must be litigated on the basis of state constitutional provisions. "In retrospect, *Rodriguez* may have served a very useful function by blocking a facile federal solution to a quite complex problem, the origins of which are to be found in state capitals (Jennings 1979: 403).

The basic precedent for the recent wave of school finance reform may be found in the *Serrano* (1971) decision by the California

Supreme Court. In the original decision, the court ruled on the basis of the equal protection clause of the California Constitution and provisions in that constitution related to education. Rather than relying upon the ruling that the state school support system should be rational, as had been the case in previous decisions, the court declared that education was a fundamental interest for pupils and was to be protected by the constitution. The court indicated that the level of funding for a child's education should not be dependent upon the wealth of the local school district.

The principal point in the first decision was that spending per pupil did not have to be equal, but that available revenues could not be dependent upon the wealth of the child's parents and neighbors. Further, the court did not prescribe the remedy, but left this decision to the legislature. As *Serrano* evolved since the original 1971 decision, the court has indicated that significant disparities in spending per pupil are not to be permitted. Subsequent passage of Proposition 13 in California resulted in a further closing of the gap in spending among California school districts. The combination of the court decision and the constitutional amendment restricting property tax revenues appears to have contributed to California's making significant strides in attaining a higher level of equity, as determined by a reduction in the degree of expenditure disparity among school districts.

Provisions of state constitutions related to education typically refer to a system of schools to be maintained by the state in which education is to be "free" and contain provisions calling for the state to provide a "thorough and efficient system." This latter constitutional provision served as the basis for the often-quoted *Robinson* (1973) case in New Jersey, which was decided at the lower court level shortly after the U.S. Supreme Court ruled on *Rodriguez*. The basic difference between the two cases was that *Robinson* was initiated in the state courts on state constitutional grounds and *Rodriguez* was litigated in the federal courts on federal constitutional provisions. Original plaintiffs prevailed in *Robinson*, and New Jersey's system for financing schools has been revised; however, plaintiffs did not prevail in *Rodriguez*, and the issue has not been litigated on the basis of the Texas state constitution.

In *Robinson*, the court relied upon the wording in the New Jersey Constitution that indicated that the legislature was to provide for the maintenance and support of a thorough and efficient system of free schools for the instruction of all children in this state between the ages of five and eighteen years. The court dismissed the argument that educational quality could not be measured by differences in educational expenditures and indicated that the state's fulfillment of its constitutional obligation would be determined in large measure by the amount of funds available for the education of children in the local school districts of the state.

In most of the litigation, the courts have been rather patient with the legislatures, giving consideration to ways in which state school support programs could be revised to meet the requirements of the court. However, national attention was focused on New Jersey when that state's supreme court ordered schools closed when the legislature was unable to enact a school finance reform measure. With the closing of the schools, the New Jersey legislature enacted a tax reform measure to fund school finance reform legislation that met the court's minimum requirements, and the schools were then reopened.

Even though *Robinson* has received considerable national attention, earlier decisions may be found in Ohio (*Miller* 1923) and in Oklahoma (*Miller* 1924). The court in Ohio stopped short of requiring the legislature to revise the state school support program so that "a thorough and efficient system of common schools" was provided, but did note that "educational need" could be a factor used in allocating funds to local school districts. The same pattern was followed in Oklahoma, but the court placed a "duty" on the legislature to furnish a "degree of uniformity and equality" of education and to afford as "far as practical, equal rights and privileges to all its youth" for education. Even though the court went beyond the positions stated in the earlier cases that established the power of the state to use the equalization approach in funding education, these two cases did not require the state to fund schools in a particular manner.

In another decision, *Horton v. Meskill* (1977), the Connecticut Supreme Court followed the *Robinson* precedent and relied upon language of the state's constitution. However, the court went further and also followed some of the *Serrano* precedent in finding that a child's "right to an education is so basic and fundamental that any infringement of that right must be strictly scrutinized." The court found that more funds were available for the education of children in property-rich towns than in property-poor towns and that the present system favored the property-rich districts. As with the original

Serrano ruling, the *Horton* ruling indicated that absolute equality in spending was not required and that the property tax could still be used as a means of providing revenue for schools.

A recent ruling by the Washington Supreme Court (*Seattle* 1978) has questioned the use of special local access levies, or leeway taxes, as a means of supporting education. The ruling indicated that the Washington Constitution was clear in placing primary responsibility on the state to fund schools and found that the level of funding provided by the state was not sufficient to fund a basic education for the children attending all public elementary and secondary schools in Washington. The legislature was charged with devising a system of funding schools that would assure that each child attending the public schools was provided with a basic education. This is the first instance in which a court has charged the legislature with assuring adequacy in funding, and the decision may be a forerunner of future litigation depending upon specific provisions of a state's constitution.

Considerable attention was given to recent litigation challenging the school-financing system in Ohio on the grounds that the constitutional requirement of a "thorough and efficient" system was not being provided. The original plaintiffs prevailed in the lower state court (*Cincinnati* 1978) and at the appeals level, but lost with the Ohio Supreme Court (*Board of Education* 1979). In its ruling, the court relied heavily upon the *Rodriguez* precedent and ruled that Ohio's school finance system had its faults but did meet the rationality test.

Litigation has also occurred in New York and Colorado. The New York *Levittown* (1978) case raised additional issues relating to "educational overburden" and "municipal overburden." The concept of educational overburden refers to additional funds required by school districts with large numbers of handicapped, disadvantaged, or non-English-speaking students. The lower court accepted the contention that higher levels of expenditures are required to provide adequate services to these children. Plaintiffs also argued that the state financing program should recognize the local tax burden that accrues to certain school districts because of the necessity to provide additional police and fire protection services. This case is somewhat unique in school finance litigation because of the support given in the decision to this latter contention. However, the case is being appealed, and it remains to be seen if the lower court's *Levittown* decision will be upheld.

In Colorado, the *Lujan* (1979) plaintiffs relied upon the equal protection clauses of the state and federal constitutions. In view of the disparities in expenditures associated with differences in wealth per pupil, the court found that this disparity was suspect. Further, the court ruled that the state's constitutional provision requiring a "thorough and uniform" educational system was being violated. As with New York, this decision is being appealed.

The *Levittown* case is not the first instance in which the educational overburden issue has been raised. In two earlier federal court cases, *Burruss* (1970) and *McInnis* (1969), plaintiffs contended that additional educational need existed in school districts with high incidences of low income families and that the state should recognize this condition in the state school support program. In both instances, the Court decided against the plaintiffs. The Court recognized that the condition might exist, but denied the action because of the absence of "judicially manageable standards." Both cases were litigated in the 1960s, and some observers speculate that outcomes might be different in the current judicial arena because of the considerable amount of school finance research that had been conducted during the intervening period.

As illustrated in the previous discussion, the concept of equity may be considered from a variety of perspectives. During the reform decade of the 1970s, major efforts have been devoted to assuring equal access for all children to fiscal resources within a state irrespective of local school district level of wealth. Differential treatment of school districts has become the reform goal, with only limited attention being given in reform efforts to differential treatment of pupils.

Judicial decisions provide general principles relative to the concept of equity but fail to provide concise definitions or guidelines sought by instigators of the legislation. From the various court decisions, the following minimum observations seem pertinent:

1. Redress for the inequities in state school support programs is like to be found in state rather than federal courts.

2. Technical wording of the state constitution appears to have become increasingly important in guiding the decision of the court.

3. Courts have established that the state legislature can enact state school support programs that provide for equalization in state funding for schools and can provide different levels of funding per child based on variations in educational needs of students.

4. Equity has been interpreted in terms of equal levels of fiscal resources rather than equality of educational process or outcome.

5. Courts have not stipulated precise remedies, but have left corrective action to the legislative process.

6. Even though the issue has only been raised in the Washington case (*Seattle* 1978), the next wave of litigation may be to identify the educational program and service components or funding level required to meet state constitutional provisions.

PROGRESS IN ATTAINING SCHOOL
FINANCE EQUITY

At least nineteen states are considered to have enacted school finance reform legislation since the early 1970s, usually with the intent of providing for increased equity in the funding for elementary and secondary schools in the state (Berne and Stiefel 1979: 10). In instances such as California and New Jersey, action was required to meet the mandate of the state supreme court, but in other states such as Kansas, Michigan, Colorado, Florida, Illinois, Minnesota, New Mexico, Utah, and Wisconsin, the legislative action was a result of educational, social, economic, and political pressures. In the following discussion, attention will be given to several research studies that have attempted to measure relative progress toward equity that has resulted from legislative actions.

Problems emerge from efforts to ascertain the increased equity that has resulted from school finance research efforts. First, states exhibited different levels of equity before enacting reform legislation. In some instances, a state may have already had a relatively equitable program; therefore, limited progress may have resulted from the "reform" legislation. However, the state may rank rather high among all states in terms of the level of equity in the state school finance program.

Second, various equity measures are based on different assumptions concerning what constitutes a desirable level of equity. States have had varying goals as they have enacted school finance reform legislation. The result is that a state may not have improved its ranking on the expenditure disparity measure, but if the state enacted a reward for effort program that encouraged greater disparity, one would not have expected a reduction in disparity to occur because of the enactment of the reform legislation. In view of the lack of a universally accepted operational definition of equity and variations in state intent, it would seem that efforts to measure equity in a state should be tailored to the legislative intent in that state, rather than applying standards that are inappropriate in terms of state policy.

A third possible problem area is that currently available data do not permit recognition of factors such as differences in level of funding required to provide adequate educational programs for students with special needs or allow for necessary adjustments in expenditure data to cope with cost variations that may be associated with population density or sparsity or differences in economic conditions among local school districts within a state. Legal theorists, researchers, and practitioners appear to be in general agreement that equal expenditures per pupil among all school districts within a state will not support an equivalent quantity and quality of educational programs and services for all pupils. This problem is further compounded by lack of agreement concerning (1) the amount of additional funds that should be provided for pupils with various special needs—for example, handicapped, disadvantaged, limited English-speaking ability—and (2) acceptable techniques for allocating funds in a manner that will neutralize the effect of different economic conditions among local school districts.

To further add to the frustration related to equity determination, a fourth problem is that the goal of the state in the reform effort may not have been to address the issue of pupil or educational equity, but rather to provide for greater taxpayer equity without equal regard for the impact upon the level of spending for education programs among school districts. An interesting aspect of this problem is that advocates of taxpayer equity have often sought some type of expenditure or revenue controls and the result has usually been a reduction in expenditure disparities among local school districts. Of course, such decisions have often been made without regard for the impact upon the ability of the school district to address the educational needs or economic conditions that may require additional funds.

The discussion of these four problems illustrates the complexities involved in conducting statistical analyses of a state's current equity level or progress in achieving equity over a period of years. Especially evident is the difficulty in conducting such analyses independent of the implicit or explicit policy goals of the decisionmakers. The two major efforts to assess the equity level of a national sample of states (Berne and Stiefel 1978–1979; Brown, Ginsberg, Killalea, Rosthal, and Tron 1978) did not compare the policy goal(s) of the states with the equity standard to ascertain if the result of the legislation had been congruent with intent. The same basic point may be made concerning the Rand study (Carroll 1979) of five "reform" states. Most of the research assumed that "a pupil is a pupil" and did not include intrastate economic data; consequently, differences in educational need and economic conditions were also ignored. In view of the current state of the art in school finance research, the studies referred to in the following discussions have limitations that circumscribe their validity or usefulness.

Equity research efforts in the 1970s have been characterized by extensive use of statistical measures of the impact of state school finance programs upon individual school districts. The unit for analytic purposes has been per pupil expenditures or revenues in the district, but data have been aggregated at the district rather than the pupil level. Aggregation at this level ignores intradistrict variation in resources per pupil, but these latter differences have not been analyzed because of the lack of sufficient data. However, district analyses do represent an advancement over the work of Johns and Salmon in which state and local revenues for each state were analyzed for comparison of equity positions (Johns, Alexander, and Stollar 1971: ch 4).

A recent effort exploring measures of equity has been sponsored by the National Institute of Education, Ford Foundation, and Education Commission of the States (Odden, Berne, and Stiefel 1979). Absence of data on a national basis has been one of the severe restrictions in efforts to study equity on a multistate basis, but the cooperative sought to solve this problem through involvement of school finance researchers from throughout the nation. As possibly the most comprehensive effort from the standpoint of exploring alternative statistical techniques to measure equity, based on the earlier work of Berne and Stiefel, this effort will likely serve as the departure point for additional refinements in equity measurement techniques.

Across the equity measures, Odden, Berne, and Stiefel found that only a few states ranked consistently at the top or the bottom of the equity rankings related to revenue disparities and relationship between revenues and wealth. In this analysis, they also found that none of the high-ranking (i.e., most equitable) states had a state school support program that used a guaranteed yield or power equalization state school support plan (1979: 42–46). This was to be expected, since both of these approaches to school support contain elements that equalize state funds on the basis of the level of wealth and effort, thereby making these equity measures somewhat inappropriate in terms of the policy goals inherent in the state school support program.

In an analysis of the pattern in twenty-one states over a time period, Odden and his colleagues found that nine of the states had reduced their revenue disparities on two equity measures. The interesting point is that all nine of these states were among those that had been classified as reform states. In a somewhat cautious analysis of the findings in the study, the authors reviewed the tendency of states to move in the same direction over time on equity measures that considered revenue disparity and the relationship between revenues and wealth. Their findings were that of the twenty states, seven moved the same way on all four measures related to wealth disparity and the revenue–wealth relationship, sixteen moved the same way on three of the four measures, and only three states moved in opposite directions on the measures (Odden, Berne, and Stiefel 1979: 42–46). However, in view of the lack of complete agreement of the data, a case study approach might be used to isolate factors that contributed to the differences in outcomes on the four equity measures related to revenue disparities and wealth–revenue relationships. Findings suggest that movement in a positive direction on the revenue disparity and wealth–revenue equity measures can result from school finance reform.

In contrast to other studies reviewed later in this discussion, Odden and his colleagues made efforts to include state funding adjustments that recognize the special needs of high cost students in calculating equity in ten states. The equity measure improved in some instances, and the authors indicated that inclusion of student needs could affect equity statistics (Odden, Berne, and Stiefel 1979: 47–53). Rather than including a uniform factor for all states, revenues were adjusted in terms of the state funding mechanism. The authors did not discuss inadequacies of the approach but noted that further research would be needed before an adequate picture could be presented of school finance equity measures that recognized variations in student need among local school districts.

In a more technical discussion of the research, Berne and Stiefel (1979: 19) noted that horizontal equity of school children had been improved in school finance reform states, but that data were not available to determine if vertical equity or equalization of educational opportunity had been enhanced by reform efforts. This analysis used multiple measures of equity and included nonreform as well as reform states so that group comparisons could be made. Berne and Stiefel called attention to complexities in the equity determination when they indicated that reform had made a difference, but that research must consider the applicable equity principle and appropriate measures for that principle in determining equity progress resulting from implementation of school finance reform legislation (Ibid.).

Persons seeking universally applicable strategies for bringing about reform will receive little help from Berne and Stiefel's conclusions, for they suggest that variables that influence reform are not easily manipulable by policymakers. However, they did indicate that the likelihood of reform was greater when inequity was great (Ibid.). This latter point illustrates why it is somewhat difficult to determine progress being made in a state in which inequity is not great and in which legislative intent is to address intricacies of vertical equity and equalization of educational opportunity. Traditional equity measures and available data often do not lend themselves to the type of analysis required in the states that have moved to more advanced stages in the quest for equity.

The experience of school finance reform in New Jersey does not appear to have achieved the results that some anticipated. In an analysis of the results of the New Jersey school finance legislation, Goertz has indicated that the "new school finance law in New Jersey is no more equalizing than the old one, despite a 50% increase in state aid dollars" (1978: 6). The interaction of mandatory budget "caps" or limits, local choice, and use of some of the new state funds for property tax relief contributed to the lack of impact on the reduction in expenditure disparities among local school districts (Goertz 1978: 14). Use of the expenditure disparity approach to determine progress toward equity in New Jersey contained inherent limitations. The state had enacted a school finance formula using a guaranteed tax base. The effect of this approach is to base the amount of state funds on the level of effort being made by the local school district. The equity goal is to equalize on the basis of wealth neutrality rather than expenditure disparity; consequently, policies inherent in the legislation were not consistent with those that under-lie use of expenditure disparity as the measure of equity.

As emphasized earlier, resolution of the school finance search for equity is being found in the state legislatures, and the New Jersey action is illustrative of the manner in which the art of legislative compromise results in meshing of values rather than in an immediate attainment of the level of equity sought by legal theorists. Also, this instance provides an example of the importance of using multiple equity measures in analyzing the effect of school finance reform leg-islation. The point of debate is related to whether or not the intent of the court was followed in the type of legislation used to resolve the legislative–judicial impasse, and some type of judicial challenge may be required to secure the answer (Jennings 1979: 395–414).

Carroll (1979) studied the impact of school finance reform efforts in five states in terms of taxing and spending in local school districts, use of funds in local school districts, and reasons why reforms did not achieve equalization aims. Among the findings were that district revenues had increased in all five states, some progress had been made in attaining a more equal distribution of revenues per pupil, and greater progress had been made in bringing about equalization in tax rates among school districts in the five states. In addition, many advantages previously enjoyed by wealthy districts had been elimi-nated by the reform. Carroll indicated, however, that reforms had "not much affected the distribution of revenues between poor chil-dren and rich children, while the tax rates levied by disproportion-ately poor districts increased relative to those levied by districts serving higher-income populations" (1979: vi).

Reform efforts purportedly did not achieve their objectives be-cause of the diversity of objectives and the difficulty in meeting objectives that were often in conflict. An example of the inadequacy of current equity measures was illustrated in the Florida cost of liv-ing adjustment, which was considered to have a disequalizing effect. The current state of the art in measuring equalization does not per-mit consideration of intrastate cost differences than an adjustment purports to accommodate (Carroll 1979: vii). Therefore, its equaliz-ing impact cannot be determined. This latter point is also relevant to attempts to measure the level of equity that has been attained in those states that have levels of population sparsity that result in "necessary" small schools and school districts.

As with the discussion of New Jersey, a further problem was related to the legislative intent, for some states may have sought to attain equity in one step while others viewed the activity as evolutionary or did not enact legislation that would bring about reduction in expenditure disparities among local school districts. A recurring point in the quest for equity is emphasized by one of Carroll's (1979: 17) conclusions: equalization, if it is to be attained, comes about by leveling the distribution of revenues and increasing the share of state revenues, rather than by a redistribution of existing revenues.

In congressional testimony, Ginsburg relied on a study of the changes in disparity among all of the states between 1970 and 1975 (Hearings 1977). Among the findings were that regional patterns were not found among states with the greatest disparity, more populous states tended to have greater disparity, and less populous states tended to have less disparity. States with relatively few school districts also tended to have less disparity. No allowance was made for the level of disparity, or equity, in 1970, but the study indicated that only about one-third of the states had made observable progress during the five years. One interesting point from the study was that states with the reputation of being a "reform state" had not uniformly reduced their within-state disparity in revenues among local school districts. However, such states as Illinois, Michigan, Iowa, Kansas, Wisconsin, New Mexico, and Florida reduced their level of disparity, and these states are usually found on the list of "reform" states. In the discussion, the study noted that variations in special needs of students had not been recognized in the analysis nor had efforts been made to measure equity on other measures (Hearings 1977: 282).

These research efforts illustrate the difficulties in conducting multistate studies of school finance equity. One of the basic difficulties is lack of comparable data among states; efforts are underway to resolve this problem. The National Center for Education Statistics (NCES), under Section 1201 of Public Law 95–561, has been given responsibility for developing biennial profiles of the level of equity for all states. Even though all factors related to equity will not be encompassed in the reports, they may provide the impetus for assembling a more comprehensive data base. However, these studies will merely report the status of the states on selected equity measures. They will not relate those measures to the school finance program in each state and the degree to which stated and implied goals of that program have been attained in terms of appropriate equity measures. Statistical expressions cannot provide the answer to this latter question; consequently, additional research in the form of case studies may be required to provide a more adequate picture of the equity in a given state.

PROSPECTS FOR THE 1980s

When one contemplates possibilities of the 1980s and beyond regarding financing of public elementary and secondary schools, various scenarios can be proposed. Extremes range from a return to the pre-Cubberley days of wide variations in expenditures per pupil and in educational opportunity to an era in which fiscal allocation decisions are made in a manner that assures complete equity (horizontal and vertical) for pupils, school districts, and taxpayers. The likelihood is that neither of these will materialize and that the situation will be somewhere between the two extremes. Continuing progress toward equity is likely, for, as Berne and Stiefel (1979: 19–20) have indicated, reforms of the 1970s have improved horizontal equity in approximately one-third of the states. Data and conceptual problems will continue to be challenges to the measurement of and attainment of higher levels of vertical equity.

Prospects for greater simplicity in the definition of and agreement on precise definitions of equity in school financing do not appear to be among the forecasts for the 1980s. With increased research efforts and greater involvement by state courts and state legislatures, there may be some sharpening in the definition of equity. Support for this latter contention may be found in the assumption that advancements in research efforts and greater judicial activity will reduce the number of preferences; therefore, a consensus on the meaning of equity may be reached more easily. That position may be applicable to court efforts and researchers; however, such may not be the case with legislatures because of the larger number of persons involved in the decision situation and because of diverse public interest goals and pressures.

In the absence of a uniformly accepted definition of the concept of equity as related to the funding of education, one is left with the contention that equity is the dream of the idealist, a term so complex that it virtually defies a singular definition. Thus, the challenge for the school finance professionals is to identify and explain school finance public policy choices. Even though a measure may be uniformly accepted as an expression of theoretical equity from a research standpoint, the measure may not be appropriate from a public policy analysis perspective because of a lack of congruence with public policy. The stated or implied goal in a particular state's legislation may be in opposition to or irrelevant to underlying equity measure assumptions. Contrary to the desires of various interest groups, in the absence of a direct mandate from the courts, a state legislature can enact and implement school finance legislation without considering theoretical equity implications.

Evaluation of the equity in school finance programs on a national basis could appropriately be based on a set of "standard" equity measures to provide theoreticians and national policy figures with interstate comparison. However, as stated previously, such comparisons may be of questionable validity. This latter point is especially critical in view of the federal position on school finance indicated in the *Rodriguez* decision of the Supreme Court. Consequently, under the governance system for education in the United States, it would appear to be equally important that a program's evaluation be in terms of those equity measures that are congruent with policy goals of the legislation, so long as those goals have a sufficient level of social acceptability. Thus, the ideal system would involve a continuing linkage from the macro or national principles to the state's goals or intent so that interested public policy figures would have maximum information.

Unless there is a significant movement toward greater centralization of management and decisionmaking in education, it is likely that the concept of equity will continue to focus on allocation of funds in a manner that will equalize inputs for education. To attain this first level goal, the demographic diversity of pupils, schools, and school districts dictates that equity measures give attention to such concerns as the following:

- The optimal levels of funding required to assure that each child has access to an appropriate educational program that recognizes differences in psychological, physical, emotional, and cultural conditions and occupational aspirations; and

- Variations in the cost of delivering equivalent educational programs and services that are attributable to differences in the prices of goods and services among local school districts or to the sparsity or density of population and/or enrollment among districts.

The assumption underlying these two major areas for concern is that equity for the taxpayer will be addressed from the perspective of assuring equal treatment for legislatively or judicially prescribed classes. Equity in the taxation system is a concern that relates to revenues for the full range of governmental services. The uniqueness of the concern for taxpayer equity in education relates to education being a state function; therefore, taxation systems for education should not have an unequal impact upon similar taxpayers among the school districts in a state.

Two strong traditions of public education in the United States have been decentralization and diversity rather than uniformity. A major reason for the evolving interest in equity has been the inequities and inadequacies resulting from diversity. The ultimate hope is that the concept of pareto optimality will prevail in the political system, to assure that equality of educational opportunity is provided for all children in a public school system that receives its equitable share of public funds.

NOTES TO CHAPTER 3

1. Arrow, Kenneth J., *Social Choice and Individual Values* (New York: John Wiley & Sons, 1951). Arrow specified five reasonable conditions under which groups make rational decisions: (1) There are at least three possible outcomes, and at least two individuals are involved in the decision situation. (2) If one outcome is preferred to another for a set of individual preferences, the preference does not change when other outcomes are considered. (3) If there exist other alternative outcomes, the original preferences do not change when the other alternatives are considered. (4) For each pair of alternatives, there exists some grouping of individual preferences such that society prefers one alternative. (5) There is no dictator. For a more complete discussion of this phenomena, see Luce and Raiffa (1958: ch. 14).

2. Due (1968: 37–38) has noted that it is not necessarily in the best interests of individuals to reveal their preferences, if their tax burden is dependent upon the preferences they indicate, especially since most individuals lack adequate information upon which to reach a decision. Benson (1975: 7) additionally notes that individuals will not necessarily voluntarily contribute (tax themselves) to provide societal benefits nor let their preferences be known.

REFERENCES

Atkinson, A.B. 1970. "On the Measurement of Inequality." *Journal of Economic Theory,* p. 245.

Bell's Gap Railroad Company v. Pennsylvania, 134 U.S. 232 (1890).

Benson, Charles. 1975. *Education Finance in the Coming Decade.* Bloomington, Indiana: Phi Delta Kappa, Inc.

Berne, Robert. 1979. "Alternative Equity and Equality Measures: Does the Measure Make A Difference?" In *Selected Papers in School Finance.* Washington, D.C.: USDHEW.

Berne, Robert, and Leanna Stiefel. 1978–1979. Working Papers No. 6–16. New York: Public Policy Research Institute, Graduate School of Public Administration, New York University.

_____. 1979. *State School Finance Reform: Some Optimistic Findings.* Working Paper No. 16. New York: Public Policy Research Institute, Graduate School of Public Administration, New York University, June.

Board of Education of City School District of City of Cincinnati v. Walter, 58 Ohio St. 2d 368, 390 N.E. 2d 813 (1979).

Bowman, Mary Jean. 1945. "A Graphical Analysis of Personal Income Distribution in the United States." *American Economic Review* XXXV (March): 607–28.

Brown v. Board of Education of Topeka, 347 U.S. 483 (1954).

Brown, Lawrence L. III; Alan L. Ginsburg; J. Neil Killalea; Richard A. Rosthal; and Ester O. Tron. 1978. "School Finance Reform in the Seventies: Achievements and Failures." *Journal of Education Finance* 4 (Fall): 195–212.

Burke, A.J. 1957. *Financing Public Schools in the United States.* New York: Harper and Bros.

Burruss v. Wilkerson, 310 F. Supp. 572 (W.D. Va. 1969), *aff'd per curiam* 397 U.S. 44 (1970).

Carroll, Stephen J. 1979. *The Search for Equity in School Finance: Summary and Conclusions.* Santa Monica, California: The Rand Corporation, R–2420–NIE, March.

Cincinnati v. Walter, 10 003D 26 (1978).

Cubberley, Ellwood P. 1906. *School Funds and Their Apportionment.* New York: Teachers College, Columbia University.

Daly, G., and F. Giertz. 1972. "Welfare Economics and Welfare Reform." *American Economic Review* (March): 131–38.

Dalton, H. 1930. "Measurement of the Inequality of Incomes." *Economic Journal* XXX: 348–61.

Dean v. Coddington, 81 S.D. 140, 131 N.W. 2d 700 (1964).

Dorfman, William B. 1978. *Educational Opportunity* (Washington, D.C.: NCES U.S. Dept. of HEW, 1978).

Due, John F. 1968. *Government Finance, Economics of the Public Sector.* Homewood, Illinois: Richard D. Irwin, Inc.

Garms, W.I.; J.W. Guthrie; and L.C. Pierce. 1978. *School Finance: The Economics and Politics of Public Education.* Englewood Cliffs, New Jersey: Prentice-Hall, Inc.

Gini, C. 1921. "Measurement of the Inequality of Incomes." *Economic Journal* XXXI: 124–26.

Goertz, Margaret E. 1978. *Where did the 400 Million Dollars Go? The Impact of the New Jersey Public School Education Act of 1975.* Princeton, New Jersey: Education Policy Research Institute, Educational Testing Service, March.

Hearings before the Subcommittee on Elementary, Secondary and Vocational Education, Committee on Education and Labor, House of Representatives, 95th Cong. 1st sess., p. 13. 1977. *School Finance Act of 1977 and Equalization Efforts.* Washington, D.C.: U.S. Government Printing Office.

Horton v. Meskill, 172 Conn. 615, 376A. 2d 359 (1977).

Indiana School Finance Study. 1979. *Final Report of the Foundation Program Sub-Study.* Indianapolis.

James, H.T.; J.A. Thomas; and H.J. Dyck. 1961. *School Revenue Systems in Five States.* Stanford, California: Stanford University School of Education.

Jennings, John. 1979. "School Finance Reform: The Challenge Facing Connecticut." *Journal of Education Finance* (Spring): 398.

Johns, R.L. 1972. "The Coming Revolution in School Finance." *Phi Delta Kappan* 18, 20.

Johns, R.L., and E.L. Morphet. 1952. *The Problems and Issues in Public School Finance.* New York: Teachers College, Columbia University.

_____. 1960. *Financing the Public Schools.* Englewood Cliffs, New Jersey: Prentice-Hall.

Johns, R.L.; K. Alexander; and K.F. Jordan. 1972. *Financing Education: Fiscal and Legal Alternatives.* Columbus, Ohio: Charles Merrill Publishing Co.

Johns, R.L.; Kern Alexander; and Dewey H. Stollar, eds. 1971. *Status and Impact of Educational Finance Programs.* Vol. 4. Gainesville, Florida: National Educational Finance Project.

Kassouf, Sheen. 1970. *Normative Decision Making.* Englewood Cliffs, New Jersey: Prentice-Hall.

Kuznets, S.S. 1933. "National Income." In *Encyclopedia of the Social Sciences,* vol. XI, pp. 205–24. New York: The MacMillan Co.

Lane, R.P., ed. 1964. *Special Educational and Fiscal Requirements of Urban School Districts in Pennsylvania.* Philadelphia: Fels Institute of State and Local Government.

Levittown v. Nyquist, Index No. 8208/74 (Nassau County Supreme Court), June 23, 1978.

Lorenz, M.C. 1905. *Publications of the American Statistical Association* (New Series) 9: 209–19.

Luce, R., and H. Raiffa. 1958. *Games and Decisions.* New York: John Wiley and Sons.

Lujan v. Colorado State Board of Education, Civil Action No. C–73688 (District Ct. Col.), March 13, 1979.

McLure, W.P. 1964. *The Public Schools of Illinois.* Springfield, Illinois: Office of the Superintendent of Public Instruction.

McInnis v. Ogilvie, 293 F. Supp. 327 (N.D. Ill. 1968) *aff'd sub. nom.* 394 U.S. 322 (1969).

Menges, G. 1973. *Economic Decision Making: Basic Concepts and Models.* London: Longman, Kropp, Ltd.

Miller v. Korns, 107 Ohio St. 287, 140 N.E. 773 (1923).

Miller v. Childers, 107 Okla. 57, 238 P. 204 (1924).

Morphet, Edgar L. 1958. *Financial Equalization in the Public Schools of California.* 1959 Legislative Problems No. 1. Berkeley: Bureau of Public Administration, University of California.

Morrison, Henry C. 1930. *School Revenue.* Chicago: The University of Chicago Press.

Mort, Paul R. 1924. *The Measurement of Educational Need.* New York: Teachers College, Columbia University.

Mort, P.R. and F.G. Cornell. 1941. *American Schools in Transition.* New York: Teachers College Press.

Mort, P.R., and W.C. Reusser. 1941. *Public School Finance, The Background, Structure, and Operation.* New York: McGraw-Hill.

Musgrave, R.A. 1970. "Pareto-Optimal Redistribution." *American Economic Review* 60 (December): 991–94.

National Center for Educational Statistics. 1978. *Educational Opportunity, The Concept, Its Measurement, and Application, Highlights.* Washington, D.C.: U.S. Government Printing Office.

Odden, Alan; R. Berne; and L. Stiefel. 1979. "Equity in School Finance." Report No. F79–XX, Education Commission of the States. Denver, Colorado, July. Unpublished.

Pareto, V. 1897. *Cours d'economie politique.* Lausanne.

Robinson v. Cahill, 62 N.J. 473, 303 A.2d 273 (1973).

San Antonio Independent School District v. Rodriguez, 411 U.S. 1 (1973).

Sawyer v. Gilmore, 109 Me. 169, 83 A 673 (1912).

Seattle School District No. 1 v. State of Washington, 585 P.2d 71 (1978).

Serrano v. Priest, 96 Cal. Rptr. 601, 437 P. 2d 1241 (1971).

Strayer, George D., and R.M. Haig. 1923. *The Financing of Education in the State of New York.* Report of the Educational Finance Inquiry Commission. New York: The MacMillan Company.

Superintendent's Advisory Committee on School Finance. 1972. *Definition, Measurement, and Application of the Concept of Equalization in School Finance.* Springfield, Illinois: Office of the Superintendent of Public Instruction, August.

Theil, H. 1958. *Economic Forecasts and Policy.* Amsterdam: North Holland Publishing Company.

Updegraff, Harlan, and Leroy A. King. 1922. *Survey of the Fiscal Policies of the State of Pennsylvania in the Field of Education.* Philadelphia: University of Pennsylvania.

U.S. Advisory Commission on Intergovernmental Relations. 1969. *State Aid to Local Governments.* Washington, D.C.: April.

Yntema, Dwight. 1933. "Measures of the Inequality in the Personal Distribution of Wealth or Income." *Journal of the American Statistical Association* 23: 423.

Young, Allyn A. 1917. "Do the Statistics of the Concentration of Wealth in the United States Mean What they are Commonly Assumed to Mean?" *Journal of the American Statistical Association* XV (March): 471–84.

4 CAN EDUCATION BE EQUAL AND EXCELLENT?

*John E. Coons**

From its infancy the rule in *Serrano v. Priest* (1971) has been widely misunderstood as a norm of equality in educational spending. *The New York Times, The Wall Street Journal,* and the media in general persist in this delusion; even some California legislators remain innocent of the truth. Nor is the judiciary itself immune; the New Jersey Supreme Court has been suffering this fantasy version of *Serrano* since 1973. Maybe there is no cure for this egalitosis, but one last time recall that the decision tolerates differences in spending of any magnitude.

The rule in *Serrano* —commonly known as "fiscal neutrality"— holds that spending may not be affected by the amount of available taxable wealth per pupil. Dollars for a child's education may not be made to differ according to the presence in his district of oil wells or shopping centers. Why such a rule? Because the proximity of oil wells is irrelevant to both the child's needs and to any other legitimate policy goal of education. That is all *Serrano* says.

This conclusion need not interfere with spending $5000 of tax money per child in Beverly Hills, if someone could suggest a reason for doing such a thing, and in fact someone has. That reason is local

*John E. Coons, Professor, Boalt School of Law, University of California, Berkeley.

The editor and the officers of the American Education Finance Association wish to express their appreciation to the *Journal of Education Finance* and to the author for permission to reprint this article. This article was originally prepared for presentation to the Woodrow Wilson Center and to the American Education Finance Association.

131

willingness to sacrifice for education. There are finance systems available that stress local preference. They are called "power equalizing" and make it possible for high-rolling lighthouse districts to exist, imposing the sole condition that such districts bear a local tax rate commensurate with that borne historically by their poorer neighbors. All *Serrano* forbids is high spending with a low tax rate. It would not cramp the style of anyone who cares enough to spend the very most.

Consider the following fiscally neutral system for a state. It comes in three parts. First, the state gives each district $1000 per pupil from general revenue. Second, from the same source come varying amounts for high cost areas, vocational schools, bilingual instruction, the gifted, desegregation—indeed, for anything rational. Third, the state invites the districts to add on whatever they like according to the following formula: each mill of locally voted property (or income) tax authorizes the district to spend an additional $50 per pupil. If one mill raises less than $50 in District X, the difference is subsidized by the state; if one mill raises more than $50 in District Y, the difference is recaptured. The result, in compliance with *Serrano*, is full local control of the budget above the state subvention; all districts enjoy equal power to add on, and as between two districts with equal state categorical aid, the one taxing the hardest spends the most.

The rich districts say that *Serrano* is intended to darken their lighthouse. No taxpayer, they argue, would ever vote to send money out of his district. Hence the opportunity to add on is, for his constituents, theoretical only. This response, common among the members of the association of rich districts, represents a form of kamikaze politics. It counts upon persuading legislators that they must continue forever to cheat in favor of rich districts. The risk of this strategy is that one day *Serrano* will be enforced, and their constituents' nerve to tax themselves will have been paralyzed by all the metaphors of Robin Hood and migratory dollars.

A strategy less grounded in self-pity and more responsible in fact would stress that what counts in the local voting booth is not the mobility of dollars but the tax to be borne by the homeowner in relation to the benefit to be enjoyed by the schools. The local taxpayer-voter in a neutral system of add-ons faces a price measured as a tax rate on his house, and that price is standard throughout the state in districts rich and poor. Every taxpayer can buy as many extra dollars for his local schools as he pleases at the same tax price.

Hence, what the pessimist critics must argue is that living in a rich district has sapped the fiber of voters, leaving them incapable of bearing loads long familiar to the voters of poor districts. This is doubtful, but if so, it may mean only that the lighthouse districts will now be those of low property wealth where voters are ready to sacrifice for children.

Another canard of rich district public relations men is that the "Serraniks" originally intended to help poor minorities but forgot to see where they lived before pulling the legal trigger. The truth of this may be judged by the following pro-*Serrano* statement in which race was used as a proxy for poverty:

> If racial discrimination were measured by the percentage of all minority students who reside in districts below the statewide median (property wealth), California would manifest inverse discrimination. Fifty-nine percent (683,919) of minority students live in districts above the median. (Coons, Clune, and Sugarman 1970: p. 357).

This is partly a statistical curiosity. Los Angeles, with 15 percent of the state's public school children, is only slightly above the median and skews the figures. *Serrano* is unlikely to have the slightest impact on Los Angeles or any other district of near-average wealth. The ultimate point is that *Serrano* is and was intended to be neutral by income class, though it is clear that low income families living in low wealth districts were the worst hurt by the old system and now will be the big winners. The demographic pattern in other states is mixed, but it appears that a majority of the poor do live in poor districts. Again, however, there is nothing in *Serrano* to prevent a state spending as many extra dollars on the disadvantaged as it thinks appropriate.

May districts, then, at last inter the specter of spending equality stemming from *Serrano*? Again, this is doubtful. It is tactically too useful for rich districts as the threat from some imagined "left." Even worse, they have some excuse for their paranoia. So much of the recent reform and so much redistribution has proceeded in the name of equality that it may be that we are to be forever under its spell. Even among the reformers the sin persists; in truth, a good many of the lawyers involved merely tolerate *Serrano* as a handy cudgel to promote a wide variety of ends to which the case is wholly irrelevant. Their behavior and their rhetoric help maintain the equality myth.

A primary complaint with equality has nothing to do with the educational substance of new spending programs, state or federal. Even some that failed in the last decade were worth a try. What deserves no one's support is the notion that headstart, bilingual, urban factors, and compensatory education can be justified in terms of equality. To the contrary, the dependence on this rhetoric has rendered such laudable experiments incoherent and thereby exacted a stiff price in public confidence. No one understands why equality is the goal—and nobody should. Equality is not an appropriate purpose for education, even if it is often a useful diversion for politicians and litigators.

THE EQUALITY PROBLEM

Equality has had two general meanings. One is aspirational or normative, as in the phrase, "The principle of equality implies that all schools should have comparable facilities." So used the word serves no function but to confuse. One could as well say, "The principle of equality implies that all of us should be dead." Comparable facilities may be a good thing and annihilation a bad thing, but it is not their perfect equality that makes them so. There is no denying equality's power to move the human heart; what it lacks is a capacity to move the head. It fails as an intelligible aspiration or value because it lacks substantive content. It is no virtue simply to achieve equality in facilities or in anything else; indeed, it may be a very great vice to do so where individual needs or preferences differ. It is those needs and preferences that are important, and equality does not always serve them. Indeed, it tends to be an arbitrary master. If an equal solution is a good solution, often this is so only by accident.

If equality fails as aspiration, it might be useful as description. Some physical things are equal, and that is important for physicists and engineers to know. People, however, are not so readily equated. If there is one salient feature of the human scene, it is the diversity among individuals. People differ in abilities, age, size, wealth, and intelligence—and they also want different things. True, they all have bodies, eat, and move about. These common features, however, are not sufficient grounds for an ethic of equality, unless we are willing to include cows, spiders, and frogs. Most egalitarians are crusading only for human rights. Presumably this requires them to determine what it is to be human. This special quality must also be something relevant to a theory of justice. A common vestigal appendix will not do as the ethical motor for policy reform.

Further, that little difference, whatever it is, cannot consist in some quality that is inevitably present in a specific final form in all humans; if it were, there would be no issue of policy. We would simply all have it, and that would be the end of the matter. What egalitarians need to identify is some common aspect of humanity that is itself aspirational. It must be capable at least in principle of both fulfillment and frustration. Furthermore, it must allow forms of perfection that differ from person to person. The favorite candidate of the philosophers for this role is man's moral nature. As Rawls (1971:505) stated it, "The capacity for moral personality is a sufficient condition for being entitled to equal justice."

Basing educational entitlements upon moral capacity would raise two policy implications: One is substantive and very important, having little to do with equality. If our humanity lies in the exercise of moral freedom, it should be the business of government to enhance the scope of choice for all. The chief task of education becomes the nurture of moral autonomy. This is a grand and, of course, traditional perception. The second implication for policy displays at least an egalitarian surface. Descriptive equality suggests that in fostering autonomy or any other good for the child, society may not without reason augment the opportunity of X and neglect or frustrate that of Y. It is the familiar principle of nondiscrimination. Though commonly stated as egalitarian, it would be better understood as a criterion of minimal rationality in government. It forbids only distinctions *without reason*. It does not seek equality as such between X and Y and achieves it only in the limited and instrumental sense that, given a particular objective (e.g., reading), if there is no rational justification for treating X and Y differently, they must be treated the same.

This is the formal and feeble equality of traditional Fourteenth Amendment jurisprudence—feeble precisely because becoming "entitled to equal justice" tells one nothing about the substance of his entitlement. For practical purposes this debility continues even when the purpose of the entitlement is specified. If, for example, the autonomy of the child were to become accepted as education's substantive goal, it could be sensibly pursued in many different ways for every child; our ability to predict the outcomes of intervention in children's lives is often minimal, and rationality would be an easy criterion to satisfy. Suppose that John complains because he has been sent to a military school while Michael gets to attend art school. The most that equal justice can require is that the decision for each child be not wholly capricious in the light of the objective. But who is to say that military school is an irrational path to autonomy?

Even where it succeeds in undoing some distinction, the presumption of equal treatment is often of little consequence as a remedy because it is essentially negative. In our example, what is John's remedy? That both children go to military school, to art school, or to no school at all? The presumption of equal justice can end discrimination, but it cannot start anything sensible. Equality is never the active element in educational policy.

Jefferson held that God created men equal; but the Declaration of Independence is the last reference to equality. When it came to defining inalienable rights, Jefferson turned to liberty, a word to which he could give positive content. It would be clarifying if our society, like Jefferson, were to abandon the rhetoric of equality and turn to serious subjects. In education issues of discrimination could be handled adequately under a rationality criterion, while issues of educational style and substance could at last be debated in terms of specific educational purposes. Instead of asking whether a policy promotes equality, the legislator would ask whether it promotes literacy, respect for law, upward mobility, high consumption, better workers, aggressiveness, pacifism, patriotism, personal liberty, or the class struggle. Take your choice of purposes and then draft your policy.

There, of course, is the rub. The purposes that have been noted are not all consistent—yet all have substantial political support. There is little consensus about the ultimate aims (or, indeed, the means) of education. This is one reason that equality has been a popular medium of discourse for the fraternity. Being essentially meaningless but broadly benign in tone, it has permitted public education to proceed on a grand scale without the need for an identifiable purpose.

POLICY IN THE FACE OF PLURALISM

There are two alternatives to this form of drift. One is to muster a consensus for particular purposes or—what may be the same thing—

to identify amid the equality rhetoric something that amounts to a present consensus concerning desirable outcomes of education. To a degree this is possible. There is broad support for the ideas that education should serve the best interest of the child and that it should promote social and racial harmony. Unlike equality there are positive objectives, with concern not merely for the poor but for all. These objectives can even be made specific to a certain extent. For example, it is agreed to be in the best interest of every child to read, write, and do arithmetic; nor does anyone doubt that producing adults committed to tolerance and civil order would benefit society as a whole. There exists, then, a certain consensus on minimum goals or "basics" of education.

Such agreement, however, is superficial and, like equality, masks gross indeterminacy. For example, concerning the method of instruction in these basics, there is either rampant disagreement or utter inability to predict outcomes, or both. There is certainly in the present scene no rational ground for the law's choosing any particular structure or style for the delivery of education. More importantly, beyond the agreed basics, there is wholehearted pluralism even on what a child is supposed to become in his "best interest." As a consequence of such indeterminacy of means and ends, it seems impossible to establish any meaning for excellence in education.

This, however, is only because of the dependence upon the metaphors of society and state. We reify the sovereign, then imagine that, whenever his "mind" is schizophrenic or ignorant, policy cannot be made; some political scientists even blame the people themselves for blocking the possibility of a rational order by their dissensus. In fact, of course, all policy questions do receive an answer, even if government knows or does nothing. Children do experience one thing or another in education either because or in spite of specific governmental programs.

The point is that the absence of accepted knowledge or of value consensus at the macropolitical level does not mean a similar vacuum among flesh and blood persons and organized private groups. These do not lack views of the child's interest or of how to teach social harmony. They do, of course, disagree with one another, and why this is evil has not been discovered.

The real question for legislators, when faced with indeterminacy at the macrolevel, is which of these constituent units of society shall the law empower to decide about the education of individual children. Whose private views shall be given the force of law? Historically, our governments have located authority over the child's formal learning in the bureaucratic structures of "public" education. It has been the private views of the members of the public education fraternity, modified by circumstance and local politics, that have determined the character of Mary's education—unless her family could afford the alternative known as private education.

This subordination of the average family to the education fraternity may be wise, but it has not been the fruit of measured policy debate or even rational argument. It has been, in Mancur Olson's words, "The logic of collective action" (1965). Interest groups such as teachers and welfare workers can be effectively organized to obtain from government legal dominance over their "clientele"—an authority supported by hard cash and all in the name of child welfare. Children and families are by contrast ineffective lobbyists, both because the interest of their children differ from one another and because it is seldom efficient for a family to use its limited resources to support a lobbying vehicle on which other families can ride free. This explains why foundations are currently spending large sums to support family and children's interest lobbies that cannot support themselves.

Is there a rational approach to the question of who decides for the child, or is everything to be left to the flux of interest group politics? Can we begin to build a theory about the relationship of adults to children that would help us pursue their individual interest, assuming that to be one important goal of education? This would be possible, but first there must be agreement on the characteristics of good paternalism. In the author's opinion, three related conditions prevail. First, the dependent person—here the child—must be extended the maximum opportunity to be heard in the process by which his or her education is to be designed. This may be called voice. Second, the adult or adults who decide for him should be linked to the child by bonds of affection. This may be called caring. Third, the deciding adult should also be linked to the child by bonds of mutual self-interest. This may be called responsibility.

Among the potential deciders, who best embodies voice, caring, and responsibility? The viable contestants ultimately boil down on the one hand to some version of a well-organized education bureaucracy and on the other to the family. But before you judge between them, note how narrow the contest. No one is suggesting that the child be relegated to his family for his formal education. The practical proposition, rather, is a subsidized system of family choice with a scholarship for every child restricted only by important minimal criteria.

The bare minimums would include a *Serrano* rule insuring access to every school in a manner unaffected by family wealth; this means both no tuition add-ons and free transportation where necessary. Where applications to a school exceed places, admissions would be by random selection, with a possible tilt toward racial integration. Not only would private and public schools be subject to the same admission rules but a system of minimal due process would protect children in all schools from academic or disciplinary discrimination. A system of information would assure that families knew their options irrespective of the parents' literacy and that they had access to counselors who would be independent of the schools. Finally the state would insure the maintenance of minimum standards—that is, would enforce that portion of education as to which there is a consensus concerning means and ends.

The picture here is scarcely that of a head-on collision of parent and public educator. The parent has the last word, but the educator has the first and retains a powerful position; he is there at every point to support, caution, and inform parental judgment. In this context the separate capacities of school and family for voice, caring, and responsibility are put in synergy rather than conflict.

It is conceded, however, that sometimes parent and educator would conflict. However, if the criteria for paternalism are sound, the parent should prevail in such cases. Arguments about voice, caring, and responsibility may well apply. To the parent, the child is no stranger who appeared in September at the call of a computer. To the parent the child is unique, not one of twenty-five, each with clamant needs and wants. The relation is intimate and direct; it is voice in its fullest manifestation.

And it is caring in the richest sense that word can bear. It is not implied that teachers do not care; they are teachers and should care in the manner of professionals. They will know the child for nine months as one of a large transient group. Affective involvement is not to be expected or even desired. But it is desirable that someone who does care be ultimately responsible.

As for responsibility, it is not necessary to dwell upon the statistics of teacher discipline; there would be little enough to note. It is sufficient to observe that the educator need not live with the child. The essence of responsibility is in the permanent intertwining of human fates that is the family. When the child is hurt, the parent is hurt.

Giving the nonrich family its choice might at last make a profession out of education. There has been nothing so corruptive of excellence in teaching as the mandarin posture forced upon creative teachers by the present structure. Public teachers are not by nature so feckless and so repugnant to children as to need this crutch (though, as Acton long ago observed, ultimately they may become so). By shifting the states' economic support to the family instead of the monopoly, teachers could both gain and deserve the respect of those who would now be self-determining clients instead of impotent subjects.

Choice could have other beneficial consequences. One might be a decreasing number of academic "failures" who do not achieve the minimum. Children now driven to actual or intellectual truancy by an imposed arrangement might find in a chosen school sufficient interest to maintain the effort toward literacy. Likewise, the introduction of choice would provide new physical opportunities for racial integration. Here there is immediate hope for policy change. Courts today are at last being asked to order the provision of scholarships and transport to provide inner city children with an integrated education in either a private or out of district public school. Hearings were held in 1977 in California on a bill designed to make interdistrict transfers economically attractive, with state dollar bonuses where the result is integration. The bill as originally drafted permitted integrative transfers to private schools where there is today substantial space waiting for minority students.

In the pursuit of integration our notions of excellence become more complex. They include more than the best interest of the child, for they directly implicate the full society. But there need not be conflict between the individual and society. Far from it. Insofar as social harmony is an objective of education, choice is the ideal mechanism. It is a statement in cash that society perceives all of us to be as fully human as are the rich. Trusting the preferences of minorities is not a bad way to win their loyalty. In the bargain something might be learned about alternative definitions of excellence.

LIBERTY AND EDUCATION

Finally, consider the case that public education ceases to be indeterminate in its goals. Specifically, suppose that a majority were to accept the Jeffersonian position that the only relevant equality of mankind is its original moral liberty and that the humane policy is to foster that liberty through government. Excellence then is to be measured by the contribution of the educational process to the child's developing autonomy. What forms of finance and governance would such an objective imply?

There is a threshold problem of definition. The liberty of children can mean three things—the provision to the child by adults of a range of choice, always revocable; the subjective capacity of the child to criticize choices made for him; and the capacity to lead the life of a self-determining adult. Various schemes of finance and governance might be argued to promote one form of liberty but not another. For example, some believe that adult autonomy is the fruit of strict childhood discipline—the temporary frustration of autonomy.

It will be assumed, however, that the achievement of adult autonomy requires some measure of liberty even in childhood—indeed, that children are no less moral beings than adults and that they require liberty for their human function. Yet it is also naive to imagine that young children can be truly free. The ideal is a dominion adaptable to the growing competences of a child, giving each capacity scope as it appears. It is likely to be a regime characterized by voice, caring, and responsibility.

It is not necessary to repeat in full the argument for the family. Instead, it should be emphasized that it is in the family's self-interest that the child becomes autonomous. In prior ages—in an agrarian economy—the family's interest was quite different; a "dependent" child meant another pair of productive hands and security for old age. In an industrial age, continued dependence is a heavy burden to the family. The welfare of the public school system as presently structured is by contrast linked to the dependency of the child. The worse his troubles—the more pitiable his performance—the more the system is needed, and, in turn, the more resources the system needs to solve his problems—a happy spiral of successful failure.

The argument is not that the fox has been set to guard the chicken house. Teachers do not devour children, and they are very good at guarding them. The problem is that children are not chickens and keeping them in one coop when they prefer another may be bad for their autonomy. This strategy does, however, maintain a state of restless malaise, justifying the hiring of more guards and specialists.

Would family choice tend to produce autonomous adults even among lower income families? There is, of course, no direct experience to support this conclusion. Families have never been asked what school they would prefer for their children. It is known that most adults were themselves the products of a choiceless education. If one felt them deficient in autonomy, it would be hard to see why he would impose the same experience on yet another generation.

Yet he might, for he could imagine that the family would make choices even worse than that imposed upon him. No doubt some families would. It is quite plausible that, stripped of choice, the family's functions atrophy. Only by choosing does one develop and retain capacity for choice.

A dilemma of our own creation seems to have developed. Responsibility would be good for the low income family, but its exercise bad for the child. Must society sacrifice one generation to make the next autonomous? It is doubtful. This disparagement of ordinary families is, of course, plausible; however, it is unconvincing, expecially considering the record of the systems on their own. If there is a gamble in empowering the common parent, the odds are for change. It would be hoped that a people serious about democracy would at some point begin to trust themselves.

REFERENCES

Coons, John E.; William H. Clune III; and Stephen D. Sugarman. 1970. *Private Wealth and Public Education.* Cambridge, Massachusetts: Harvard University Press.

Olson, Mancur. 1965. *The Logic of Collective Action.* Cambridge, Massachusetts: Harvard University Press.

Rawls, John. 1971. *A Theory of Justice.* Cambridge, Massachusetts: Harvard University Press.

Serrano v. Priest, 96 Cal. Rptr. 601,437 P.2d 1241 (1971).

THE PURSUIT
OF EFFICIENCY

5 ISSUES IN EDUCATIONAL EFFICIENCY

J. Alan Thomas[*]

Three criteria should underlie development of a system for financing education – the system should be equitable, it should be efficient, and it should permit students and parents to select from among a variety of ends and means those that most closely approximate their own preferences.[1] While this chapter deals primarily with the efficiency criterion, the other values cannot be ignored. The terms are reciprocal, so that the definition of each sets limits on the degree to which the other values can be realized. For example, while freedom of choice is a deeply held value, by imposing compulsory education, state legislators require some parents and students to invest in or consume more education than they would if free to make their own

[*]J. Alan Thomas, Professor, Department of Education, University of Chicago, Chicago Illinois.

The research reported herein was performed pursuant to a grant with the National Institute of Education, U.S. Department of Health, Education and Welfare. Contractors undertaking such projects under government sponsorship are encouraged to express freely their professional judgment in the conduct of the project. Points of view or opinions stated do not, therefore, necessarily reflect official National Institute of Education position or policy.

Professor Susan S. Stodolsky is co-principal investigator of the project that gave rise to this chapter. Teresa Ferguson, Frances Kemmerer, and Robert Wimpelberg, my colleagues at the Educational Finance and Productivity Center, provided helpful drafts on an earlier version, and Robyn Beatty was responsible for its preparation. The errors and flaws are, of course, my own.

choice. Also, despite a general commitment to equality of educational opportunity, there are few proposals to eliminate parents' options to send their children to private schools, even though the latter can be costly and are believed by many to be superior to public schools. Efficiency may not be as appealing a concept as equality and freedom, and it usually does not warrant the same attention. In fact, research dealing with efficiency issues is sometimes mislabeled as if it treated the issue of equal education opportunity.[2] Like other value considerations, efficiency is difficult to define, and overly simple views are misleading.

The history of educational finance in the United States is an account of a persistent attempt to reconcile conflicting values of equity, freedom of choice, and efficiency. School finance experts advocated for many years employing a mixture of state and local funds to support school systems: it was argued that raising funds locally would enhance efficiency, since local residents would insist that care be exercised in the manner in which locally collected monies were spent.[3] Freedom of choice would also be served, since localities would select curricula that would be appropriate for their own students. In short, each community would base its procedures to financing schooling on a continuing comparison of costs and benefits.[4] At the same time, equality would be enhanced through use of state funds to guarantee a "foundation level" of expenditures, although an increase in equity through centralized financing might endanger efficiency and might diminish local communities' ability to make choices about their educational programs.[5]

However, whether and in what manner locally financed educational programs were actually efficient was never demonstrated: within a financial system in which expenditure levels and programs were determined locally, there were still many students who did not have access to educational programs serving their needs and interests. Furthermore, it was clear by the early 1970s that heavy dependence on the local property tax, which decentralized financing, resulted in substantial inequalities among districts in both tax rates and expenditures. The *Serrano* (1971) decision attempted to deal with this issue, although the manner in which the court addressed interdistrict inequalities was ambiguous and within-district inequalities were ignored.[6]

The decision of the *Serrano* court that expenditures for education should not be a function of wealth, except the wealth of the state as a whole, left open the possibility that inequalities among districts would be acceptable if they were a function, not of local wealth, but of other district characteristics such as shared educational aspirations. The response to this possibility was district power equalizing, which thus represents the most recent attempt to balance the equity criterion with a concern for freedom of choice and efficiency.[7] However, while controversies over school finance have focused on inequalities among districts, it is increasingly recognized that inequalities within districts in the resources available to students may constitute an equally important problem.[8]

If the political will to do so existed, states could ensure equality in expenditure levels among school districts. However, it seems reasonable to assume that state and federal governments have neither the information nor the insights into local preferences to ensure that money be spent wisely and that students and parents be provided with appropriate choices among curricula and teaching methods. It is assumed, then, that a major role of the higher levels of government is to establish, through their financial and legal procedures, a context within which fair access to schooling is provided for students of varying backgrounds, while the details of this access are determined by local agencies.[9]

A central purpose of this chapter is to examine the roles of parents, students, teachers, administrators, school boards, and legislatures in addressing issues of efficiency and, in a peripheral way, equal opportunity and freedom of choice. Since many of the inequalities that persist despite efforts to eliminate them result from differences in students' home backgrounds, a commitment to equal opportunity implies in part an attempt to utilize schools as society's agents in reducing home-based inequalities. Due partly to the development in the home of values and preferences, students arrive at school with varying interests, differing levels of ability, and motivational structures that vary across students and, for a given student, across elements of the curriculum. Local school boards and administrators are, it is assumed, partially influenced by demands placed on them by parents and students: the important aspects of freedom of choice are those that affect the latter.

The following section of this essay provides a general discussion of the efficiency concept as it applies to education and also discusses the most common empirical models for studying the efficiency of educational systems. Section three contains basic arguments for examining the relevance to educational efficiency of decisions made in homes and classrooms. Finally, the fourth section summarizes the discussion.

EFFICIENCY IN EDUCATION

The major concern of the school finance reform movement of the 1970s was how best to bring about equity in the distribution of public school benefits and tax burdens (Garms, Guthrie, and Pierce 1978). A persistent minor theme was how to preserve the freedom of local educational agencies to define appropriate educational programs for their clientele (Coons, Clune, and Sugarman 1970). Efficiency is not as appealing a notion as the other two since it is, as will be seen,[10] difficult to define and operationalize, and narrow definitions of efficiency may imply policies that are distasteful to many.[11] Similarly, broad general definitions of efficiency appear to be lacking in focus.[12] It may in part be the case that because definitional issues are generally avoided, much of the research designed to promote greater efficiency has only limited value.[13] Defining efficiency carefully has merit, not merely as a corrective for overly narrow approaches to research and policy, but also as a basis for clarifying the process of decisionmaking in the systems within which education is produced.

The popular definition of efficiency is that it means making the best use of scarce resources to achieve given ends (see, for example, Koopmans 1957: 69–70). Obtaining and distributing money is a central and sensitive role of government, and this definition emphasizes the idea that a system is efficient if no possible reallocation among inputs of a given amount of money would improve goal attainment. In practice, then, an increase in efficiency may result from procedures that increase goal attainment with no increase in cost, reduce cost without reducing goal attainment, or enhance goal attainment while also reducing costs.

In the multigoal, multiclient organizations that produce education, two corollary definitions are also important. A system is said to be efficient if (1) there is no way to reallocate resources among inputs so as to produce more of one output without producing less of another and (2) there is no way to reallocate benefits among recipients that will make some better off without making others worse off (Rawls 1971: 66–70).[14] Classroom examples of these approaches to defining efficiency are readily identified. For example, if in social studies classes students are taught to improve their reading skills or to acquire values associated with citizenship in a democracy, without a loss in their learning of social studies facts and skills, the system is more efficient than if available resources were used only for the latter purpose. Second, a gain in efficiency will result if a teacher reorganizes the classroom so as, for example, to provide direct instruction to a group of slower students while assigning more able students to library research and if, as a result, slower students gain while more able students suffer no loss.

The popular definition of efficiency provides a useful guide to administrative decisionmaking. It calls for a clarification of goals, an identification of relevant resources, and a "rational" approach— based, for example, on an analysis of costs and effectiveness—for selecting the best means to attain given ends. Procedures stemming from this definition include Program Planning Budgeting Systems and management by objectives. However, using these management methods, implementing accountability systems, and researching the input-output relationship all depend heavily on a careful examination of goals, resources, and the models that link inputs and outputs. Finally, since the search for efficiency implies a decisionmaking policy, we must ask, Who are the relevant decisionmakers?

Whose decisions affect educational efficiency? In factory production, both raw materials and finished products are inanimate objects. In education they are human beings who have their own goals and dreams and can be expected to act so as to further their own welfare.[15] While traditional approaches to studying efficiency in education are based on the idea that efficiency results from decisions made by administrators, school board members, and legislators, it is apparent that parents also have goals and aspirations for their children and that they allocate resources so as to attain these ends. Children also allocate their own time, both at home and in school, and may be thought of as sometimes actively pursuing their own learning.

Defining Educational Goals

The concept of efficiency depends on the idea that ends and means of schooling are separable. In fact, ends are sometimes embedded in means. Particular approaches to schooling, such as those represented by church-related schools, military academies, and open classrooms, are sometimes valued for the methods they employ rather than for the results they achieve.

Finally, parents and students have educational goals that may not coincide with those of the school system. Current efforts to develop systemwide preference functions on the basis of the priorities expressed by clients are not convincing; Arrow's famous treatise (1963) proves that it is not possible to develop a social preference function that reflects preference functions of individuals. Furthermore, the social benefit approach to goal definition, which might otherwise serve as a justification for setting goals on a systemwide basis, has been widely criticized as lacking an empirical foundation.[16] It might, of course, be argued that the state has a responsibility for setting goals for those students whose parents are lacking in knowledge and political power, but assigning this role to the state incorporates the danger that centralized decisionmaking will be extended beyond its legitimate boundaries.[17]

These problems can not be dismissed as mere nit-picking; they go to the heart of the concept of schooling in a democratic society. In a centralized society in which specialized agencies define goals of schooling, efficiency is a more meaningful concept than in a society that values individuals' freedom to choose goals. Equity is also hard to define when individuals have different objectives. It may seem to some that decentralized decisionmaking is sloppy and results in inefficiency from the point of view of the total society. However, it may also be the case that if individuals possess the necessary information about the educational system and the labor force, they can make better choices than social agencies.[18] They may therefore make decisions that, from the point of view of both individuals and society, are preferable to those made by centralized agencies.

This is not necessarily to advocate greater decentralization of decisionmaking through voucher systems or similar schemes. Rather, it is to explain some of the complexities of educational systems in which decisions are made by parents, pupils, and teachers as well as by administrators and legislators. These complexities, in turn, create problems in defining and researching efficiency issues.

Resources Used in Learning

Because the influence of government on ensuring equity, efficiency, and, to a degree, freedom of choice in the educational system is exerted primarily through the manner in which money is raised, distributed, and spent, studies of educational efficiency have concentrated on availability and use of purchased resources. Existing studies of efficiency in education have included such topics as space utilization, class size, teacher qualifications and pay systems, and utilization of library books. Statistical "production function studies" have concentrated on determining the marginal effects of various types of purchased resources on students' learning.

The enthusiasm that policy analysts, administrators, and researchers have displayed in their search for the effect of school resources on achievement has had to be modified, for two reasons. First, studies have frequently failed to find any consistent relationship between resource allocation and achievement (Averch et al. 1972; Jencks et al. 1972). Second, and more importantly, there is no logical or pedagogical reason why, for example, teachers' demographic characteristics will have an effect on students' learning. It has therefore been suggested that flows rather than stocks of resources may be relevant variables (see Monk 1979). It may be more important to observe how a teacher's behavior affects individual students than to take account of the teacher's age, sex, experience, and training. Also, it is more important to observe how the library is used by students of different levels of ability and with different interests and motivations than to count the number of books it contains.

Accounting for stocks or even flows of purchased resources does not exhaust the inventory of resources used in a classroom. Students' time is also a resource that (because it has alternate uses) is valuable and that is combined with purchased resources in the production of learning. In fact, students' time may be the most important resource of all. While learning can take place without books and, conceivably, without teachers, it generally cannot take place without an investment by students of their own time. Furthermore, students' time is supplied to learning activities in the home as well as in the classroom. In the former context it is combined with other resources such as the time of parents, space, books, and even television, which affect learning but are not purchased by the school district.

Including students' time as a resource has important implications for research and practice. In the research context, placing a value on students' time implies the importance of careful studies of how students allocate time to learning in homes and classrooms. From the point of view of educational practice, it is worth reflecting on Schultz' comment that "It is plausible that all too little has been done to economize on the time that students put into education" (1961: 82).

Modeling the Relationship between Means and Ends in Education

The model on which most empirical studies of educational efficiency are based is called the production function. This formulation is a mathematical representation of a postulated relationship between the resources used in education and the resulting outcomes. These models are based on well-developed economic procedures that have been found useful in industry.

Basic to the production function concept is the notion that learning results from the effect of a number of conditions or variables that induce learning. Some of these variables are related to school characteristics; others describe home and community characteristics assumed to affect learning and the characteristics of students' peers. Among those items or conditions typically included as independent variables or "inputs" in the production function are:

School Effects
    Class size
    Average salaries of teachers
    Teachers' experience, sex, and age
    Number of books in the school library
    Presence of a science laboratory in the school
    Age of school building

Background Effects
    Parents' education
    Parents' income
    Urban or rural background
    Books and other resources in the home

Peer Group Effects
  Home background of other students in the class
  Racial composition of the classroom
  Average ability level of students in the classroom

The production function itself is a mathematical equation that represents a hypothesized relationship between "inputs" and "outputs." The most general form of this equation is

$$O_i = g\ (S_i,\ H_i,\ P_i,\ u) \qquad (5.1)$$

where O_i is the ith output variable; S_i is a vector of school related variables assumed to affect O_i; H_i is a vector of home and other background variables; P_i is a set of peer group characteristics; and u is an error term (see Katzman 1971: ch. 3).

The objective of researchers is to isolate the marginal effect of school variables when background and peer group effects are controlled. The purpose of such research is to determine how a fixed amount of money can best be allocated among a variety of purchased school inputs in order to maximize attainment of a given outcome.

The underlying notion is that money should be divided among inputs in such a way that the last dollar spent on one input will provide the same addition to knowledge as that provided by the last dollar spent on each other input. Take the case where a given output is produced by two inputs, x_1 and x_2, which might represent, for example, teachers' time and the time of teachers' aides. If we assume that, beyond a given point, additional increments of each input produce successively smaller additions to outputs in accordance with the "law" of diminishing returns, the substitution possibilities are represented by a line that is convex to the origin, as illustrated by AB in Figure 5–1. The slope of AB at any point is equal to the ratio between the marginal product of x_2 and that of x_1. Now let XY be one of a family of parallel lines whose slope represents relative prices of two inputs. Since XY is tangent to AB at Q, slopes of the two lines are equal at that point:

$$\frac{MPx_1}{MPx_2} = \frac{Cx_1}{Cx_2}$$

or, by cross-multiplying,

$$\frac{MPx_1}{Cx_1} = \frac{MPx_2}{Cx_2}$$

—that is, the last dollar spent on input x_1 provides the same con-tribution to the given output as the last dollar spent on x_2 and each other input. This is the condition for optimality or maximum efficiency.[19]

Even this simplified explanation suggests that the approach is a potentially powerful one. Reservations expressed in the literature are for the most part minor. For example, while there is some concern over whether the relationship expressed in equation (5.1) is additive or multiplicative, attempts to resolve this question through empirical means have not demonstrated that either approach is superior (Katz-man 1971: 194–203). Second, and more basically, it has been sug-gested that it is meaningless to use this approach for determining allocative efficiency unless it can be assumed that schools are tech-nically efficient—that is, that the most effective technologies are selected. Since private sector incentives are largely absent in educa-tion, it cannot be assumed that schools are technically efficient. The main problem with the production function approach is that it is basically a factory model that has not adequately addressed ques-

Figure 5–1.   Conditions for maximum efficiency.

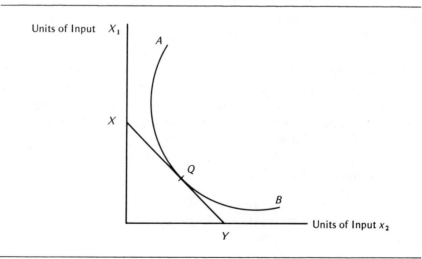

tions concerning multiplicity of decisionmakers, diversity of goals, complexity of educational inputs, and intricacy of relationships at the classroom and home level.

Despite the fact that these studies have not provided consistent approaches for improving educational efficiency, they have provided the basis for new and more promising lines of research. Coleman's finding that "differences between schools account for only a small fraction of differences in pupil achievement" has turned researchers' attention to explaining within-school differences in achievement (1966: 22). Heyns, for example, examined differences among students in "access to resources within schools" (1974: 1435). Tracking, especially, was seen as a mechanism for assigning "better teachers, counselling, and highly motivated, academically talented peers" (Ibid.) to some students. She found that high socioeconomic status (SES) students tend to demonstrate high achievement and therefore to be assigned to a college-related curriculum, while curriculum placement in turn gives students unequal access to school resources and personnel. In a related study, while Alexander and McDill found evidence of "considerable status ascription in curricular sorting," (1976: 24) their findings tended to agree with those of Heyns.

Tracking is an excellent example of within-school differences in resource allocation in secondary schools. Other more subtle mechanisms also exist, especially in elementary schools. It remains for a new generation of researchers to attempt to identify phenomena that explain within-school variance in attainment.

In critique of the Coleman study, Bowles and Levin (1968) pointed to the importance of multicolinearity between school and background variables. Because these variables are intricately associated, controlling for the latter tends to remove much of the statistical explanation that would otherwise be attributed to school effects. These school and background interactions were explored by Summers and Wolfe (1975), who examined the effect on students' performance of interactions between student characteristics and school resource variables.

Coleman's finding that "a pupil's achievement is strongly related to educational backgrounds and aspirations of the other students in the school" (1966: 22) has led to a renewed interest in what sociologists call peer group effects and what economists might term externalities.[20] More especially, it has contributed to advances in statistical methodologies designed to deal with data at different levels of aggregation (see Burstein 1980).

Approaches traditionally used in the study of efficiency in education focus on decisions made in legislative halls and administrative offices. A broader view of the process of allocating resources in education recognizes that parents and students allocate resources in homes and schools and that these decisions are important determinants of both efficiency and equity. A full discussion of the topic must, therefore, include a consideration of decisions made in homes and classrooms.

Education in Homes and Classrooms

Extent studies of educational efficiency have been remiss in examining only a part of the total system within which learning is produced. A broader perspective that includes the home as well as the school is likely to be rewarding. This is particularly the case because of the existence of home-school interactions. Competences produced in homes contribute to students' ability to benefit from classroom instruction, while once children enroll, their home activities are affected by their learning experiences in school.[21]

A broad approach to the study of efficiency in education will therefore include an examination of decisions made in homes and schools by teachers, parents, and students. Teachers structure activities in classrooms in part according to their own preferences and in part, we postulate, in response to their students' characteristics.[22] Decisions made by administrative officials at the school and school district level may also be sensitive to learning activities that take place in the home.[23]

One way to describe classroom learning effects of parents' decisions to influence their children's capabilities is to make use of the idea that students' time is a resource analogous to purchased resources and that the value of time can be measured in terms of the amount of human capital (or learning) that students embody at a given time.

There are three reasons why the time of children, even at an early age, has value. The first reason depends on the so-called "foregone learning" argument: the time of children has value because by studying one curriculum, using one technology, or being involved in a given topic within the curriculum, a child is prevented from simultaneously being involved in a different learning activity.[24] This perception is, in part, the foundation of curriculum theory, since development of a curriculum must take into consideration that the costs of providing time for, say, mathematics, consist in part of the foregone opportunity to use the same time for study of other subjects—for example, reading and science.

The other reasons why students' time has value are related to human capital theory. In the first place, individuals at any age embody a set of capabilities that have been developed through past investments of their own time, the donated time of others such as their parents, and purchased goods and services. Human capital possessed by students thus represents earlier investments; students' time has a value that is roughly proportional to their ability. The other viewpoint is that students' time has value because time may be used to obtain additional learning that may be utilized in obtaining further education and, ultimately, gainful employment. Again, the value of students' time is obviously proportional to the amount of human capital that has been accumulated—or in other words, to ability.

The learning and motivations that children develop in their homes both before and during their period of schooling may affect both equity and efficiency in classroom instruction. Some students are more able than others to transform their time into learning, and some students are more willing than others to allocate their time to learning activities. Unless schools find a way to help those students who have been less advantaged in their homes to develop learning skills and to improve their motivation, differences in school learning may result from home differences, even if the educational programs that students experience are essentially the same. Also, additional learning that results from resources provided by the school system may be less in classrooms that are composed of students who have not developed basic competences in the home than in classrooms composed of students whose time value reflects greater home investments in learning. Differences within classrooms in competences developed in the home may also result in systematic within-classroom differences in students' productivity.

Complexities exist that result from expanding the view of learning and teaching to include the home and the classroom, as well as higher levels at which decisions are made. For example:

1. The system within which learning-related decisions are made has several levels, including the federal and state government, school districts, schools, homes, and classrooms. Efficiency and equity in the production of education can best be considered by examining these levels separately and in interaction.

2. Interactions between levels can be considered from several points of view; there are statistical approaches to the use of multilevel data; there is the behavioral approach that examines how teachers and administrators respond to the presence in school of students with varying levels of ability; there is also the political approach that studies how parents attempt to influence the ends and means that are embedded in their children's education and how schools attempt to influence the manner in which parents allocate resources for children's learning after the latter enroll in school.

3. Since no two homes are alike in their effects on students, the latter come to school with greatly differing abilities, interests, aspirations, and motivations.

4. Regardless of the resource mix that is available for use within classrooms, flows of resources to students depend in part on decisions made by teachers and in part on the decisions of students to allocate their own time to education. Students' time is therefore an important element in the system within which learning is produced, and students' time is allocated by students themselves as well as by parents and teachers.

5. The manner in which students are combined for instruction is an important determinant of learning. Grouping of students depends on decisions made at several levels that include, for example, drawing of district and school attendance boundaries, transportation of students for the purpose of school integration or curricular diversity, tracking, and grouping within classrooms. Parents' choices of a place of residence also affect peer group composition, as does a student's choice of friends.

It is platitudinous to state that while learning is an individual phenomenon, some of the variables that affect learning can best be observed at the classroom, school, or district level. However, earlier studies did not always distinguish between levels, so that, for example, districtwide figures for per pupil expenditures were used to explain variance in student achievement. What is called for is a careful examination of the levels at which data are collected so that, for example, when individual achievement is used as the dependent variable, resource variables that are observed are as much as possible specific to each student. Under some circumstances, of course, structural variables (such as classroom technologies) or peer group effects (calling for an aggregation of individual properties) are introduced as explanatory variables, and the problems inherent in cross-level inference must be kept in mind (Burstein 1980).

While most research concentrating on cross-level influences has been statistical, it is also necessary to examine behavioral and political aspects of the phenomenon. Behaviorally, the important phenomenon is the manner in which the composition of a class or groups of students affects the manner in which teachers structure and pace their educational activities (Barr 1975). Political influences are also important, since it appears that parents may affect both the goals and the procedures selected by schools and school districts.[25] Furthermore, school teachers and principals, as well as superintendents, may utilize a variety of approaches to influence homes.

As a result of investments made in the home, students arrive in school with vastly different capabilities. For example, some can already read when they arrive in school. These differences may persist after students enroll in school and are not readily overcome by compensatory education programs.[26] Furthermore, many educationally advantaged children come from high status homes in which parents may use economic and political power to secure a resource-rich school environment for their children.[27]

Within classrooms, activities or technologies selected by teachers, including, for example, supervised seatwork, lecturing, class discussion, group projects, and individual tutoring, mediate between resources available in classrooms and the manner in which these resources are combined with the time of individual students. Actual measurement of the value of resources that are received by students in a classroom presents difficult conceptual and measurement problems (Monk 1979). It is not clear at this point that differences in the dollar value of resources flowing to individuals represent differences in educational opportunity. Teachers have many alternative ways to combine purchased resources with students' time in classrooms, and the particular combinations that are selected are relevant to questions of efficiency[28] as well as of equity. Finally, it is assumed that the manner in which teachers structure learning activities in classrooms is, to a degree, sensitive to the mix of students' abilities, so that these activities are, in combination, both a result and a cause of differences within classrooms in students' performance levels.[29]

Finally, sociologists have for some time been interested in peer group effects on acquisition of attitudes, values, and learning (see, for example, Coleman 1966). The concept of peer group effect has an analogy in economic theory, since the effect on student B of learning produced in the home of student A is an example of an externality or third person effect. Policies related to such issues as homogeneous and heterogeneous grouping within and among classrooms, tracking, integration, comprehensive high schools, and separation of technical from academic systems of education all are affected by considerations of the effect on a student's learning peer characteristics. Paralleling the work of sociological researchers, methodologists have given attention to the manner in which data aggregated to the level of a group or classroom interacts with other school effects and background data in affecting individuals' performances (Burstein 1980).

SUMMARY

This chapter has followed four trains of thought in its examination of efficiency applied to education. First, the manner in which efficiency is defined was examined and analyzed. Both a broad and a narrow definition of the term were identified because educational practices that are justified by a narrow definition of the term may appear inappropriate when efficiency is more broadly defined. Second, the relationship between the concept of efficiency and the reciprocal criteria of equity and freedom of choice were discussed. Third, the chapter concentrated on implications for improvement of efficiency, narrowly and broadly defined.

The narrow definition of efficiency reflects an effort to apply the so-called methods of rational analysis to the improvement of educational practice. The definition calls for (1) definition of goals and, where multiple goals are sought, setting priorities among them; (2) identification of available resources; and (3) identification of various procedures for using resources at hand to reach desired goals, selecting the "best" of these procedures by comparing costs and benefits associated with each alternative, implementing the procedure, and evaluating the results. In practice, a narrow range of goals is often selected. These goals are usually cognitive rather than affective, and standardized tests of achievement or, at best, specially constructed criterion referenced tests are selected to measure goal attainment. Educational practices that implement this definition of efficiency include program planning budgeting systems (PPBS), management by objectives (MBO), and in the field of research, the so-called production function approach.

While the broader view of efficiency recognizes the validity of the rational model, it also emphasizes the multiplicity of goals, while stressing the apparent impossibility of completely separating ends from means in the case of education. Furthermore, the broader definition emphasizes that parents and students as well as educators are involved in setting goals and selecting means for attaining them, that learning takes place in home as well as at school, and that parents and teachers as well as students are involved in the allocation of resources. Finally, the broader definition of efficiency is based on a realization of the complexity of the multilevel systems within which education is produced.

Paradoxically, efficiency in the narrow sense may imply inefficiency if the term is more broadly defined. Suppose, for example, a school district adopts a management by objectives system that focuses on the improvement of scores in reading and mathematics. The welfare of parents and students interested in other educational outcomes, such as competence in music, art, science, and foreign languages, may in fact diminish. Therefore, while mathematics and reading test scores improve, total utility may decline. This result may persist even if the district-defined preference function is broader than the basic skills, since no districtwide set of priorities will correspond to those of individual parents and students.

This paradox is reinforced when we examine relationships between efficiency and concepts of equity and freedom of choice. The narrow definition of efficiency may result in setting of goals by a central agency that may seek to enhance equity through bringing about a reduction of variance in test scores. However, if students and parents have goals that do not correspond to those of the district, interpersonal comparisons become meaningless, and equity cannot be measured through statistical means. Finally, an increased centralization of the process of selecting ends and means will automatically mean a reduction of freedom of choice at classroom and home levels.

Some recent authors have concluded that freedom can best be implemented through replacing present methods of financing education with a voucher system.[30] However, considerable choice in selection of educational goals and means to attain them is available in the present system, especially for parents who can afford to select a place of residence where schools are to their liking. On the other hand, the move to implement accountability systems at state and district levels may imply a centralizing of decisionmaking and a reduction of alternatives presently available, thus strenghthening the position of voucher advocates.

If an alternative financial system were introduced, certain problems would still require careful examination. Consider, for example, the following statement.

1.   Learning occurs in homes as well as in schools, and parents make decisions that affect their children's learning and their ability to profit from an educational program. Concerns for equity, efficiency, and freedom of choice are all related to the role of the home as well as to that of the school.

2.   In addition to parents and teachers, students also make decisions about their involvement in learning. Students' decisions include the manner in which they allocate their time to learning by, for example, being on task in school, reading for recreation and for information, being involved in hobbies, and doing homework. Homes affect classrooms indirectly through the effect of home-developed competences on teachers' behavior. It is also postulated that, through political means, parents influence the type of education that is provided in schools and in classrooms and that teachers are able, to a degree, to affect the home-based learning activities of their students.

3.   Teachers structure classroom activities in ways that may reflect such diverse influences as their own training and preferences, the influence on them of preferences of administrators, the capabilities and motivations of their students, and the preferences of parents. Since classroom activities constitute means by which available money is transformed into flows of resources to students, classroom structure has implications for equity and efficiency.

4.   The system in which learning takes place consists of several levels, with different types of effects being exerted at each level.

Examination of the efficiency of the system requires obtaining information about learning activities in the home, close observation of teachers' selection of educational activities and of students' time allocation in classrooms, and an examination of the effects of decisions made at higher system levels.

NOTES TO CHAPTER 5

1. Cubberley (1906) provided an insightful discussion of many of the problems in educational finance that have plagued analysts in the ensuing decades. James (1961: ch. 1) traced key issues in educational finance from a historical perspective.

2. So-called production function studies are primarily aimed at improving efficiency, although several of them, such as Coleman et al. (1966) and Summers and Wolfe (1975), include "equality of educational opportunity" in their titles. This is not to criticize the authors, since equity and efficiency are closely related.

3. Among the writers who relate local control to fiduciary responsibility are Johns and Morphet (1960: 198) who wrote: "There are a number of reasons why some local school financial support should probably be provided. Many . . . assert that since local people pay a part of school costs directly, they insist upon more economical and efficient administration than they would if all funds were provided by the state and Federal governments."

4. Johns and Morphet (1960: 198) also wrote that "local freedom encourages local initiative in finding new and better solutions to the educational problems. . . . "

5. This statement is implied in the preceding quotations.

6. It has been pointed out since the *Serrano* decision that many poor and educationally disadvantaged children live in districts which did not benefit from school finance reform.

7. District power equalizing, one response to *Serrano* and related decisions, is a financial system whereby the state matches local contributions according to a ratio that takes local property wealth into consideration, with the aim of making possible equal expenditures for districts that levy the same rate of taxation. For a discussion of school finance reform see Garms, Guthrie, and Pierce (1978: 215–47).

8. See Sexton (1961), Greenberg and McCall (1974), Wiley and Harnischfeger (1974), Heyns (1974), and Monk (1979) for evidence of variations in resources available to students within districts or within schools. Sexton deals with differences in expenditure among schools in a school district, Greenberg and McCall with teacher migration in an urban school district, Wiley and Harnischfeger with variation in the amount of time provided for

       schooling to students in a single school district, Heyns with tracking, and Monk with differences in resource flows within classrooms.

9. Decisions of the Supreme Court dealing with fairness in access to schooling are, for example, Brown v. Board of Education of Topeka, Kansas (1954), Tinker v. Des Moines (1969), and Goss v. Board of Education (1975), which deal respectively with school desegregation, free speech, and student suspensions.

10. Equity depends on efficiency, since it rests to some degree on the development of efficient methods for educating low achievement students. Also, whether resources can be spared for providing freedom of choice for students and parents in the selection of goals and means for attaining them depends in part on efficient use of resources.

11. State accountability systems that define success in terms of performance on a narrow band of test outcomes are distasteful because they focus the attention of teachers and students on the items included in the tests, which are usually based on lower order cognitive processes.

12. Broad definitions lack focus because efficiency is defined in terms of the attainment of a variety of outcomes, which may vary for each student.

13. After a careful review of the literature, Averch et al. (1972: x) conclude that "Research has not identified a variant of the existing system that is consistently related to students' educational outcomes." In retrospect, it appears likely that this lack of consistent findings may result partially from the fact that production function research is not grounded in either sociological, economic, or pedagogical theory. On the other hand, some recent work, such as Heyns (1974) and Bidwell and Kasarda (1975), provides a theoretical base for school effects research.

14. Brown and Saks (1980) appear to combine (1) and (2) by regarding students as well as subject areas as goals among which teachers distribute resources.

15. Brown and Saks (1980) refer to the analogy between classrooms and "job shops." If, however, students and parents as well as teachers are regarded as decisionmakers who help determine specific goals and procedures, factory analogies may be misleading.

16. See, for example, Windham's (1978: 103−21) analysis of the social benefits of positive externalities, which some claim are associated with provision of higher education.

17. It does, however, seem appropriate that special programs be developed and special resources allocated for education of those who, for one reason or another, are not mastering basic skills needed for survival in our society. In this case, previous arguments about decentralized decisionmaking should probably give way to the narrow definition of efficiency.

18. Windham 1978: 4) writes:

> Planners, no matter how much discretionary power they have, never determine the actual outcomes of policy. They can only set in action forces which they anticipate, with or without rational justification, will have certain effects. The effects themselves are the result of the millions of micro-decisions made by individuals who are responding to the planners' policies in terms of (1) the actual pattern of rewards (positive or negative) which their decision matrix presents and (2) their perception of this pattern.

While this statement was written in the context of higher education, it may apply to education at all levels.

19. MP indicates "marginal product," so that MPx_1 is the increment in learning that results from a small increment in input x.

20. Peer group effects are externalities, since learning produced by children in one home has indirect effects on students from other homes.

21. For example, children who learn to read in school may also read at home for recreation or for knowledge in the home.

22. Barr (1975) found that teachers' grouping decisions are affected by ability distribution of their students.

23. Attendance lines may be drawn and special schools (for example, academic and technical high schools) may be created in response to abilities and motivations developed in homes. Within schools, tracking may incorporate differentiated programs that respond to differences in the abilities and motivations of students.

24. The concept of "foregone learning," along with some other notions that are incorporated in this chapter was suggested by Mary Jean Bowman.

25. In a dissertation currently under way, Robert Wimpelberg is assessing the manner in which parents express educational preferences within the public school system.

26. Bloom (1962) found that children's aptitudes are formed at an early age.

27. James, Thomas, and Dyck (1962) found a strong correlation between community SES and expenditures for education from local revenues.

28. Current research at the University of Chicago's Educational Finance and Productivity Center focuses in part on the structuring of classroom activities.

29. For example, teachers may group students for instruction in response to perceived distribution of students' competences. Grouping patterns may in turn have an effect on how well students of different ability levels learn.

30. Coons and Sugarman (1978) provide a cogent argument for vouchers. They do not adequately discuss the trade-offs between freedom of choice, equity, and efficiency that are implied by major reorientation of the educational system.

REFERENCES

Alexander, Karl L., and Edward L. McDill. 1976. "Selection and Allocation Within Schools: Some Causes and Consequences of Curriculum Placement." Report No. 213, Center for the Social Organization of Schools, The Johns Hopkins University, May.

Arrow, K. J. 1963. *Social Choice and Individual Values.* 2nd ed. New York: Wiley.

Averch, Harvey A.: Stephen J. Carroll; Theodore S. Donaldson; Herbert J. Kiesling; and John Pincus. 1972 *How Effective is Schooling? A Critical Review and Synthesis of Research Findings.* Santa Monica: RAND.

Barr, Rebecca. 1975 "How Children are Taught to Read: Grouping and Pacing." *School Review* 83, no. 3 (May): 479−98.

Bidwell, Charles E., and John D. Kasarda. 1975. "School District Organization and Student Achievement." *American Sociological Review* 40 (February): 55−70.

Bloom, Benjamin S. 1962. *Stability and Change in Human Characteristics.* New York: Wiley.

Bowles, Samuel S., and Henry M. Levin. 1968. "The Determinants of Scholastic Achievement: An Appraisal of Some Recent Evidence." *Journal of Human Resources* 3 (Winter): 3−24.

Brown v. Board of Education of Topeka, Kansas, 347 U.S. 483 1954.

Brown, Byron W., and Daniel H. Saks. 1980. "Production Technologies and Resource Allocation within Classrooms and Schools: Theory and Measurement." In *The Analysis of Educational Productivity*, Vol. I: *Issues in Microanalysis*, edited by Robert Dreeben and J. Alan Thomas. Cambridge, Massachusetts: Ballinger.

Burstein, Leigh. 1980. "The Role of Levels of Analysis in the Specification of Educational Effects." In *The Analysis of Educational Productivity*, Vol. I: *Issues in Microanalysis*, edited by Robert Dreeben and J. Alan Thomas. Cambridge, Massachusetts: Ballinger.

Coleman, James S.; E. Q. Campbell; C. J. Hobson; J. McPartland; A. M. Mood; F. D. Weinfield; and R. L. York. 1966. *Equality of Educational Opportunity.* Washington, D.C.: Government Printing Office.

Coons, John E., and Stephen D. Sugarman. 1978. *Education by Choice.* Berkeley: University of California Press.

Coons, John E.; W. A. Clune, III; and S. D. Sugarman. 1970. *Private Wealth and Public Education.* Cambridge, Massachusetts: Harvard University Press.

Cubberley, Ellwood P. 1906. *School Funds and Their Apportionment.* New York: Teachers College, Columbia University.

Garms, Walter I.; James W. Guthrie; and Lawrence C. Pierce. 1978. *School Finance: The Economics and Politics of Public Education.* Englewood Cliffs, New Jersey: Prentice-Hall.

Goss v. Board of Education, Lopez 419 U.S. 565 1975.

Greenberg, David, and John McCall. 1974. "Teacher Mobility and Allocation." *Journal of Human Resources* 9, no. 4 (Fall): 480–502.

Heyns, Barbara. 1974. "Social Selection and Stratification within Schools." *American Journal of Sociology* 79 (May): 1434–51.

James, H. Thomas, J. Alan Thomas, and Harold Y. Dyck. 1961. *School Revenue Systems in Five States*. Stanford, California: School of Education, Stanford University.

Jencks, Christopher; M. Smith; H. Acland; M.J. Bane; D. Cohen; H. Gintis; B. Heyns; and S. Michelson 1972. *Inequality: A Reassessment of the Effect of Family and Schooling in America*. New York: Basic Books.

Johns, Roe L., and Edgar L. Morphet. 1960. *The Economics and Financing of Education*. Englewood Cliffs, New Jersey: Prentice-Hall.

Katzman, Martin T. 1971. *The Political Economy of Urban Schools*. Cambridge, Massachusetts: Harvard University Press.

Koopmans, Tjalling C. 1957. *Three Essays on the State of Economic Science*. New York: McGraw-Hill.

Monk, David H. 1979. "An Economic Analysis of Resource Allocation within Classrooms." Ph.D. dissertation, Department of Education, University of Chicago.

Rawls, John. 1971. *A Theory of Justice*. Cambridge, Massachusetts: Harvard University Press.

Schultz, Theodore W. 1961. "Education and Economic Growth." In *Social Forces Influencing American Education, The Sixtieth Yearbook of the National Society for the Study of Education*, edited by Nelson B. Henry, pp. 46–48. Chicago: University of Chicago Press.

Serrano v. Priest, 26 Cal. Rptr. 601, 437 P.2d 1241 (1971).

Sexton, Patricia Cayo. 1961. *Education and Income: Inequalities of Opportunity in our Public Schools*. New York: Viking.

Summers, Anita A., and Barbara L. Wolfe. 1975. *Equality of Educational Opportunity Quantified: A Production Function Approach*. Philadelphia: Department of Research, Federal Reserve Bank of Philadelphia.

Tinker v. Des Moines, Independent Community School District, 393 U.S. 503 1969.

Wiley, David E., and Annegret Harnischfeger. 1974. "Explosion of a Myth: Quantity of Schooling and Exposure to Instruction, Major Educational Vehicles." Chicago: University of Chicago, 1974; Mimeograph. rptd. *Educational Researcher* 3 (March 1974): pp. 7–12.

Windham, Douglas M. 1978. "Incentive Analysis and Higher Educational Planning: Alternatives in Theory, Research, and Policy." Paris: International Institute for Educational Planning.

6 A NEW VIEW OF SCHOOL EFFICIENCY
Household Time Contributions to School Achievement

Charles S. Benson*
Elliott A. Medrich**
Stuart Buckley***

In recent years educators have rediscovered families. For some decades policymakers had argued that schools could equalize children's educational attainment and, indeed, their life chances. Researchers, on the other hand, have offered more recent evidence indicating that everything else aside, a child's prospects for educational success are largely a function of his or her family's social class position and socioeconomic status. In other words, what children take away from the classroom reflects fundamental differences in what they bring to the classroom in the first place.

In their important studies, Coleman (1966) and Jencks (1972) conclude that the environments in which children are raised and their away from school experiences probably hold the key to their prospects in traditional educational terms. In his report on educational

*Charles S. Benson, Professor, Graduate School of Education, University of California, Berkeley.

**Elliott Medrich, Project Director, Childrens Time Study Project, Boalt School of Law, University of California, Berkeley.

***Stuart Buckley, Research Associate, Childrens Time Study Project, Boalt School of Law, University of California, Berkeley.

Charles Benson and Elliott Medrich are co-principal investigators of the Children's Time Study, Schools of Law and Education, University of California, Berkeley. Stuart Buckley is research sociologist at the project.

opportunity Coleman (1966: 73–74) wrote:

> The sources of inequality of educational opportunity appear to lie first in the home itself and the cultural influences immediately surrounding the home; then they lie in the school's ineffectiveness to free achievement from the impact of the home and in the school's cultural homogeneity which perpetuates the social influences of the home and its environs.

Policymakers have been slow to respond to these kinds of findings, choosing instead to focus their efforts to raise student performance on time-tested, school-based intervention strategies. Benson sums up the issue this way:

> The Coleman Report states: "Studies of school achievement have consistently shown that variations in family background account for far more variation in school achievement than do variations in school characteristics." Bowles, in extending the analysis of the Coleman data, indicated that such variables as reading material in the home and family stability have a strong positive correlation with school achievement of children. Given these well supported findings, it is somewhat ironical that the main efforts in the United States toward overcoming school failure are still thought to be concentrated in schools and in programs, such as Headstart, that are based primarily on the school model. (Benson 1980: 31)
>
> It is a curiosity in educational policy that policy makers at both federal and state levels attribute power to reform in the distribution of educational resources that Coleman (and subsequent) evidence would appear to deny. So far at least, Coleman, not the reformers, is winning. Neither federally-financed compensatory education nor the rather ambitious efforts of a large number of states to reduce the effect of disparities in locally-taxable wealth on school district expenditures have served to remove the baleful influence (certain success stories excepted) of family background on performance of students in school. (Benson 1980)

Most researchers now recognize the powerful impact of home life on school performance. Models of efficiency in educational production, for instance, reflect this perspective. In Chapter 5 of this volume, J. Alan Thomas argues that "a broader view of the process of allocating resources in education recognizes that parents and students allocate resources in homes and schools and that decisions are important determinants of both efficiency and equity." He views the school as part of a broader educational context, and he notes that time and how it is spent in school and away from school by the student is a fundamental resource that must be taken into account.

Accounting for stocks or even flows of purchased resources does not exhaust the inventory of resources used in a classroom. Students' time is also a resource that (because it has alternate uses) is valuable and that is combined with purchased resources in the production of learning. In fact, students' time may be the most important resource of all, since while learning can take place without books and conceivably without teachers, it cannot take place without an investment by students of their own time. Furthermore, students' time is supplied to learning activities in the home as well as in the classroom; in the former context it is combined with other resources such as the time of parents, space, books, and even television that affect learning but are not purchased by the school district. (Thomas 1980)

The time use factor was introduced into the literature on education production in the 1960s, some three decades after the pioneering work by Strumilin (1960) and Walsh (1935) on the value of education. These early studies provided intellectual underpinnings for an emerging field of inquiry concerned with the issue of earned income differentials associated with increments of formal education. This notion was seized upon by Theodore Schultz (1961), who popularized the concept of "investment in human capital" in the 1950s. The investment idea came from the fact that one could translate differentials in earnings to a rate of return on costs of acquiring successive increments of formal education. Of course, lifetime income streams of different individuals take different shapes, and it was necessary to establish a common denominator of value to account for these differences. This is done through the process of discounting. Discounted values of incremental return were equated with discounted values of incremental costs to estimate an "internal rate of return." The rate of return for education could then be compared to rates of return for investments in physical capital and investments in other forms of human capital, such as health and nutrition.

Though it might appear that human capital theory evolved under a common set of social values, this was not the case. Walsh (1935) was concerned with a question of equity: Would the operation of the market economy bring about an equilibrium, or point of equality, between prices charged for a given set of human services and costs of producing additional units of those services? Or did market imperfections allow those who possessed certain kinds of human capital to extort a monopoly price for their services? In short, Walsh would have preferred the market rate of return to education to become equal in different lines of work and to become stabilized at the going rate of interest. On the other hand, Schultz (1961) and his followers appeared to extol high and rising rates of return to education. The worth, indeed, of a national system of education was to be found in the fact that returns to education exceeded returns to investment in physical capital. It goes without saying that high rates of return to education are grounded in a markedly unequal distribution of earned income.

In the 1960s and 1970s, theorists came to recognize that human capital is created not only in institutions of formal education but also in the workplace. It became fashionable to compute returns to "on the job training." The leading economist in this line of inquiry is Jacob Mincer (1962). More to the point of this study, another group of economists, those working in particular with Gary Becker, turned their attention to a relatively unexplored set of issues—the production of human capital in the family (Becker 1965). This new way of viewing the creation of value in persons became established in the mid-1960s as a question of the "economics of time." Becker's own work is almost entirely theoretical. He constructs economic models based on standard kinds of assumptions such as diminishing rates of return to portray, for example, how adult family members will allocate their time, scarce by definition, to various of their children in order to maximize the whole family's lifetime income.

It should be noted that Becker's work associated him with the tradition, on the empirical side, of time budget studies, a form of investigation most commonly practiced by sociologists. However, human capital economists quickly recognized the utility of this mode of research. For instance, out of the James Morgan team at the University of Michigan, Hill and Stafford (1974) analyzed the amounts of time adult members of families in different SES categories devote to the care of their children. The basic assumption is that greater time allocations to children translate into a higher level of development in children. Using different data sets, Arleen Leibowitz (1977) sought to assess effects of "home investments" on childrens' IQ. She examined mothers' time inputs to children, exploring the impact of different kinds of activities and interactions. Ruben Gronau (n.d.) studied the effects of husbands' and wives' market wage rates on allocation of time to market production, home production, and leisure. As these references suggest, although connections between time uses of different members of families and children's educational attainment have been an issue of concern to researchers, few have demonstrated clear linkages. Our objective here is to approach this question more deliberately and to analyze time contributions of family and parents to children's schooling success.

As the relationship of educational attainment to school and family inputs has received more attention, economic and sociological perspectives have moved somewhat closer, and the confluence of perspectives has had an impact on policymakers. Hence, in the 1970s it is not surprising to find educators concerning themselves with "proeducational" contributions of the family. Today, the language of collective responsibility—school and family working together in support of educational objectives—is commonplace. Educators no longer wish to go it alone. Similarly, policymakers no longer expect that finance reform in and of itself, or any sort of school-based resource allocation, will create significantly different outcomes for those who have achieved poorly in the past. Even parents, while they still value the role that schools can play in children's lives, no longer view the institution as all powerful, able to assure every child's future and certain to equalize life chances among children whose backgrounds are fundamentally unequal to begin with (see, for example, Gallup 1969, 1973, 1976; *Phi Delta Kappan* 1978).

Reasonably enough, these developments promote interest in nonschool inputs that might have an effect on educational attainment. These inputs involve values and attitudes as well as "proeducational" behaviors. It is presumed that families support or fail to support traditional learning to varying degrees and that this variation in inputs has some impact on a child's educational experience and school performance.

Much of what is thought to matter about the family's contribution to school achievement rests at the level of informed speculation rather than systematic inquiry. For instance, many policymakers and educators are promoting parent-school "contracts," agreements calling for parents to take specific actions that may help children at school—controlling TV viewing, maintaining quiet "study hours" in the home, helping children with homework, reading together, and more. In a similar fashion, the Elementary and Secondary Education Act (ESEA) compensatory program contends that certain types of out of school enrichment activities represent important proeducational experiences. Title I of that statute makes available enrichment services because it is believed that these kinds of activities may not be occurring in the homes of eligible children. Clearly there are contrasting expectations here. Where the contract assumes that parents can promote educational support, Title I suggests that parents cannot or will not become direct participants in their children's educational development. Both are efforts largely aimed at children from families of lower social status who are achieving less well at school. The messages, however, are contradictory. We must ask what we want or expect from families, particularly from families whose children are not doing well in school; and we must ask a more central question: If family inputs matter, which ones matter and in what ways and to what degree can particular actions overwhelm the "handicaps" of social class position, which so significantly dominate school performance equations?

In our research we have had an opportunity to study facets of children's daily life outside of school. Here it is possible to identify behaviors that may represent effective educational support—effective in the sense that they are associated with superior school achievement. By studying how children use time, we can examine the incidence of particular behaviors among children of different backgrounds performing at different levels in school. The link between these behaviors and school performance may be direct, indirect, or part of a more complex home-school-community dynamic. It may even be the case that activities do not matter individually—that there is some larger "support environment" in the home that simply cannot be captured by calculating the incidence with which behavior or sets of behaviors occur.

With this caveat in mind, in this chapter we will analyze data from the Children's Time Study's survey of 764 eleven and twelve year old (sixth grade) children and their mothers living in Oakland, California.[1] With time study data it is possible to examine the extent to which parent inputs and parent–child interactions are associated with school performance.[2] In other places we have described ways in which this type of analysis contributes to our understanding of these school-related issues.

> Each year children attend school, they bring with them a lot of "baggage:" their health, energy levels, knowledge of skills acquired in formal learning and in informal activities, tastes, attitudes, and expectations. Presumably, some of this baggage is helpful to a given child in his schoolwork, and some is not helpful. We know very little about how the baggage is acquired by a child or, in some cases, forced on him. What we do know is that the differences in

school performance of children is greater than can be explained by the initial intellectual endowments and that the gap in performance tends to get wider the longer children attend school. (Benson 1977: 12)

Benson argues for focusing on home-based family inputs in the following way:

> The chief thing we know about determinants of school performance is that it is closely associated with differences in "home background," where home background is measured by parental income, educational level, and occupation. It is not possible easily to change the levels of parental income, education, and occupation in the short run—nor is it at all certain that changing such description of family life would have any desirable effects on the child in the short run. So public policy, as it has shaped up, seeks to "compensate" for deficiencies in home background, but this compensation is offered in the absence of knowledge of precisely what is lacking in the home, toward which compensation should be made.
>
> Now, if it is parental behavior that affects school performance, we would expect some of the achievement-stimulating kinds of behavior to be in the grasp of parents of whatever level of SES. This seems to be the assumption underlying parenting education. But we cannot be certain that given types of parental behavior will work well with all types of children. More important, we do not know much about how different kinds of parental behavior are reinforced or cancelled by different kinds of neighborhood conditions and by different kinds of institutional behaviors. In the absence of such information, policies toward children are fragmented—and, in attacking the problems of school failure, ineffective. A more comprehensive approach to studying the out-of-school environment might allow us to design a better integrated and more effective set of policies toward youth. (1977: 14–15)

In the context of educational production, families as well as schools create human capital, and human capital is surely affected by interactions between home and school and among home, family, and neighborhood. However, one should not expect to find simple relationships. Home and family inputs may be mediated by other factors such that they are not directly reflected in school achievement or vice versa. Although we intend to focus on parent and family inputs, it is essential to recognize that there are competing models that "spotlight" different factors affecting school performance. These have been reviewed elsewhere by Benson (1980). He has addressed the following question: Recognizing the strong influence of socioeconomic status (SES) on student achievement, can some of the variation be explained by looking at differences in parent–child interactions? One might find, for example, that higher SES parents did more things or different kinds of things with their children than lower SES parents. Then, controlling for SES, one might find an association between different forms of parent–child interaction and success in school. The assumption that parent–child interaction is the primary determinant of differences in school attainment is what Benson calls the "parent-dominant model." Benson also recognized other possibilities by means of which SES could effect school attainment. Characteristics of the school, which is not to say just the quantity of purchased inputs, could bear a relationship to family SES and be the primary determining influence. Under the "school-dominant model," groups of lower SES children attending higher SES schools would, on average, be expected to display a higher level of attainment than lower SES children in low income schools, regardless of observed differences in parent–child interaction in the family. Finally, Benson suggested that SES factors might operate within the neighborhood and within the class structure itself. On the latter point, he noted that, for example, negative attitudes toward the importance of school attainment could be generated by high rates of youth unemployment in inner cities and that these attitudes could filter downward from adults and from older siblings and friends to affect adversely even the performance of elementary school students.

The conclusions in Benson's first paper on this topic suggest that the parent-dominant model is relatively weak. School performance of upper SES children and lower SES children, though substantially different, showed rather minimal influence of parent–child interactions in individual families. However, the several models are not mutually exclusive. In fact, collectively they probably describe the real complexity of the school achievement dynamic.

Benson's earlier writings raised many of the theoretical issues, with a small amount of empirical inquiry. This chapter offers a more detailed analysis of data from the Children's Time Study field survey. Here we will continue this mode of inquiry, focusing on the import of proeducational parents inputs to children as well as inputs at school—this in an effort to describe their contributions, individually and collectively, to school achievement.

Several constraints affect our analysis. To begin with, we are limited by the nature of our data. We have surveyed children and families in one community and at one specific time. In fact, there may be more or less congruence between parent inputs and parent–child interactions over time. A family directing high levels of inputs at a child now may or may not have done so in the past. School achievement data, on the other hand, represent an "accumulated history" of sorts. That is to say, it is an evaluation of a child's schooling success over a period of many years. This against our "specific time" survey data.

Second, we have data only on eleven and twelve year old children (sixth grade). It may well be the case that the most salient inputs, from a perspective of school achievement, took place (or failed to take place) years before and that high or low inputs now are much less important than high or low levels of inputs in the past (that we do not know about). Finally, we are making assumptions about which kinds of inputs matter in the traditional educational sense. We are, in effect, selecting certain behaviors for close examination and assuming that these activities, per se, make a difference.

With these cautionary notes in mind, we turn to an exploratory analysis of several kinds of family inputs. Our intention is to examine the association of these inputs with school achievement. While we will devote much of our attention to the family, we will also explore the combined impact of family and school inputs. Given earlier work, we would expect to find that both affect children's school performance, and accordingly, we shall try to determine the degree to which their cumulative power exceeds their individual contributions.

INPUTS AND INTERACTIONS—
SELECTED MEASURES

Our analysis utilizes data collected in Oakland, California, in 1976. The field survey, as noted previously, involved 764 sixth grade public school students and their parents. The nature of the sample makes clear the inner city nature of the respondent population.

Let us briefly describe how we shall proceed. First, we explore time constraints on parents. At the outset we must establish some parent input "parameters"—limits on their availability to their children. While this is not to say that their available time is a measure of the quantity or the quality of actual inputs, it does provide a way of approximating the highest possible level of interaction. We then explore the link between this measure of time availability and children's school achievement.

Next, we select several specific parent–child interactions that we would expect, given existing literature, to be related to school performance. From this long list of items we select a subset for detailed analysis. This subset, in our sample, is statistically linked to achievement—that is, children from families in which these inputs occur are likely to do better in terms of their school performance. We link the interactions first to SES and then, within SES groups, to achievement. We also establish a "summary input" variable across all these measures and explore their cumulative effect on achievement.

The last part of our analysis focuses exclusively on our low SES sample. Here we attempt to relate findings regarding level of parental inputs among these low SES children to characteristics of the school each child attends and to achievement.

As a prior matter, readers should note that among children in our sample, expected relationships between SES and achievement are clearly in evidence. Table 6–1 displays proportions of each SES group in each achievement quartile. Low SES children are over-represented among low achievers, while high SES children are over-represented among high achievers. This basic distribution will be referred to at several points in our analysis, so we believe that it is important to introduce it before we turn to the data themselves.

PARENTS' TIME AVAILABILITY TO CHILDREN

From the time study survey we used detailed information on parents' work schedules to calculate number of waking hours per week not spent at work or traveling to and from work. For our purposes, however, this was not a sufficiently precise estimate of time available to children, since much nonworking time is spent on personal and household maintenance and is not even potentially available for the kind of (presumptively) enrichment activities in which we were interested. Moreover, such maintenance is in part a function of number of children in the family and of the number of parents. The mother in a large family, for example, is likely to have less time to do things that may have educational payoffs with her children simply because of the many demands made upon her. To refine our calculation we used

Table 6—1.   Socioeconomic status and achievement (*percent*).[a]

	Achievement in Quartiles				
	Low			High	
Socioeconomic Status[b]	(1)	(2)	(3)	(4)	(N)[c]
High	10	18	20	52	(87)
Middle	19	23	23	35	(206)
Low	35	29	26	11	(284)
Totals	25	25	25	25	(635)

$$X_6^2 = 81.257$$
$$p < .001$$

a. In all tables, "achievement" refers to performance on the sixth grade English–Verbal section of the California Test of Basic Skills (CTBS).

b. In all tables, SES categories are defined as follows:

High = Family income $20,000 or more, and mother at least a high school graduate;
Middle = Family income $10,000—19,999 without regard to mother's education;
Low = Family income below $10,000, and mother's education less than college graduate.

Families on which full income and education data are not available were excluded from the analysis.

c. In all tables, children attending schools that did not administer the CTBS to sixth grade students were excluded from the analysis.

data derived from Vickery (1977) and from Walker and Woods (1976) and deducted from our gross estimate of parents' nonworking hours the amount of time typically spent in day-to-day care and maintenance in families with different numbers of children and parents.

Time availability is significantly related to SES, if not in an entirely straightforward way (Table 6—2). Taking the time of all parents in the household, we found that although high amounts of time were not systematically distributed by SES, the overall tendency showed a positive relation. In particular the proportion of families short on time, measured in this way, was strongly related to SES. To some extent this pattern has to be ascribed simply to number of parents present in the family, but in muted form similar patterns reappear when we consider only mothers' time (Table 6—3). Here, however, distribution of both low and medium SES mothers' time is bimodal, in contrast to that of high SES mothers. What this suggests

Table 6-2.   Parental time availability (*percent*).[a]

| Socioeconomic Status | Time Availability[b] | | | |
| | Low | | | High |
	(1)	(2)	(3)	(4)
High	7	24	50	19
Middle	26	19	27	28
Low	41	33	8	18
All Children	28	27	23	23

$$X_6^2 = 129.62$$
$$p < .001$$

a. Calculated as nonworking (waking) hours per week less maintenance time on the following schedule (see Vickery 1977):

| Number of Parents | Number of Children | | | |
	1	2, 3	4, 5	6+
1	57	61	63	69
2	62	66	68	74

b. The categories, designed to divide the sample into four comparably sized segments, were from low to high—less than or equal to 52 hours per week; 53–72 hours per week; 73–112 hours per week, and 113 hours per week or more.

is that only more affluent mothers are likely or able to work on a flexible schedule (if they work at all). Others, it appears, must choose between either working full time such that they have less nonwork time for their children or not working at all. This suggests that aggregated time availability in and of itself might not be closely related to achievement.

We were not surprised, therefore, to discover that although parental time as a whole did show a slight and positive statistically significant relation with achievement, this was almost entirely a function of the relation of the variable to SES and vanished when controls for the latter were applied. This is not a matter of inadequate measurement. It reflects an empirical feature of the relationship between time availability and achievement. When we assessed achievement levels of children who came home from school to a house with no adult present, although we had thought that we might find at least some evidence of deprivation here, in fact those children, in all socio-

Table 6–3. Mothers' time availability (*percent*).[a]

| | Time Availability[b] | | | |
| | Low | | | High |
Socioeconomic Status	*(1)*	*(2)*	*(3)*	*(4)*
High	12	46	13	30
Middle	28	19	17	37
Low	25	12	27	36
All Children	23	20	21	36

$$X^2_6 = 71.36$$
$$p < .001$$

a. Calculated as nonworking (waking) hours per week less maintenance time on the following schedule (see Vickery 1977):

| Number of Parents | Number of Children | | | |
	1	*2, 3*	*4, 5*	*6+*
1	57	61	63	69
2	62	66	68	74

b. The relevant intervals in this case are 20 hours a week and below, 21–36 hours, 37–56 hours, and 57–74 hours.

economic groups except the highest, showed slightly higher achievement levels. We were thus led to conclude that to the extent that parent inputs may influence children's success in school, in many homes this happens in spite of relatively severe time constraints. On this basis we devoted the remainder of our analysis to an examination of specific uses of time rather than to absolute amounts or aggregate availability during the out of school day.

PARENTAL INPUTS—TYPES OF TIME AND ITEMS ANALYZED

Many items in our survey were used to measure parent–child interactions. In search of a relationship between parental inputs and achievement, we began our analysis by selecting a wide variety of variables that might be expected to affect performance.

First we examined items representing everyday kinds of interactions. These included whether

- Parent and child eat dinner together;
- Parent and child do housework or yardwork together;
- Parent and child shop together;
- Parent and child watch TV together;
- Parent and child go places like restaurants, movies, parks, or sports events together; and
- Parent and child do things together on weekends.

Next we considered parental control over children's activities. Here we intended to identify a different kind of input—strength of the parent's role as a socializing agent, directly influencing the child's time use. We selected another broad set of measures:

- How free the child is to move around neighborhood and city on his or her own;
- Rules about bedtime and chore performance;
- Rules about doing homework and watching TV;
- Rules about allowances; and
- How "pressed" the child felt outside of school.

The first three measures were constructed on the basis of mothers' responses to the question, At what age will your child be ready to make decisions regarding each of these matters on his or her own? The last measure was derived from the child's interview—their response to a question regarding whether or not they felt that they "have to do" many things they would rather not do.

Our third set of items considered activities specifically oriented toward educational or cultural enrichment:

- Whether or not parent and child go to cultural activities together;
- Whether or not parent and child play games together;
- Whether or not parent encourages child to pursue a hobby;

- Whether or not parent and child go to church, libraries, museums, plays, and concerts together; and

- Whether or not the parent and child read together at home.

Finally, we considered the parent's involvement with the school—in terms of volunteering, PTA membership, and attendance at school functions and events.

Many of the individual items listed above displayed a relationship to SES, and a few were associated with achievement. When we summed the items and created additive indexes for each category, our findings offered more interesting analytical possibilities. Two summary indexes—everyday activities and control—yielded no strong relationships to achievement. Cultural activities and parental involvement, on the other hand, were significantly associated with the child's achievement level. The relationship of these two measures to achievement is presented in Table 6–4. Though suggestive, the association is far less robust than might have been anticipated, and indeed, when controls for SES were applied, the relationships virtually vanished for both high and medium SES families.

The pattern remained, however, among low SES families with respect to cultural activities, leading us to conclude that the kinds of parent input influence we hoped to find did indeed exist. But they were not strong. This might be because such causal linkages are difficult to find with a survey instrument. Or it might be that the effect of our variables are too indirect to expect to see any relationship to school performance per se, or that our age group is beyond the point of significant impact. We therefore determined to pursue our analysis in two directions—first by observing the "fine grain" of the specific items we knew to be achievement related, and second by looking at the interaction of parental inputs with the school itself so that we could address the issue of whether these inputs were simply attributes of individual families or interactions that had some larger relationship to the school environment.

Table 6-4. Achievement, cultural activities, and parental involvement (*percent*).

| | Achievement Quartile | | | | |
| | Low | | | High | |
Summary Input Measure	(1)	(2)	(3)	(4)	(N)
Level of cultural activities together					
0 (low)	35	26	20	19	(112)
1	31	33	19	18	(171)
2	16	29	27	29	(161)
3	20	13	32	35	(112)
4 (high)	28	19	29	24	(78)
All children	25	25	25	25	(635)

$$X^2_{12} = 42.474$$
$$p < .001$$

Level of parental involvement in school activities					
0 (low)	23	29	24	24	(108)
1	32	31	20	17	(181)
2	27	25	23	26	(163)
3	22	18	32	28	(111)
4	14	18	28	40	(73)
All children	25	25	25	25	(635)

$$X^2_{12} = 32.013$$
$$p < .01$$

PARENTAL INPUTS—ANALYSIS OF THE ACHIEVEMENT-RELATED MEASURES

Of the individual items described above, we selected five for further analysis, because not only was the relative strength of their association with school achievement apparent, but each could also be attached to a specific theory concerning power and import of pro-educational activities in the home. These items are:

- Child and parent visits to cultural centers together,
- Child and parent doing hobbies together,
- Parent facilitating child's participation in organized activities,
- Dinnertime eating patterns, and
- How frequently parent and child did things together on weekends.

Each of these items seems to be a proxy of some sort—a way of measuring some genuine proeducational input. Visits to cultural centers like museums is a traditional enrichment activity, a valuable kind of exposure to unconventional learning environments. Doing hobbies together represents parent support and encouragement of the child's interests and efforts to learn skills or sharpen competencies. Parent facilitation represents a commitment (at a personal, if not a material, cost) to helping the child develop his or her potential in ways that require professional expertise. Eating dinner together is an important socializing experience, for this is perhaps the only time of day that parents and children can really talk together and share and learn from one another. Weekend activities tap the degree to which parents choose to be involved with their children during nonwork time. Parents may or may not treat these precious hours as "their time" and may be more or less receptive to "doing things" with their children— this being the most general measure of input in this analysis. Taken together, these items tap some of the many ways in which parents seem to enhance children's educational prospects either directly and deliberately or indirectly and perhaps unconsciously. In the following pages we shall analyze these items individually in relation to achievement and as part of an additive index.

Table 6−5 displays the manner in which these items are related to our achievement measure. Table 6−6 illustrates the relationship of the same items to SES. In some cases (weekend activities and dinnertime patterns), high-achieving children who are from low SES fami-

Table 6−5.   Parental time inputs related to achievement (*percent*).

	Achievement Quartiles				
	Low (1)	(2)	(3)	High (4)	(N)
1. Family visits to cultural centers in area[a] during sixth grade					
Family has visited at least one	23	25	12	40	(87)
None	26	25	27	22	(548)
2. Parent engages in hobbies with child					
Ever	20	28	24	28	(237)
Never	29	24	25	23	(398)
				$X_3^2 = 7.204$	
				$p < .2$	
3. Parent facilitates[b] child's participation in organized activities−lessons					
High degree of facilitation	17	21	23	38	(153)
Some facilitation	26	22	27	26	(201)
No facilitation	30	31	24	16	(281)
				$X_6^2 = 31.296$	
				$p < .001$	
4. Family eating patterns					
All eat together	22	21	27	30	(333)
Some eat together	23	28	25	24	(158)
Each eats when wants to	37	33	19	12	(144)
				$X_6^2 = 32.244$	
				$p < .001$	

Table 6-5. continued

	Achievement Quartiles				
	Low (1)	(2)	(3)	High (4)	(N)
5. Frequency of activities together (parent and child) on weekends					
Every weekend	18	26	28	28	(92)
Most weekends	25	20	28	28	(178)
Some weekends	26	27	23	24	(231)
Hardly ever	30	30	21	19	(134)
				$X^2_9 = 11.484$	
				n.s.	
Number of inputs (summary of items 1-5 above)					
0-1	33	28	22	17	(288)
2-3	19	23	29	30	(291)
4-5	21	26	14	39	(56)
				$X^2_6 = 32.687$	
				$p < .001$	

a. Cultural centers: museum, aquarium, planetarium, hall of science, exploratorium.

b. Components of facilitation: seeks out activity for child, drives child to and from activity, signs child up for activity.

lies have patterns of behavior across these items that approximate patterns of children from higher SES families (Table 6–7).

Looking closely at the relationship between these five variables and achievement within SES groups (we do this in order to determine the extent to which they have an independent impact on achievement and the extent to which they can explain SES differences), we find differing patterns, none indicating a strong independent effect but, on the contrary, suggesting a relationship subordinate to SES itself. In the case of visiting cultural centers, although there may be some impact on achievement among middle and high SES children, there is no evidence that this has any impact on achievement among lower SES children (Table 6–8). In contrast, hobbies

Table 6–6. Parental time inputs related to achievement (*percent*) (*percentaged vertically where applicable*).

	Socioeconomic Status		
	High	*Middle*	*Low*
1. Family visits to cultural centers in area[a] during sixth grade			
Family has visited at least one	30	19	11
			$X_2^2 = 23.217$
			$p < .001$
2. Parent engages in hobbies with child			
Ever	47	40	31
			$X_2^2 = 11.179$
			$p < .01$
3. Parent facilitates[b] child's participation in organized activities–lessons			
High degree of facilitation	52	35	14
Some facilitation	30	32	33
No facilitation	18	33	53
			$X_4^2 = 86.771$
			$p < .001$

Table 6–6. continued

	Socioeconomic Status		
	High	Middle	Low
4. Family eating patterns			
All eat together	67	59	53
Some eat together	28	21	22
Each eats when wants to	5	20	25

$$X_4^2 = 25.195$$
$$p < .001$$

5. Frequency of activities together (parent and child) on weekends

	High	Middle	Low
Every weekend	18	18	14
Most weekends	31	28	25
Some weekends	40	36	37
Hardly ever	11	17	24

$$X_6^2 = 13.793$$
$$p < .05$$

Number of inputs (summary of items 1–5 above)

	High	Middle	Low
0–1	22	35	51
2–3	59	52	43
4–5	19	13	6
(Total N)	(129)	(234)	(333)

$$X_4^2 = 45.271$$
$$p < .001$$

a. Cultural centers: museum, aquarium, planetarium, hall of science, exploratorium.

b. Components of facilitation: seeks out activity for child, drives child to and from activity, signs child up for activity.

Table 6–7.   Parental time inputs, family SES, and achievement (*percent*).

Number of Inputs	High–Middle SES Families	Low SES Families	
		Child in Highest Achievement Quartile	Other Children
0–1	30	42	35
2–3	55	55	39
4–5	15	(1)	5
(N)	(254)	(30)	(363)

$$X_4^2 = 45.27$$
$$p < .001$$

Table 6–8.   Achievement, SES, and family visits to cultural centers during sixth grade (*percent*).

Socioeconomic Status	Achievement Quartile				
	Low (1)	(2)	(3)	High (4)	(N)
High					
At least one visit	11	5	18	67	(19)
No visits	10	22	20	48	(68)
					(n.s.)
Middle					
At least one visit	21	26	5	48	(37)
No visits	19	23	26	33	(169)

$$X_3^2 = 8.200$$
$$p < .05$$

Socioeconomic Status	Low (1)	(2)	(3)	High (4)	(N)
Low					
At least one visit	36	38	17	9	(26)
No visits	34	28	27	11	(258)
					(n.s.)

Table 6–9. Achievement, SES, and working at hobbies with parents (*percent*).

| | Achievement Quartile | | | | |
| | Low | | | High | |
Socioeconomic Status	(1)	(2)	(3)	(4)	(N)
High					
Ever work at hobbies					
with parent	10	15	17	58	(39)
Never do	10	21	22	47	(47)
					(n.s.)
Middle					
Ever work at hobbies					
with parent	22	25	15	38	(85)
Never do	17	22	28	34	(122)
					$X^2_3 = 5.239$
					$p < .2$
Low					
Ever work at hobbies					
with parent	19	34	37	10	(90)
Never do	42	26	21	11	(194)
					$X^2_3 = 16.997$
					$p < .001$

show a relationship for the low SES group. This, however, mostly reduces the proportion of low achievers; it does not increase the proportion of highest quartile achievers (Table 6–9). Facilitation appears to increase the number of high achievers at all SES levels, and it reduces the number of low achievers, but it does not significantly close the performance gap among SES groups (Table 6–10).

Weekend activities have an important effect (Table 6–11). Lower SES children whose parents do things with them often on weekends have an achievement profile significantly different from the rest of the low SES group. The proportion of low SES children with low achievement and high weekend activities is comparable to that of middle SES children generally. The proportion of low SES high achievers approaches the level of the middle SES group as well. This is a definite effect but hardly one that enables us to explain the over-

Table 6–10. Achievement, SES, and parental facilitation of organized activities (*percent*).

	Achievement Quartile				
Socioeconomic Status	*Low (1)*	*(2)*	*(3)*	*High (4)*	*(N)*
High					
High degree of facilitation	8	14	26	53	(41)
Some facilitation	5	24	15	56	(27)
No facilitation	23	19	14	44	(18)
					(n.s.)
Middle					
High degree of facilitation	16	18	22	44	(68)
Some facilitation	21	18	22	39	(67)
No facilitation	21	32	23	24	(72)
					$X_6^2 = 9.087$
					$p < .2$
Low					
High degree of facilitation	30	31	24	15	(39)
Some facilitation	35	24	30	11	(89)
No facilitation	35	31	24	9	(156)
					(n.s.)

all SES gap. Dinnertime patterns also have fairly substantial effects (Table 6–12). Children from low SES families who eat together are less likely to be in the lowest achievement quartile than children from either middle or upper SES families who do not eat together. However, those low SES families are still far less likely to have high achieving children than the middle SES family that does not eat together.

In summary, we do find some evidence that particular behaviors and interactions reduce the achievement deficit of low SES children when compared with the upper SES peers. This is an important point that deserves considerable attention. However, we also find that high levels of inputs are not strongly related to high achievement within

Table 6-11.   Achievement, SES, and frequency of child's weekend activities with parents (*percent*).

Socioeconomic Status	Achievement Quartile				
	Low (1)	(2)	(3)	High (4)	(N)
High					
Every weekend	16	12	31	41	(12)
Most weekends	6	14	17	63	(27)
Some weekends	11	25	22	42	(36)
Hardly ever	13	13	5	69	(11)
					(n.s.)
Middle					
Every weekend	19	25	21	35	(37)
Most weekends	23	21	16	41	(59)
Some weekends	15	25	28	33	(73)
Hardly ever	22	22	25	32	(37)
					(n.s.)
Low					
Every weekend	19	32	30	20	(36)
Most weekends	34	18	39	9	(75)
Some weekends	37	28	21	14	(101)
Hardly ever	39	39	18	5	(72)
					$X^2_9 = 23.693$
					$p < .01$

the low SES group and that on balance, parental inputs aside, their performance remains well below that of both middle and upper SES children (Table 6-13).

Table 6–12.   Achievement, SES, and family eating patterns (*percent*).

Socioeconomic Status	Achievement Quartile				(N)
	Low (1)	(2)	(3)	High (4)	
High					
All eat together	8	13	19	59	(50)
Some eat together	13	26	19	41	(32)
Each eats when wants	13	14	27	47	(5)
					(n.s.)
Middle					
All eat together	16	19	27	38	(114)
Some eat together	16	20	20	44	(47)
Each eats when wants	31	35	14	20	(46)
					$X_6^2 = 14.004$
					$p < .05$
Low					
All eat together	31	24	30	15	(142)
Some eat together	30	35	27	7	(65)
Each eats when wants	44	32	19	6	(77)
					$X_6^2 = 12.315$
					$p < .1$

Table 6-13. Achievement, SES, and number of parental inputs (*summary measures; percent*).

	Achievement Quartile				
Socioeconomic Status	Low (1)	(2)	(3)	High (4)	(N)
High					
4-5	18	7	16	60	(12)
3-2	5	15	20	60	(51)
0-1	17	29	22	32	(24)
					$X^2_6 = 8.630$
					$p < .2$
Middle					
4-5	20	19	11	50	(25)
2-3	16	24	24	36	(103)
0-1	23	23	24	30	(77)
					(n.s.)
Low					
4-5	21	50	23	6	(14)
2-3	28	23	35	14	(118)
0-1	41	32	20	8	(153)
					$X^2_6 = 15.950$
					$p < .02$

CUMULATIVE IMPACTS—PARENT-CHILD INTERACTION AND THE SCHOOL ENVIRONMENT

In this section we focus on the cumulative impact of parents and schools on the performance of the 284 children from low SES families in our sample. In varying numbers, children from low SES families in our sample attend schools throughout the city. Although low SES children are concentrated in fairly homogeneous settings, this is not entirely the case. For a number of reasons, low SES children can be found living in relatively high income neighborhoods and attending higher income schools (we classify each school in our sample on the basis of the median income of residents in the school attendance area).

With regard to our low SES sample, note first that the achievement profile of these children is markedly different, depending on the income level of the school they attend (Table 6-14). However,

Table 6-14. Achievement of children from lower SES families attending schools of different income levels (*percent*).[a]

	Achievement Quartile				
	Low (1)	(2)	(3)	High (4)	(N)
Children attending high or middle income schools	24	24	28	25	(58)
Children attending low income schools	37	30	26	7	(227)
				$X_3^2 = 17.244$	
				$p < .001$	
Variation among low income schools[b]					
High achievement: School A	29	35	24	12	(32)
B	24	23	41	12	(40)
Low achievement: School C	37	37	19	7	(40)

a. School income categories (high, middle, low) were created with 1970 census data. The median income for each school attendance area was calculated and all schools in the sample were then ranked and clustered into three groups.

b. Of the eight low income schools, schools A and B had the highest proportion of high achievers; school C had the lowest proportion of high achievers.

Type of Input	Child Attends High/Middle Income School	Child Attends Low Income School	Low Income School[a]		
			High Achieving		Low Achieving
			A	B	C
Takes child to cultural centers	11	11	29	5	7
Hobbies together	34	30	48	11	18
Family eating patterns					
All eat together	61	51	52	53	48
Each eats when wants	23	26	19	16	26
Frequency of weekend activities with child					
Every weekend	15	13	29	5	7
Hardly ever	20	25	24	26	37
Facilitates organized activities–lessons					
To a high degree	28	9	5	5	11
Some	31	33	14	47	53
Never	42	58	81	47	56
Number of inputs (summary of items above)					
4–5	4	6	19	0	4
2–3	54	40	24	32	37
0–1	41	54	57	68	59

a. Of the eight low income schools, schools A and B had the highest proportion of high achievers; school C had the lowest proportion of high achievers.

Table 6–16. Parental inputs, income level of school, and lower SES children's achievement (*percent*).

Parental Inputs	School Income Level	Percent of Low SES Children		
		Achieving in Lowest Quartile	Achieving in Highest Quartile	(N)
Cultural activities				
Visits to cultural centers	High/Middle	(1)	(2)	(3)
No visits	High/Middle	24	23	(53)
Visits to cultural centers	Low	42	0	(21)
No visits	Low	37	8	(206)
Hobbies				
Hobbies with parents	High/Middle	10	24	(21)
No hobbies	High/Middle	30	27	(37)
Hobbies with parents	Low	21	6	(69)
No hobbies	Low	44	7	(157)
Facilitates organized activities–lessons				
Facilitation	High/Middle	13	33	(30)
No facilitation	High/Middle	33	19	(27)
Facilitation	Low	40	5	(98)
No facilitation	Low	35	8	(129)
Family eating patterns				
All eat dinner together	High/Middle	21	29	(34)
Each eats when wants	High/Middle	33	25	(12)
All eat dinner together	Low	35	11	(107)
Each eats when wants	Low	46	2	(65)

Frequency of weekend activities with child				
Activities most/every weekend	High/Middle	23	23	(26)
Activities some weekends or hardly ever	High/Middle	26	29	(31)
Activities most/every weekend	Low	17	16	(27)
Activities some weekends or hardly ever	Low	41	6	(200)
Number of inputs (summary of items above)				
4–5	High/Middle	(0)	(1)	(2)
2–3	High/Middle	16	28	(32)
0–1	High/Middle	35	17	(23)
4–5	Low	24	0	(12)
2–3	Low	32	8	(85)
0–1	Low	42	7	(129)

it is also the case (Table 6–15) that there are only modest differences in parental inputs by low SES parents regardless of the income level of the child's school. Facilitation is the only low SES parent input that demonstrates a significant difference across low, middle, and high income schools. Since input levels are generally similar, inputs by low SES parents do not seem to be significantly linked to the school environment itself.

The second part of Table 6–15 adds an important dimension to this discussion. Here we compare three individual low income schools that we categorized as low or high achieving depending upon the proportion of high achievers at the school. As the data show, among high-achieving children attending these schools, parent input levels (individually and cumulatively) differ dramatically. In school A, high achievement is clearly associated with high parent inputs. In school B it is not. This suggests that the attitudes and behavior of low SES parents that appear similar in the aggregate may be mediated by other factors at the school level—factors that may affect the way parents interact with their children outside school.

Table 6–16 takes the analysis one step further, comparing parental inputs from low SES samples at different income level schools. Two points are of note. First, expected interaction between parental inputs and school income level does not invariably occur. Second, children who went to low income schools and had high parent inputs were sometimes less likely to be low achievers than children who went to higher income schools and had low parent inputs. However, these children, in the aggregate, never had rates of high achievement even approaching those who attended higher income schools.

Table 6–16 compares the achievement of low SES children receiving low parental inputs and attending high or middle income schools with that of low SES children receiving high parental inputs and attending low income schools. Taking our summary index (bottom of Table 6–16), the following points can be made: High parental inputs reduce the proportion of low SES children in low income schools who are in the lowest achievement quartile to levels comparable to that of low input, low SES children attending higher income schools. These inputs, however, do not appear to raise the proportion of high achievers, under any circumstances. As the table indicates, this pattern is repeated for each individual input.

With regard to our low SES sample, our conclusion, as in the previous section, is that parental inputs do matter. While they do not seem to increase the proportion of high achievers, they clearly do reduce the proportion of low achievers. But in general, parental inputs do not seem to overcome the disadvantages associated with attending a low income school. This is evident, given that low SES children not attending low income schools perform better than their SES peers who do attend low income schools, levels of parental input aside. In other words, a low SES child is relatively advantaged by attending a middle or upper income school—much more so than the child is advantaged by a high level of parental inputs.

CONCLUDING OBSERVATIONS

Our data refer directly to a rather short span of time—parent inputs during the year the child was in sixth grade. It may well be true that the basis for success in school is set at an early age, and among our respondents, we know nothing about parent-child interactions during, say, the first three years of life. This reservation aside, we note that family conditions display a certain stability. Our data reveal a great deal of the nature of these conditions during the period of elementary schooling of our children.

Our results attribute only a modest amount of power to parent-child interactions in determining school achievement. This is not to say no power. Indeed, specific kinds of behavior (such as "spending time together on weekends") have significant effects on achievement of all children and, most notably, children from low SES families. No group of parents, hence, should regard their efforts toward their children as foreordained to failure. The involved parent is much more likely to prevent low levels of school performance than is the inattentive parent. Nevertheless, even strong commitment toward children does not readily avail the low SES family of any reasonable assurance of high school achievement. If our data indicate that parent power is modest, they attribute a surprising degree of apparent influence to the SES composition of the school. Low SES children appear to be almost literally buoyed up in performance by attending a high income school, even if they receive few parent inputs. Contrarily, low SES children from high input families who attend low income schools do not do well, on the average.

Our chief measure of school level differences is composition of the student body by SES. Nothing we found could be interpreted to say that Coleman's results regarding the insignificance of variations in quantity of purchased inputs is wrong. In fact, in our sample, schools with lower performance had greater quantities of purchased inputs on the average (given that these are the schools receiving ESEA Title I monies, bilingual education support, etc.).

It is difficult precisely to interpret the meaning of these inter-school differences in socioeconomic status, but there are at least three possibilities: First, the influence on low SES children flows directly from contact with high SES youngsters and affects the atti-tudes and behavior of low SES children in school. This is a pure con-tagion effect and is apparently what Coleman had in mind in his use of peer variables. Second, the influence of high income schools on low SES children might be felt through teachers. Teachers may estab-lish their own commitment to work and their own attitudes toward acceptable levels of performance based on the SES composition of the school. In this circumstance, more is expected of the low SES child because more is expected of all children in the school. Third, low SES children in high SES schools may be different from low SES students in low income schools because the former spend their out of school time in middle class neighborhoods and somehow benefit in ways that affect many aspects of their lives, including their school performance. (This appears to be the case in Oakland, where children attend neighborhood schools—that is, schools near to where they live. There is no busing and little "open enrollment.") This third possibility suggests that the school effect in our study may reflect larger neighborhood or class factors acting on children outside of school itself.

These explanations are not mutually exclusive. They may even reinforce one another. In any case, given our findings, it would be interesting to know more about the extent to which teacher behavior can offset the influence of neighborhood and social class. Although in our sample there was not much evidence of a teacher effect, we do not exclude this possibility. In fact, from our data one might suspect that dedicated teachers could have at least as much of an impact on a child's school achievement as dedicated parents.

Our analysis is too rudimentary to serve as a basis for policy, but the line of inquiry is sufficiently provocative to warrant further attention. If other research also reveals that student body composi-tion is a central factor contributing to the success or failure of chil-dren in school, implications are profound both in terms of school finance reform and general social policy. For if this is the case, the focus of our efforts would necessarily shift from redistributing resources among school districts to integrating schools by socioeconomic status within metropolitan areas.

NOTES TO CHAPTER 6

1. A detailed description of the sample is available from the authors.
2. To measure school performance we will use data on each child made available to us by the school district. Oakland, like many other districts, measures achievement with the California Test of Basic Skills (CTBS), English and mathematics competency examinations that are administered to children at several elementary and secondary grade levels.

REFERENCES

Becker, Gary. 1965. "A Theory of the Allocation of Time." *Economic Journal* 75 (September): 493–517.

Benson, Charles S. 1980. "Time and How it is Spent." Working Paper, Children's Time Study, School of Law, University of California, Berkeley. Rptd. in Charles S. Benson and Michael Kirst, eds., *Future Research Directions for the Federal Government in Education.* Washington, D.C.: Government Printing Office.

Benson, Charles S. 1980. "Household Production of Human Capital: Time Uses of Parents and Children as Inputs." In Walter W. McMahon and Terry Geske, eds., *Toward Efficiency and Equity in Educational Finance.* Boston: Allyn and Bacon.

Coleman, James S. et al. 1966. *Equality of Educational Opportunity.* Washington, D.C.: Government Printing Office.

Gallup, George. 1969. *The Gallup Opinion Index, #47.* May.

_____. 1973. *The Gallup Opinion Index, #119.* May.

_____. 1976. *The Gallup Opinion Index, #135.* October.

Gronau, Reuben. n.d. "Leisure, Home Production and Work–The Theory of the Allocation of Time Revisited." Stanford, California: National Bureau of Economic Research, Working Paper #137.

Hill, C. Russell, and Frank P. Stafford. 1974. "Allocation of Time to Pre-School Children and Educational Opportunity." *Journal of Human Resources* IX (Summer): 323–41.

Jencks, Christopher et al. 1972. *Inequality.* New York: Harper & Row.

Leibowitz, Arlene. 1977. "Parental Inputs and Children's Achievement." *Journal of Human Resources* XII (Spring): 242–50.

Medrich, Elliott A.; Judith Roizen; Victor Rubin; and Stuart Buckley. 1980. *The Serious Business of Growing Up: A Study of Children's Lives Outside of School.* Berkeley: University of California.

Mincer, Jacob. 1962. "On the Job Training: Costs, Returns, and Some Duplications." *Journal of Political Economy* LXX, pt. 2 (October): 50–79.

Phi Delta Kappan. 1978. *A Decade of Gallup Polls of Attitudes Toward Education 1969–78.* Bloomington, Indiana.

Schultz, Theodore W. 1961. "Education and Economic Growth." In National Society for the Study of Education, *Social Forces Influencing American Education*, pp. 46–88. Chicago: University of Chicago.

Strumilin, S.G. 1960. "The Economic Significance of National Education." Translated from an article in *Ekonomiski Truda* (based on papers appearing in the Soviet Union in 1929).

Thomas, J. Alan. 1980. "Issues in Educational Efficiency." In James Guthrie, ed., *School Finance in the 1980s: A Decade of Conflict.* Cambridge, Massachusetts: Ballinger.

Vickery, Clair. 1977. "The Time-Poor: A New Look at Poverty." *Journal of Human Resources* XII, no. 1 (Winter): 27–48.

Walker, Katheryn, and Margaret E. Woods. 1976. *Time Use: A Measure of Household Production of Family Goods and Services.* Washington, D.C.: American Home Economics Association.

Walsh, J.R. 1935. "Capital Concept Applied to Man." *Quarterly Journal of Economics* XLIX (February): 255–85.

IV THE PURSUIT OF LIBERTY

7 EFFICIENCY, EQUITY, AND THE NEED FOR A NEW EDUCATIONAL POLICY

*Jacob B. Michaelson**

Between 1970 and 1977 the school age population in the United States dropped by 4.3 percent. During this time, nonsectarian private school enrollments increased by about 60 percent.[1] Popular accounts attribute the shift more to dissatisfaction with public schools than to an increase in the quality of private alternatives.[2] While these accounts may overgeneralize, it seems likely that many families that have chosen to bear the added expense of nonpublic schools regard the decline in the public school programs as real enough. The argument in this chapter is that public schools, as presently financed and governed, suffer from a systemic incapacity to meet legitimate demands of a growing number of families and that efforts to make schools more responsive to these demands that do not take the causes of this incapacity into account are not likely to bear fruit.

Charles Wolf Jr. (1979) contends that public enterprises are subject to systemic deficiencies just as private ones are. He notes that public understanding of how markets fail is now so widespread that it has become a factor in the growth of regulation to limit environmental degradation and abate health and safety hazards. There is no similar body of widely understood analysis of nonmarket failure. Wolf believes one consequence of this gap is the enactment of public

*Jacob B. Michaelson, Professor, Department of Economics, University of California, Santa Cruz.

207

policies that treat public enterprises as virtually defect-free instruments for achieving public goals. He offers his analysis of the systemic deficiencies of public enterprise as a step toward filling the gap in public understanding on nonmarket failure and thereby improving chances for designing sound public policy.

For many of the same reasons, school districts often fail to produce efficient and effective educational programs. To be sure, efficiency is but one criteria by which public school efficacy may be judged. Equality of educational opportunity is an important criterion as well. However, neither efficiency nor equity appears to take absolute precedence as an objective of public policy toward schooling. It is important, therefore, to have a clear conception of the sources and extent of inefficiency in public schools so that the consequences of subordinating considerations of efficiency to the achievement of equity can be assessed.

This chapter begins with a review of recent work of public choice economists that bears on resource allocation and management decisions in nonmarket settings. The subsequent section adapts general features of the public choice approach to particulars of the public school setting with a view to illustrating some of its important implications for designing educational policy. The chapter concludes with a brief analysis of two current policy issues that highlight possible trade-offs between efficiency and equity that informed public policy should take into account.

THE ANATOMY OF NONMARKET FAILURE

Public choice theorists, much more than other analysts of modern bureaucracy, distinguish sharply between private, profit-seeking firms and public, nonprofit bureaus.[3] This distinction keeps in clear focus the notion of efficiency that is so central to price theory. These theorists place efficiency in the forefront of their concerns as they have adapted modern price theory to institutional arrangements of the public bureaus in which prices and markets usually play a subsidiary role. Since considerations of efficiency are central to the analysis of school districts developed below, it is important to define precisely what economists mean by the term.

Under a regime of competitive markets, and in the absence of market failure, interaction of producers and consumers attempting to promote their own material interests leads to socially optimal results in two important senses. Each good and service is produced at the lowest possible cost, and the mix of these goods and services, both with respect to quantity and quality, cannot be improved upon. No one can be made better by rearranging inputs and outputs without someone else being rendered worse. Productive activity is thus both technically and allocatively efficient. It is this twofold conception of efficiency, both more complex and more precise than popular notions of being businesslike or keeping costs down, that public choice theorists bring to the assessment of governmental enterprises.

For efficiency thus defined to have clear empirical referents, productive activity should be conducted according to canons of instrumental rationality. Goals of producing organizations should be unambiguous, and means of achieving them should be reasonably well understood. When ends are ambiguous and means uncertain, the empirical meaning of efficiency becomes problematic. Under such circumstances, standard economic analysis alone cannot maintain efficiency as a criterion for assessing efficacy of organizational conduct. In the sections that follow, economic analysis is extended to accommodate situations in which obstacles to instrumental rationality are inherent and substantial. This extension is particularly important in the present context, since public school aims are the subject of continuing controversy, and there exists so little agreement about what is sound educational technology.[4]

Most public enterprises are monopolies whose budgets are funded not from sales to customers, but from direct grants generated through a political process. In competitive markets, customers dissatisfied with a firm's performance have two avenues by which to seek remedies: they can attempt to influence the firm's behavior by voicing complaints, thereby directly influencing the organization's decision processes, and they can turn to alternative suppliers.[5] Since the latter, exit option reduces the firm's budget and exercise of voice presages the possibility of budget reductions, these options together place the firm's managers under considerable pressure to attend to customer demands. Because public bureaus are seldom faced with alternative suppliers, bureau clientele must rely mainly on the voice option to seek remedies for organizational failures. Because the bureau's budget is relatively secure in the absence of the exit option, voice alone is not likely to be a powerful remedy in the public context. One way to view the public choice approach is as a theory of the behavior of modern organizations subject primarily to constraints of clientele voice and only minimally to those of clientele exit.

Principal features of the public choice approach are (1) separation of factors determining level and character of the bureau's activities into traditional categories of demand and supply: (2) a theory of demand that incorporates results of work on the economic theory of democracy and interest group politics and on institutional arrangements of representative government including congressional committee appropriations review process; (3) a theory of supply that recognizes possibilities for self-interested action by bureaucrats who enjoy a monopolistic position relative to the bureau's sponsor—the body of elected officials—and implications of depending on grants from taxes, rather than per unit sales, to satisfied customers for revenues; and (4) a model of supply and demand interaction that shows that the level of quality of the bureau's activities, the magnitude of its budget, and the ways in which it conducts its productive activity systematically fall short of optimality. This shortfall may be characterized as a twofold departure from efficiency norms. Compared to output level production costs that would obtain if the activity were conducted under a regime of competitive markets, the bureau's output is too large and its costs of production too high—that is, the bureau is inefficient both allocatively and technically.

Allocative efficiency is a much more complex matter than technical efficiency. Overproduction by individual organizations will lead to an inappropriate mix of output at the macrolevel, since if the output of some units is excessive, that of at least some others must be less than optimal. It is also possible for the output mix to be inappropriate at the microlevel. To illustrate, individual school districts may fail to meet needs and interests of some of their clients even though they meet those of others. Put differently, it is possible for a bureau to produce the wrong output as well as too much output. We shall be concerned with inefficiency chiefly as nonoptimal output mix at the organizational level when we turn to modeling school district behavior.

These departures from efficiency norms arise in the following way. The bureau faces an elected government or sponsor; together they constitute a bilateral monopoly. The sponsor expresses demand for the bureau's output as it is generated through its appropriations review process and voting procedures in the budget it allocates to the bureau. This demand can be conceptualized by analogy to the traditional market demand schedule that reveals successive funding amounts the sponsor would be willing to provide for delivery of successive increments in the bureau's output. A cost schedule derivable from technical knowledge of how inputs are transformed into outputs and from prices of inputs is attributed to the bureau. Following standard price theory, the demand schedule slopes downward and the cost schedule slopes upward, the two intersecting at what would be a market-clearing equilibrium level of output and budget were the activity conducted under competitive market conditions. A key contribution of the public choice approach is to show why the level of output and budget are greater than this competitive standard.

The crucial factor leading to this result is the imbalance in bargaining power in favor of the bureau over the sponsor owing to the bureaucrat's superior knowledge of the bureau's cost schedule. Bureaucrats, like managers of private firms, are assumed to act self-interestedly and hence will exploit this superiority. They do this by maintaining as much secrecy as possible about the bureau's cost schedules. Given the absence of alternative suppliers who could offer to produce demanded outputs for a small budget or provide the sponsor information on costs of production, bureaucrats exploit the sponsor's relative ignorance by proposing excessive output and funding levels.[6]

Why is it in the bureaucrats' interest to obtain budgets and output commitments from the sponsor that exceed levels the sponsor would choose had it the requisite knowledge to do so? The answer lies in the character of the managerial reward structure in public bureaus. In private firms, managers can be remunerated in ways that make it in their personal interest not to exceed optimal levels of output and budget. In public bureaus, gains from reducing costs and limiting output cannot, for the most part, be shared with managers in privately appropriable forms. Under these conditions, excessive budget and output levels lead to "profits" that are appropriable "in kind," as it were, internally. These "profits" can enhance managerial prestige, secure social and physical amenities, and command loyalty and cooperation from subordinates.[7] They do not, however, contribute to efficient production of government services.

To use economic theory in this way requires a number of simplifying assumptions. Thus, output was taken as an ambiguous and presumably objectively measurable quantity. Requisite technology for producing this output was taken as existing independently of participant needs and interests and objectively knowable by at least some of them.[8] Bureaucrats were taken to be primarily self-interested, if not single-mindedly self-serving, leaving little scope for altruistically motivated action. From the perspective of positive economics, the simplifying character of these assumptions is of no particular significance. What matters is whether they lead to successful predictions of relevant behavior. Recent studies provide evidence that public enterprises have excess operating budgets (Niskanen 1975; Borcherding 1977). Since work in this field has just begun, a definitive judgment about the efficacy of the model with these assumptions is premature. However, if our interest is in public schools where ambiguous ends and uncertain means are of the essence, further inquiry into the appropriateness of these assumptions is timely.

Ambiguity about goals and concomitant uncertainty about technology are probably inherent in all public enterprise. In contrast to a competitive industry where managers need only know how to operate their organization profitably for the public's interest in efficient production to be served, in a public bureau an explicit plan or understanding of how to achieve optimality is necessary, since there is no counterpart to automatic market forces to move unwilling or unknowing bureaucrats toward it. Thus, the information required about what is in the public's interest to produce and how best to produce it is much more extensive in a public setting than a private one. Because of this, public managers may only infrequently, if at all, possess an authoritative plan capable of keeping the bureau's activities focused on producing the optimal output mix at least cost.

A number of difficulties arise if an authoritative vision of the bureau's purposes cannot be firmly established. Individual bureaucrats may come to have differing and inconsistent views about the bureau's goals. Moreover, some bureaucrats may act chiefly to advance their own interests. For both reasons some key decisionmakers may pursue objectives incompatible with those pursued by others, making it virtually impossible for efficient production of the bureau's output to be achieved. Such an impasse "leads even the most selfless bureaucrats to choose some feasible, lower-level goal, and this usually leads to developing expertise in some narrow field. The development of expertise usually generates a sense of dedication, and it is understandable that many bureaucrats identify this dedication with the public interest" (Niskanen 1971: 39).

In the absence of powerful offsetting influences, displacement of goals in public bureaus is likely to be pervasive. Under such circumstances, the notions of efficiency that we have considered lose precision. To be sure, the bureau's budget can still be larger than the sponsor would choose had it means to offset the bureau's bargaining power. However, the notion of efficiency requires a known technology and identifiable input and outputs. What the bureau will be shrouding in secrecy under pervasive goal displacement is not its cost schedules, as in the analogy to market supply and demand analysis, but rather the ways it uses its budget to hold together its activities in the face of their potential and actual incoherence as an ensemble.

How useful can the public choice approach be in providing insights into organizational decisionmaking under these conditions? Organizational incoherence makes the possibility of instrumental rationality appear questionable. Economic analysis will prove useful in identifying substructures that permit instrumentally rational behavior. These substructures contribute to the maintenance of order and regularity in the face of the larger incoherence of the organization. We now turn to an examination of what public choice theory offers for developing an understanding of how this orderly structure comes to be established and maintained.

In economic theory, productive organizations are taken to be instruments designed to advance their owner's welfare. To understand ways in which instrumental rationality informs the decisionmaking process in bureaus, it will be helpful to examine the relationship between the bureau and its owners. Our procedure will be to investigate selected organizations along a continuum, identifying consequences of the separation of de jure ownership from control as we move from the classic entrepreneur-managed firm to the public bureau as the limiting case of each separation. We shall find that as the degree of separation increases, the de jure rights of those who own become increasingly attenuated, being usurped, as it were, by de facto rights of those who control. Viewed by de facto owners, the decisionmaking process may display substantial instrumental rationality even though the organization may verge on incoherence from the perspective of de jure owners.

It is helpful to distinguish between the formal and the informal decision structure in any organization (see Thompson [1974] for a discussion of this distinction in the context of modern organization theory). The former, typically explicit, displays attributes commonly associated with instrumental rationality. Thus, it establishes priorities in accord with interests of the de jure owners and calls for systematic weighing of budget alternatives in terms of their consequences for these priorities. It specifies selection of budgets that maximize owner welfare. The latter structure is implicit. It interjects interests of de facto owners into the decisionmaking processes. These two structures usually exist side by side. To the extent that the informal structure is the effective one, actual decision processes will not display attributes of instrumental rationality. Evidence of instrumental rationality in the informal structure takes quite different forms.

Let us begin with the classical entrepreneur under atomistic competition. Here there is no separation of ownership from control. The entrepreneur plans and controls the entire operation. Because he can supervise organizational processes closely, the formal structure is the effective decisionmaking structure. Given competition, both allocative and technical efficiency are achieved, the entrepreneur maximizes his or her returns and the public obtain goods and services in the appropriate mix at least cost.

Now consider a firm that is too large for any single person to exercise effective personal control. Consequently, the owner must hire managers, thus separating ownership from control and thereby giving scope to the informal decision structure. Meckling and Jensen (1976) have shown that this separation introduces special agency costs; hired managers can be expected to use the informal decision structure to divert some resources to their own purposes. While competition limits their ability to do so, they retain some residual discretion, and this, Meckling and Jensen claim, should be considered a necessary cost of doing business. When agency is necessary, owners may use stock option or other profit-sharing schemes to provide incentives for managers to reduce agency costs. By permitting a fraction of these costs to be privately appropriated by management, the remainder can be kept from dissipation within the firm and thereby appropriable by de jure owners.

If a firm is large enough to exert influence over market transactions, hired managers will have additional opportunities to divert resources for their own use. When competition is less than perfect, above average returns are available to firms in the industry if they restrict output. This, of course, leads the industry output to be less than optimal. However, de jure owners can capture the entire gain from the exercise of market power if technical efficiency is maintained. However, the informal decision structure, as with agency cost, makes it possible for the managers as de facto owners to appropriate some portion of the monopoly gains in the form of perquisites, larger staff, and perhaps, a quieter life.[9] Again, profit-sharing schemes can help to keep this organizational slack from being entirely appropriated by hired managers.

Turning now to the monopoly public bureau, we find separation of ownership from control to be virtually complete. While each member of the public possesses de jure rights in the bureau, none is in the position to exercise effective direct control, as is possible in varying degrees in private firms. Public owners have no specific claim on bureau resources that could compensate them for oversight costs. Consequently, control must be exercised by elected representatives through a process of representative government if it is to be exercised at all. As with the firm, hired managers, including all those with power to influence decision significantly, become de facto owners. However, it is apparently not possible to devise counterparts to the profit-sharing scheme used in firms so that returns to de facto ownership can only be enjoyed internally.

Because de jure rights in the bureau are exercised, however imperfectly, only by elected representatives, all others who possess power to influence the bureau's decisionmaking processes in their favor — that is, who can effectively exercise voice — should be classed as de facto owners. As in the firm, this class will include hired managers, but it may also include others who manage to make their voices heard. What determines who will possess the power to gain benefits from the bureau's resources?

To answer this question, let us posit for each group whose members share an interest in the outcomes of the bureau's decisions schedules showing the cost and benefits of the effective exercise of de facto ownership rights.[10] It has already been argued that exercise of de jure right by the public at large is precluded by the excess of exercise costs over benefits. However, both cost and benefit schedules may vary in magnitude among interest groups. Thus, for bureau employees who are connected closely to the informal decision structure, exercise costs will be relatively low. Because their major source of income is the bureau, benefits from effective exercise will be relatively high. While costs will generally be higher for nonemployees, benefits may be sufficiently high on particular issues to make possible their mobilization into effective groups.

We may now return to the question of how to understand orderly patterns of bureaucratic activity in light of the argument that public bureaus suffer from pervasive goal displacement. Even though, from the perspective of the public's interest in efficient production in public enterprises, the ensemble of the bureau's activities may appear to verge on incoherence and disorder, from the perspectives of actual and potential de facto ownership groups, norms of instrumental rationality may appear to rule. Regularities in resource allocation patterns and management of the bureau's activities should be understandable as a reflection of net benefits to the exercise of ownership rights for the de facto ownership group or groups. While this explanation may resolve the question of regularities in bureaucratic behavior under goal displacement, it raises another for de jure owners who, not being well-served, may come to question the bureau's legitimacy. We will return to the matter of legitimacy below.

To summarize, the public choice approach to bureaucracy under representative government predicts systemic departures from efficiency norms in bureaucratic production. The source of these departures is the relation of bilateral monopoly between the bureau and its sponsor in which the bureau possesses superior bargaining power because of its special access to and control over information about its production processes. Because of the inherent difficulty these circumstances create for setting goals and monitoring performance and because bureaucrats are likely to exploit their position to advance their own interests, bureaucratic decisionmaking will be marked by pervasive goal displacement. To understand patterns of resource allocation and management that arise under such displacement, the notion of de facto ownership rights with cost and benefit schedules associated with their exercise was advanced. Let us then turn from these general considerations to an examination of the public school industry.

A PUBLIC CHOICE MODEL OF SCHOOL DISTRICTS

State government remains the primary sponsor of public schooling in the United States, even though the federal government has been playing a growing role. In adapting the public choice approach to modeling school district decisionmaking, state government is conceived as the generator of the demand for schooling. The state expresses this demand in two ways. First, it establishes an education code that specifies formal goals of school districts and establishes rules and regulations for their operation. Formal goals are of a sufficiently high level of generality to command widespread assent but too high to provide direction for day-to-day conduct of schooling. Detailed rules and regulations are, in part, aimed at assuring conduct that advances these formal goals. They are also the product of extensive and continuing efforts by educators and other employees of school districts to protect and enlarge their de facto ownership rights in schools. Consequently, they may serve as impediments to realizing these formal goals.[11] In what follows we take the code as given and focus on how local districts function within constraints.

The state also grants school districts their budgets. Until quite recently, budgetary determination took the form of rules within which local authorities had discretion over local tax receipts and hence total expenditures. However, because of pressures for financial equalization among school districts, local discretion is diminishing. It will be convenient in what follows to assume full state funding of schools. Under this assumption, the school district does not propose a budgetary total and, hence, cannot influence size of its budget during the recurrent budgetary process. However, the possibility of allocative inefficiency still remains, for as we have seen, the output mix at the district level can still be nonoptimal. Also, of course, the possibility of technical inefficiency remains under full state funding.

Local governing boards do not appear in the formal public choice model. In it elected officials serve on appropriations committees that scrutinize budgets and activities of individual bureaus. However, these committees typically review appropriations of a number of bureaus, and their members participate in and have responsibility for a wider range of activities than these appropriations reviews. Because of their primary, close, and ongoing involvement in school district decisionmaking processes, it is appropriate to give these local governing boards particular prominence in modeling school districts compared to that accorded legislative review committees. Jay Chambers (1975) has done this in his adaptation of the public choice approach to school districts. His work provides an excellent point of departure from which to develop a general model of school district decisionmaking that shows why the governing board's failure as a setter of goals and as an evaluation of means is systemic.

Chambers was not primarily interested in modeling school district decisionmaking for this broad purpose. Rather he sought to understand salary differentials in the market for teachers. Interpretation of empirical results of wage and salary studies require assumptions about the motivations of the demanders of labor. When the demanders are private firms, assumption of profit maximization is quite helpful. Typically, wage differentials are seen to reflect differentials in productivity. Profit is maximized by taking these productivity differences carefully into account in constituting the firm's labor force. Recognizing that this interpretation of labor productivity becomes problematic in an industry that has an uncertain technology, Chambers proposed his model as a way to posit maximizing behavior by school districts as a basis for a stable structure of salary differentials keyed to variations in important teacher characteristics. It is this more limited effort we seek to generalize.

Consistent with the public choice approach, Chambers argued that substantial obstacles inherent in the structure of incentives in school districts as they are presently organized and governed virtually preclude overall instrumental rationality in the conduct of school districts. What then do school district managers maximize if they cannot maximize welfare of the district's de jure owners? Chambers proposed that they maximize quality of the district's activities as it is perceived, in the first instance, by the district's governing board. What is required to give this hypothesis empirical content is to show how maximization of perceived quality can lead to regularity in teacher salary differentials across districts—as well as, for our more general purposes, how maximization of perceived quality can be consistent with the maximization of the welfare of the district's de facto owners, which include, of course, the district's managers.

Beginning with the latter requirement, Chambers makes the connection between maximization of perceived quality and private interests of the district decisionmakers in the following way. He posits two main categories of district decisionmakers—trustees and high level administrators. Relying on extensive literature documenting dominance of the governing board by the superintendent, he argues that, under the superintendent's direction, school administrators

> will tend to avoid controversy and abrupt, drastic changes in policy, and they
> will manage the system in such a way as to promote the maximum amount

of reliance and trust in their personal judgments concerning the operation of the school district in order to minimize the potential for conflict. (Chambers 1975).

If they do this well, they can hope to persuade the governing board that educational activities they manage and policies and budgets they propose to support them (and which at the same time serve the interests of the de facto owners) possess qualities required by the public's interest in the efficient production of schooling.

Maximization of perceived quality is, as it were, a public cover for maximization of the private welfare of those who are in a position to influence allocation and management of district resources. As we have seen, under pervasive goal displacement and the reward system characteristic of public bureaus, maximization of private welfare can create a potential problem of legitimacy, since de jure owners interests are inherently compromised. The public side of the maximization process, then, can be viewed as an effort by school district managers to maintain and enhance legitimacy. While they create "images" of good schooling for public consumption, they do not do this out of whole cloth. To illustrate, characteristics of teachers that command salary differentials systematically across districts are likely to be those that have a common sense plausibility whether or not they contribute to student outcome in proportion to the differentials they command. The district's manager must work with the materials at hand, some of which derive from widespread public perceptions about how things ought to work and some of which are of their own making. But whatever the source of perceived quality, the major impetus for its creation arises from public school district employees' self-interest.

It might be supposed that the effort to sustain legitimacy in the face of the subordination of de jure ownership interests is undertaken in bad faith. To do so would be a mistake. As Niskanen (1971) has pointed out, the pursuit of displaced goals often leads to development of these lesser goals with the public interest. Individuals who have chosen careers in public education most likely have accepted the legitimacy of schools at the outset. If we accept the view that most persons have a deeply felt need to believe that their actions and commitments make sense, which leads them to dismiss or reinterpret dissonant evidence that might otherwise produce cynicism and bad faith, it is easy to understand why participants may not regard the creation of perceptions of quality as manipulative.[12] At the same time, it also becomes clear why the process is not likely to be altered by the selection of only "good" people to run the schools.

Chambers' (1975) characterization of school district decisionmaking as dominated by the superintendent and high level administrators serves his purposes adequately but is not sufficiently developed to serve more general ones. Other significant actors need to be identified and their interrelationships specified if we are to gain a full understanding of the systemic features of school district decisionmaking processes. We may begin by distinguishing two classes of actors—those persons employed by the district and all others. Within each of these broad classes, further important distinctions can be made. Let us turn first to district employees.

In most school districts both administrators and teachers "own" positions as tenured teachers. Only rarely do administrators own positions as administrators. Noncertified employees do not possess tenure rights, though state law usually offers substantial job protection. Since these persons do not play a critical role in the analysis that follows, consideration of them is deferred to another time. We focus, then, on the relationships between teachers, site administrators, and central administrators and the way in which their de facto ownership rights influence critical decisionmaking processes.

The bundle of rights included in ownership of a teaching position includes the right to the basic salary as long as student enrollments do not decline. Since competition from alternative suppliers is not a significant factor in enrollment decline, the budgetary base will depend primarily on demographic and other factors not closely related to individual employee or system performance. In addition to this claim on a position, teachers also possess the right to progress through the salary schedule without regard to individual merit.[13] Hence, salary will not depend on performance either.

These rights constrain the conduct of administrators in a number of important ways. Principals have very limited sanctions and rewards to support their efforts to direct the work of teachers. Because of this, teachers who do not wish direction can safely avoid it. Since the principal's tenure as supervisor depends in part on the support of his staff, teachers become the principal's primary constituency. Principals and teachers then come to develop reciprocal expectations in which the former recognize and respects the principal's need to maintain their position vis-à-vis the central administration. This mutual accommodation extends as well as between site and central administrators, since the latter are well aware of the constraints under which the former work and that condition their own scope of action. In the district hierarchy there is control up as well as down.

This system of mutual accommodation is a major determinant of the ways resource allocation and management in school districts falls short of efficiency norms. Movement toward interdistrict expenditure equalization takes the determination of total district expenditures outside local jurisdiction. As a consequence, allocative inefficiency in the form of excessive budgets will have its source in decisionmaking processes outside the school district. However, allocative inefficiency in the sense of an inappropriate mix of activities at the local level will remain subject to local determination. Moreover, existence of the de facto rights of employees will generally preclude sustained efforts to achieve technical efficiency.

The main ways allocative inefficiency arises within school districts is through preparation and adoption of budgets and policies and the development and application of working rules. Budgets and policies generally go before the governing board for at least pro forma approval. Their preparation is largely in the hands of administrative staff who can often keep their full significance hidden. District employees, in contrast to outsiders, are likely to have a keen sense of how their interests will be affected by budget and policy proposals. Moreover, employees have relatively easy access to the internal processes by which such proposals are generated. Further, if nonemployees cannot express a clear consensus about such proposals, there will be little countervailing pressure to offset the voice of employees. As a consequence, employee preferences and priorities will be regularly reflected in budgets and policies at the cost of subordinating the needs and interests of students, families, and the public at large. However, there are occasions when the needs and interest of nonemployees gain prominence over those of employees. We shall consider the circumstances later under which this reversal is likely to occur.

In any school district, rules, procedures, and understanding develop that do not come before the governing board for scrutiny or approval. In many ways these will be less visible publicly than matters that must come before the board. Because of this, public access to their formulation is even more limited than for budgets and policies. We would expect needs and interests of employees to dominate, when there is latent conflict between them and those of outsiders, more fully in these matters than in those that come before the governing board.

Turning to the question of technical inefficiency, in the absence of a well-understood educational technology, it will be quite difficult to distinguish between excessive costs and diversion of resources to serve employee interests. Nevertheless, some useful things can be said about it in connection with administrative practices. As we have seen, one result of pervasive goal displacement is for individual bureaucrats to select and pursue activities in accordance with their own preferences and priorities so that the ensemble of activities tends to lack coherence from the perspective of the organization's de jure owners. Under these conditions it will not be feasible to coordinate closely the activities of the school district and keep them focused on clear goals. Thus, the kind of tight coordination and control characteristic of organizations with clear goals and well-defined technologies will be absent from school districts, at least from those in which dissension about goals is substantial. Tight coupling of activities to each other and to the organization's goals can be taken as a necessary, though not sufficient, condition for technical efficiency.

A number of writers have commented on the "loose coupling" that characterizes school district decisionmaking (see, for example, Meyer and Rowan 1977; Cohen, March, and Olsen 1972; March and Olsen 1976). They note, for example, that teachers have control over the allocation of their own energy and attention among tasks and students within the classroom to an extent that is incompatible with the norms of instrumental rationality. I have argued that this discretion and concomitant absence of supervision and evaluation stem from the rights of teachers imbedded in tenure and the nonmerit salary schedule. These features are themselves ultimately the result of the monopoly that public schools have over public funds for education.[14] I take this loose coupling then as a necessary consequence of the systemic deficiencies of public school districts as a producer of educational services.

I do not mean to suggest that the possession of de facto ownership rights makes employment in school districts ideal or even especially desirable. Because the power to divert district resources to serve private interests and personal or idiosyncratic notions of the public interest is structural and largely implicit, it may be taken for granted.

Indeed, it may not even be seen particularly as power but as a prerequisite for effective public service. Moreover, parties to this system of mutual accommodation may find themselves in conflict: after all, resources are scarce. On occasion exigencies of image creation may entail compromise and constraint. In addition, balance in the system changes over time—witness the growth of collective bargaining—in ways that disturb existing patterns of allocation and management. If de facto rights were transferable, individuals could make fine adjustments in their situations by engaging in appropriate transactions. However, there is no market in de facto property rights. Returns can only be taken in kind within the overall resource constraints of the organization and with regard to the preferences and interests of other employees. Participants may then come to see themselves as victims of the system at the same time that they are its beneficiaries.

So far, benefits accruing to district employees from exercising ownership rights have been portrayed as greater than the cost of doing so for a wide range of decisions. This is likely to be true for the routine conduct of school and classroom activities that bulk large in the total school program. At the same time, costs are likely to exceed benefits of exercises for nonemployees in these areas for a number of reasons. First, mobilization of nonemployees suffers from the perennial obstacles to organizing collective action outlined by Olson (1965). The tendency for individuals to ride free on efforts of others is much more pronounced when the group on behalf of whom the action is to be taken is large and the members have weak interlinkages. The free rider problem is much less severe for groups like employees, which have a continuous existence for other reasons. Second, the decisions are not highly visible; at least they are much more visible, and their implication much more understandable, to employees than to nonemployees.

Nevertheless, there are other, less routine, decisions for which the impact on nonemployees is substantial and highly visible. The benefit from the exercise of ownership rights by nonemployee groups on such issues as busing for racial balance, school closings, and drastic alterations in school programs may be substantial.[15] In such instances we may expect collective actions by nonemployee groups. Further, employees may find that such actions affect their interest and can act accordingly to raise or lower cost of effective actions by outsiders. As important as such episodes may be for particular aspects of the district's operation, they are not likely to make heavy inroads into fundamental diversion of resources toward serving employee interests caused by the monopoly character of public school districts under pervasive goal displacement.

To summarize, unavoidable ambiguity of goals in public school districts and concomitant technological incoherence provide the occasion for interested groups to propose specific budgets and policies to gain commitments of resources from governing boards that, if boards had to devise concrete objectives and plans on their own, would be hard pressed to give adequate direction to district administrators. In school districts, employee groups enjoy superior access to decision processes that determine day-to-day conduct of district activities. Absence of structures, automatic or administrative, to insure that employee interest coincides with public interest in the efficient production of educational services means that budgets, policies, and working rules will favor private interests, and personal interpretations of the public interest, of employees over those of school district de jure owners. Unless a clear consensus on district goals can be reached, weak coordination and control of district activities denoted by the concept of "loose coupling" is inevitable. However inefficient the conduct of the schools may appear from a broad public perspective, from the narrow ones of the groups that have successfully exercised their voice on budgetary allocations, policies, and working rules that affect them, it is highly likely that the benefits they receive are commensurate with the costs they have incurred.

IMPLICATIONS FOR POLICY

The line of argument just developed has important implications for the design of policies to improve schools and for assessing the efficacy of past policy interventions. To be sure, the case for their importance must rest on a firm empirical base. For the most part, rigorous testing of the public choice approach in the field of public education remains to be done, though some indirect evidence bearing on it is reviewed below.[16] These implications perhaps can be most easily illustrated by reviewing briefly some of the consequences of two judicial interventions intended to make educational opportunities more nearly equal.

From the perspective of the model decisionmaking advanced here, decisions to require busing to achieve racial balance and to force revision of school finance laws to reduce expenditure disparities among school districts must have imposed substantial costs in lessened efficiency in affected school districts. Had these ramifications been anticipated, alternative policies to achieve equality might have been designed to lessen these costs. Recent work by Paul Peterson (1979) lends some indirect support to these assertions.

Peterson proposes that public education in metropolitan areas can best be understood as a dual system in which suburban and central city segments conduct their school programs in significantly different ways. He theorizes that governing boards of suburban districts are committed to fostering community's economic development. This leads them to provide the quality of education for which their constituents are willing to pay. Because families tend to select suburban residences on the basis of their incomes and their demand for schooling, school programs should tend to "reinforce and increase initial differences in child performances correlated with differences in the amount families pay for schooling" (Peterson 1979: 6). Thus, while substantial differences in program quality may be found between suburban districts, the substantial homogeneity in family constitutions within each district assures a consensus on program quality within districts. By providing a focused set of educational goals, this homegeneity would offset the tendency toward goal displacement that the public choice model predicts would, if not neutralized, lead to technical and allocative inefficiencies in suburban school districts.

Peterson argues that because central cities have quite heterogeneous constituencies, central city governing boards are unable to institute policies that contribute to the economic development of the region their district serves. Thus, rather than allocating educational resources in proportion to families' willingness to pay, these districts parcel out resources evenhandedly without regard to differences in family incomes. This redistribution should tend to diminish initial differences in child performance that suburban districts enhance. Peterson sees these universalistic rules as means that central city administrators have adopted to protect themselves from diverse interest groups pressing for special treatment.

However, the public choice model suggests another, more fundamental reason for such rules. Consider that achieving equal educational opportunity for students from diverse backgrounds is likely to require quite diverse treatment of individuals. This in turn will require quite close coordination and control of educational resources. However, such coordination and control is not possible under the kind of pervasive goal displacement from which central city districts with their fragmented constituencies are likely to suffer. Universalistic rules can serve as an excellent cover for the exercise of the de facto property rights to which these circumstances give rise.

Peterson offers two sets of findings to support his dual system hypothesis. He found property values in the Chicago metropolitan area to be positively correlated across suburban districts. He failed to find a similar relation across a national sample of central city districts. Reworking the Coleman data, Peterson found, contrary to Coleman's initial interpretation, that schools do have effects independent of family background on what students learn. These school effects appear to be most pronounced for whites, who tend to live predominantly in suburbs, and much weaker for blacks, who reside largely in central cities. Superior performance of suburban districts evident in these findings is consistent with both the dual system hypothesis and the public choice approach. While much empirical work remains to be done to firmly establish these explanations, they are not mutually exclusive; we may take Peterson's characterization of the relative effectiveness of suburban and central city schools as a point of departure in evaluating likely effects of the busing and school finance decisions on school programs effectiveness.

Busing to achieve racial balance does nothing in itself to improve school program effectiveness. Moreover, to the extent that students are transferred from districts that have reasonably focused educational goals and effective programs to larger districts with ineffective programs, the overall effectiveness of school programs will be lowered. If central city students are transferred to suburban districts, these districts will begin to suffer from the confusion created by heterogeneous constituencies. This will add to the overall deterioration of program quality.

Furthermore, consider that achieving equality of educational opportunity will require differing treatment for students from different family backgrounds. Thus, treatments may differ in resource requirements and hence in costs. Their application within districts and within schools will require precisely the kind of close coordination and control that is virtually impossible to achieve under pervasive goal displacement. Thus, the enforcement of busing under the present mode of educational finance and governance is not likely to lead to the restructuring of decisionmaking necessary to achieve increased equality of opportunity. While there are doubtless many reasons why families have abandoned districts subject to busing orders, the effects of busing on program effectiveness should provide added impetus to the flight from the public schools.

Expenditure equalization can lead to reduced program effectiveness and hence also to flight from the public schools. Consider that constraints on public resources will most likely lead to equalization of expenditures at a level below that of the higher spending suburban districts. Consequently, districts losing revenues are likely to be those with the kind of constituencies that can neutralize to some extent the inherent tendencies of public enterprises toward goal displacement. This is less likely to be true for districts gaining revenues, so that there will be a net reduction in program effectiveness. In the absence of specific reforms capable of enhancing program effectiveness, families experiencing program decline may respond in a number of ways. They can provide privately financed program supplements for their children. They can organize voluntary supplementation of district resources by families keeping their children in district schools. They can, if these alternatives are not promising, leave the public system altogether. Moreover, equality of expenditures between districts does nothing to improve access to educational opportunities within districts. Consequently, in the absence of specific reforms that direct resources toward improving access within districts, there will be little improvement in equality of educational opportunity to offset the loss in program efficiency.

The impact of the departure of any individual family on the public schools will be negligible. However, departure of substantial numbers of families will lead to a bifurcated system of education in which those who are financially able and willing to pay tuition fees will be educated in private schools and those who are not will remain behind. To be sure, some flight from central city districts subject to busing orders will be to remote suburbs not yet subject to expenditure equalization. However, public schools overall, and especially central city districts, will tend to become reservations for those who cannot flee. Families who have left may eventually organize to seek tax benefits such as tuition credits to be financed in part by reduced funding for public schools. Thus, the long-run impact of busing and expenditure equalization may be reduced program effectiveness and increased inequality for those who were intended beneficiaries of these interventions.

How, then, can access to educational opportunity be more nearly equalized?[17] The analysis advanced here suggests that attempts to achieve equality must take account of the systemic deficiencies of the public schools deriving from their present mode of finance and governance that make them defective instruments of public policy. In terms of the public choice approach, control must be wrested from those who manage schools, the current de facto owners, and returned to those who properly own them, the de jure owners. Is it likely that shifting control in this way would create equal access to educational opportunities for those who presently do not have it?

This question can only be answered fully in the context of the particular alterations in the mode of school finance and governance adopted to return control to the de jure owners of the schools. Since the public at large is too diffuse to exercise control, any change must grant substantial power to particular individuals who are in a position to exercise it effectively. These individuals may not accord a high priority to broad public goals such as equality of opportunity. As a consequence, changes that improve the efficiency with which schools serve their clientele may not fully achieve other public goals—that is, there may be a trade-off between equality and efficiency that must be confronted if gains in equality are to be achieved by these means. This possibility can be illustrated by briefly considering how educational vouchers, a reform that would shift substantial power from administrators and teachers to parents, would affect equality of access to educational opportunity.

Vouchers would make it possible for families to select educational programs for their children independently from their choice of place in residence. As in suburban districts, choice is likely to produce substantial homogeneity among school clientele regarding goals and methods.[18] This homogeneity, together with the possibility of easy exit to alternative schools for dissatisfied families, would make individual schools quite responsive to the demands of families for effective programs. Families that might otherwise have abandoned public schools would have an incentive to remain within the publicly financed system. If they do, they will also have an incentive to work for, rather than against, adequate financial support of this system, thus preventing further erosion of the possibility of equal access.

However, the clustering of like-minded families necessary to improve program quality and to prevent bifurcation of schooling into hostile private and public segments would not ensure equality of opportunity between schools. Henry Levin (1979) has argued that the differences among schools engendered by vouchers would lead to the segregation of children by family income, since preferred educational styles are highly correlated with income. He believes that such segregation would make programs in different schools inherently unequal.

As was noted above, control can be shifted from school managers only to some other individuals. It cannot be shifted to the public at large. By shifting control to families, it becomes lodged with persons who, more than any others, are likely to accord welfare of children a high priority in the conduct of schooling. However, if families seek more diligently than unrelated individuals would the welfare of their own children, there is no reason to suppose they will do the same for the welfare of children not their own. Thus, achieving equality of educational opportunity is not likely to be a primary value for key decisionmakers under vouchers, just as it is not under the present system.

This tendency for individuals to neglect the broader public interest in their own decisionmaking can be offset to some extent by designing additional resources for lower income families to be used to enrich educational programs in which their children are enrolled. However, to the extent that equality requires presence in the same classrooms of children from families with differing preferences for educational programs, methods, and styles, equality of opportunity can only be had at the cost of reduced quality. If, as I have argued, measures to achieve equality that fail to recognize this may make equality much more difficult to achieve, it appears desirable to strike some balance between equality and quality. It is not my intention here to offer a detailed consideration of how such a balance might be struck. Rather, it is to show that finding such a balance ought to be a matter of urgent public business.

NOTES TO CHAPTER 7

1. Attendance in Catholic elementary and secondary schools has been dropping in recent years due, in part, to the financial difficulties posed by the need to rely more extensively on lay staff. However, the attendance in most other denominations had been growing. See the discussion in National Center for Educational Statistics (1979: 200–203).

2. The massive commitment of federal funds since 1965 to improving public schooling attests to a widespread concern about the performance of the public schools. The efforts have not, apparently, borne much fruit. See Paul Berman and Milbrey McLaughlin (1978) for an extensive discussion of these federal efforts and their consequences.

3. An early formal effort to model nonmarket organizations in the context of representative government using price theory was made by William Niskanen (1971). His work has been catalytic, eliciting responses that have filled a number of gaps in his original model and moved the analysis in important new directions. Niskanen (1975) discusses these contributions and adapts his analysis to them. See also Margolis (1975) for a critique of the revised model.

4. Pincus (1974) emphasizes the importance of these features for modeling school district decisionmaking behavior.

5. See Hirschman (1970) for a provocative analysis of the means available to the various constituencies of modern organizations for protecting themselves from organizational failures.

6. The analysis here is the traditional one of bilateral monopoly, with one side having superior access to the relevant information. Niskanen (1971) discusses in more detail how the sponsor can develop access to this information but argues that the bureau will nearly always retain a significant residual advantage due to this superior access.

7. Orzechowski (1977) shows that Niskanen's model is closely related to the behavioral theory of the firm developed by Cyert and March (1963) and Williamson (1964). Presence of slack and the ways in which decisions about its disposition are made is quite similar in both analyses.

8. Stockfish (1976) argues that because knowledge about the bureau's production processes in the hands of outsiders can be used to reduce the bureau's budget, bureaucrats will guard it carefully. They might even avoid collecting important kinds of data. "One consequence of this behavior is that a bureau head may not be able to manage his organization even if he 'wanted' to" (p. 15). This loss of control may frustrate bureau heads at times but it keeps outsiders at bay.

9. The resources that make these appropriations possible appear as the organizational slack in the behavioral theory of the firm. See footnote 7.

10. Olson (1965) has provided a useful analysis of collective action that is pertinent here. He notes that while the good sought is the private interest of group members, it is a public good with respect to the group. My analysis follows his discussion of the costs and benefits associated with undertaking collective action.

11. Levin (1974) notes the influential role educational professionals have had in the formulation of public school legislation. In his view, this dominance of producers over consumers of educational services "raises very serious questions about the ability of present political processes to reflect true social priorities in the educational arena" (p. 378).

12. Becker (1972) makes a fascinating case that the need to believe in the sense used here is one of the fundamental human motives, more basic, for example, than Freud's libido.

13. See Staaf (1977) for a discussion of salary schedules for teachers and administrators and how they reflect de facto ownership rights.

14. West (1967) documents that up to the last quarter of the nineteenth century in New York State, schooling was provided by a substantial number of private and public schools dependent on tuition fees. Public schooling became a monopoly only after the legislature, strongly influenced by organized educational professionals, made public schools free and compulsory. Literature on the role of professionals in establishing nonmerit salary schedules and tenure is scant. In the absence of a satisfactory documentation on how these facets of current teaching positions became established, we are constrained to treat them as fait accompli.

15. Boyd (1976) provides a useful discussion of issues around which various nonemployee groups may organize and seek to express their voice in district decisionmaking processes.

16. See Michaelson (1979) for a discussion of approaches to testing the public choice model and a review of selected evidence bearing on it.

17. See Michaelson (1980) for a discussion of the requirements for the effective allocation and management of resources to achieve equal opportunity.

18. Systems of providing families choice by means of vouchers can differ in important ways. However, the possibility of clustering by preference for program goals and methods seems to be common to all such plans. Consequently, I concentrate on this feature here.

REFERENCES

Becker, Ernest. 1972. *The Denial of Death*. Riverside, New Jersey: Free Press.

Berman, Paul, and Milbrey McLaughlin. 1978. "Rethinking the Federal Role in Education." Rand Paper Series, P-6114. Santa Monica: Rand Corporation.

Borcherding, Thomas E., ed. 1977. *Budgets and Bureaucrats: The Sources of Government Growth*. Durham, North Carolina: Duke University Press.

Boyd, William L. 1976. "The Public, The Professionals, and Educational Policy Making: Who Governs?" *Teachers College Record* 77: 539–77.

Chambers, Jay G. 1975. "An Economic Analysis of Decision-Making in Public School Districts." Rochester, New York: University of Rochester. Mimeographed.

Cohen, Michael D.; James G. March; and Johan P. Olsen. 1972. "A Garbage Can Model of Organizational Choice." *Administrative Science Quarterly* 17: 1–25.

Cyert, Richard M., and James G. March. 1963. *A Behavioral Theory of the Firm.* Englewood Cliffs, New Jersey: Prentice-Hall, Inc.

Hirschman, Albert. 1970. *Exit Voice and Loyalty.* Cambridge, Massachusetts: Harvard University Press.

Levin, Henry M. 1974. "A Conceptual Framework for Accountability in Education." *School Review* 82: 363–91.

_____. 1979. "Educational Vouchers and Social Policy." Program Report No. 79–B12, Institute for Research on Educational Finance and Governance, Stanford University.

March, James G., and Johan P. Olsen. 1976. *Ambiguity and Choice in Organizations.* Bergen: Universitetforlaget.

Margolis, Julius. 1975. "Bureaucrats and Politicians, Comment." *Journal of Law and Economics* 18: 645–59.

Meckling, William, and Michael Jensen. 1976. "Theory of the Firm: Managerial Behavior Agency Costs and Ownership Structure." *Journal of Financial Economics* 3: 305–60.

Meyer, John W., and Brian Rowan. 1977. "Institutional Organizations: Formal Structure vs. Myth and Ceremony." *American Journal of Sociology* 83: 340–63.

Michaelson, Jacob B. 1979. "A Theory of Decision-Making in the Public Schools: A Public Choice Approach." Santa Cruz, California: University of California. Mimeographed.

_____. 1980. "Assessing the Efficacy of Financial Reform in California." *American Journal of Education* 88: 145–78.

National Center for Education Statistics. 1979. *The Condition of Education.* Washington, D.C.: U.S. Government Printing Office.

Niskanen, William. 1971. *Bureaucracy and Representative Government.* Chicago: Aldine-Atherton Publishing Company.

_____. 1975. "Bureaucrats and Politicians." *Journal of Law and Economics* 18: 617–43.

Olson, Mancur, Jr. 1965. *The Logic of Collective Action.* Cambridge, Massachusetts: Harvard University Press.

Orzechowski, William. 1977. "Economic Models of Bureaucracy: Survey Extensions, and Evidence." In *Budgets and Bureaucrats: The Sources of Government Growth,* edited by Thomas E. Borcherding. Durham, North Carolina: Duke University Press.

Peterson, Paul E. 1979. "Developmental Versus Redistributive Policies in Central City and Suburban Schools." Presented at the Annual Meeting of the American Educational Research Association, San Francisco, April.

Pincus, John. 1974. "Incentives for Innovation in the Public Schools." *Review of Educational Research* 44: 113–44.

Staaf, Robert J. 1977. "The Growth of Educational Bureacracy: Do Teachers Make a Difference?" In *Budgets and Bureaucrats: The Sources of Government Growth,* edited by Thomas E. Borcherding. Durham, North Carolina: Duke University Press.

Stockfish, Jacob A. 1976. "Analysis of Bureaucratic Behavior: The Ill-Defined Production Process." Rand Paper Series, P–5591. Santa Monica: Rand Corporation.

Thompson, Victor A. 1974. *The Development of Modern Bureaucracy: Tools Out of People.* Morristown, New Jersey: General Learning Press.

West, E.G. 1967. "The Political Economy of American Public School Legislation." *Journal of Law and Economics* 10: 101–28.

Williamson, Oliver. 1964. *The Economics of Discretionary Behavior: Managerial Objectives in a Theory of the Firm.* Englewood Cliffs, New Jersey: Prentice–Hall.

Wolf, Charles, Jr. 1979. "A Theory of Non-Market Failures." *Public Interest* 55: 114–33.

8 EDUCATIONAL VOUCHERS AND SOCIAL POLICY

*Henry M. Levin**

In periods of growth, social institutions rarely face major challenges to their existence. While issues of control and competition for resources may be ever present within periods of growth, there is a peculiar protection afforded to institutional forms by their sheer upward thrust. In the case of the elementary and secondary schools of the United States, the decades of the 1950s and 1960s were ones in which the major problems faced were those of rapid growth. New schools had to be constructed, teachers had to be trained, and tax burdens had to be increased to keep up with the dynamic growth of the educational sector. Like the queen's advice to Alice, educational agencies had to run as fast as they could to maintain pace with the demands for enrollment expansion. They had to run at least twice as fast to improve the quality of educational offerings.

Statistics on the growth of elementary and secondary schools over this period are spectacular. Between 1954 and 1970, the number of elementary and secondary enrollments grew from about thirty-four million to over fifty-one million youngsters, and secondary enrollments more than doubled, from about nine million to almost twenty

*Henry M. Levin, Professor, Graduate School of Education, Stanford University.

The author wishes to acknowledge the comments of Jim Catterall, Jay Chambers, Penny Howell, and Tom Parrish on an earlier version and the assistance of Sharon Carter and Mary H. Johnson in preparing the manuscript.

235

million.[1] Per student expenditures in public elementary and second-ary schools in 1976–1977 dollars doubled from $766 to almost $1500, and total elementary and secondary expenditures tripled. Since 1970, however, schools have met with significant reverses in terms of enrollments, funding, and even the prospective employment of their graduates. Demographic shifts have resulted in declines in the number of persons of school age, while inflation and slow economic growth have created pressures to reduce taxes and to divert resources to other social services. Between 1970 and 1986 it is expected that elementary and secondary enrollments will decline by six million stu-dents. At the same time there is activity at both a state and national level to reduce public spending, including public expenditures on schools (see, for example, Catterall and Thresher 1979). Further, there is evidence that young persons at all levels of education are facing inferior job opportunities when compared to those faced by similar persons in past decades, and there is also a perception of diminishing academic rigor and increasing disorder in the public schools.[2] Finally, hopes of the 1960s for obtaining greater equality of educational outcomes through compensatory educational expendi-tures and school desegregation have not been matched by ostensible progress in either greater equalization or reduced racial segregation.

To a large extent education has become a declining industry. As such, it is beset with conflicts over resources, policies, and long-term direction. Federal and state governments have increased their demands for minimum educational standards, greater equality of resource use and educational outcomes, and new programs for addressing needs of handicapped youngsters. At the same time, fund-ing for these kinds of activities has become tenuous. Parents have become increasingly dissatisfied with educational offerings and aca-demic rigor, and employers have raised serious questions regarding preparedness of secondary graduates for work roles. Schools now face a period of decline and retrenchment in which their basic capa-bility for conducting traditional roles has been challenged and under-mined by a potential loss of public support.

Among the many suggested educational reforms for addressing this malaise, perhaps the most profound challenge has been raised by those who advocate replacing the existing system of publicly oper-ated schools with "schools of choice" in which public funds would be provided to parents in the form of educational vouchers for the schooling of their children (see, for example, Coons and Sugarman

1978; Friedman 1955, 1962; West 1965; Institute for Economic Affairs 1967; Jencks 1966; Levin 1975). Under such a plan, parents could use vouchers for tuition payments at any school that met minimal state requirements. Those schools that were eligible to participate could compete for students and their vouchers and redeem vouchers for cash from the state. It is argued that a variety of alternatives would arise for each child, in comparison with the present monopoly system that generally requires attendance at a particular school based upon neighborhood residence.

Advocates of educational vouchers see the approach as one that will resolve many of the present problems faced by the public schools. Parents would be able to choose schools according to their own religious, political, and academic preferences, and schools would have to be responsive to parental and child concerns to maintain enrollments. It is asserted that such a market approach will improve efficiency of public spending on education as well as increase parental and student satisfaction. In contrast, it is argued that contemporary schools necessarily suffer from a highly centralized and bureaucratic approach that can not respond to individual needs and preferences or utilize resources as efficiently as a market-oriented approach. As a distinguished organizational analyst has stated:

> the classic antidote to monopoly is competition. By introducing alternative sources of supply, competition expands the choice available to consumers. Moreover, these alternative sources are likely to use different methods and approaches or even to develop wholly new products. Thus, greater variety makes expanded choice really meaningful. Since consumers can shift their trade from suppliers who do not please them, suppliers have a strong incentive to provide what the consumers want. (Downs 1970: 219)

By inference, if parents want to send their children to schools with greater academic rigor, with a particular political or religious orientation, with greater emphasis on the arts or sciences, or with some other specific focus, they need only use the educational voucher provided by the state to select such schools.

HISTORY OF EDUCATIONAL VOUCHERS

Although educational vouchers have become a salient topic of educational reform only in the last decade, they have a rather long history.

For example, the father of laissez-faire capitalism, Adam Smith, wrote over 200 years ago in *The Wealth of Nations* that at least part of the costs of schooling should be paid by parents because if the state were to pay all the costs, the teacher "would soon learn to neglect his business" (1937: 737). A very specific voucher approach was proposed at about the same time by Tom Paine in *The Rights of Man* (see analysis of this plan in West 1967). Under this plan, every family would receive a specified amount for each child under the age of fourteen, and children would be required to attend schools. Local ministers would certify compliance with the law.

Present discussions of voucher plans derive primarily from the provocative proposal made by Milton Friedman (1955, 1962). Friedman would give each parent of a school age child a voucher that could be used to pay a specified level of tuition at any "approved" school. Schools would become eligible to receive and redeem these vouchers by meeting requirements such as a minimum curriculum offering and safety conditions. Schools would compete for students, and they would have great incentives to meet the needs of potential clientele in order to obtain and retain enrollments. Parents would seek that school that best met their own concerns with respect to the education of their children. The role of the state would be (1) to provide funds in the form of educational vouchers for all school age children; (2) to establish criteria for eligibility of schools to receive and redeem vouchers; and (3) to assure that the educational marketplace functions efficiently and effectively by possibly establishing mechanisms for providing information on schools to parents, adjudicating conflicts between parents and schools, and ensuring that all children were enrolled in an approved school.

More recent versions of educational voucher plans build on the foundation that was laid by Friedman. For example, Jencks (1966) suggested that vouchers be provided only for children in inner cities in order to enable them to find alternatives to public schools. And in the late 1960s and early 1970s, the Office of Economic Opportunity (OEO) designed and sought to implement an experiment utilizing an educational voucher approach.[3] That experiment was aimed at testing the educational consequences of providing educational vouchers in a large, urban area, with specific foci on the nature of parental choices, the types of schools that would emerge, and the effects of these schools on student achievement and on racial and social stratifications of students. The OEO version of educational vouchers was designed to be "propoor" in providing higher or compensatory vouchers to persons from low income backgrounds and in utilizing a lottery for selecting students in schools where the number of applicants exceeded number of available places. Because of various changes in state laws that would have been required to test the voucher plan proposed by OEO, it was not possible to find a state or local school district in which the experiment could be fully implemented. A modified version was attempted in a school district located in San Jose, California; however, alternatives were restricted to public schools rather than permitting development of nonpublic alternatives.[4]

In 1979, a voucher initiative circulated in California with the aim of obtaining the required number of signatures to place it on the June 1980 ballot as a constitutional referendum. Essentially, the "Initiative for Family Choice in Education" would have modified the California Constitution in establishing three classes of schools: Public schools, independent public schools, and family choice (private) schools would be eligible to compete for students. Independent public schools would be those initiated by public educational authorities as nonprofit corporations with their own governance arrangements and would be operated according to the same laws as those affecting family choice schools. Family choice schools would need to meet only standards for private schools at present with no modifications permitted by the legislature. These requirements are rather minimal, so the family choice and independent public schools would have to meet only the most minimal curriculum and personnel requirements. Further, family choice schools would be permitted to teach any social values, philosophy, or religion, with the only qualification being that no pupil shall be compelled to profess a political, religious, philosophical, or ideological belief or actively participate in any ceremony symbolic of belief.[5]

The Family Choice Initiative was created and promoted by Professors John Coons and Stephen Sugarman of the University of California, Berkeley. Many of the basic assumptions on which it rests can be found in their book, *Education By Choice* (1978). While some of these assumptions will be discussed in a later section of this chapter, it is important to note that this initiative probably represents the leading edge of a movement to initiate voucher plans among the states. In fact, the strategy is closely modeled after the constitutional initiative to limit property taxation in California that resulted in the passage of Proposition 13 in June 1978 and that has been imitated in other states as well, providing the inspiration to reduce taxes and expenditures at the federal level (Catterall and Thresher 1979).

UNDERSTANDING VOUCHERS

One of the formidable obstacles to understanding educational vouchers is the implicit premise that this terminology refers to a single approach that will have predictable consequences for education. Perhaps this impression has been created by the discussion of educational vouchers or the voucher approach as if it were a monolithic device that differs from the present educational system in ways that are well understood. Unfortunately, the world of vouchers is far more complicated. First, there are many voucher plans, and their specific provisions can have profoundly different consequences. Second, most facets of vouchers are not well understood, because no educational voucher approach has existed previously in the United States. Thus, matters of the actual functioning of the educational marketplace and its economic and educational consequences are subjects for discussion and speculation, but the outcomes of a voucher approach cannot be predicted with certainty.

In order to promote an understanding of the nature of educational vouchers and their consequences, it is necessary to emphasize that there is not a single voucher plan. Each author or promoter of vouchers has set out a specific set of arrangements, and these often differ markedly from plan to plan. Accordingly, it is useful to refer to three major dimensions on which one might compare voucher plans in order to assess their likely functioning and results. These three dimensions are (1) finance, (2) regulation, and (3) information.[6]

Finance

The finance component of a voucher plan refers to such factors as the size of the educational voucher, what it can be used for, whether a school can charge more than the voucher or obtain additional funding through gifts, whether costs of transportation are covered, and the basic sources of funding. While we will not review all of these categories here, it is important to show how arrangements might vary considerably among voucher plans with rather different educational implications.

Under the Friedman approach, a uniform voucher would be given to parents for each child. However, parents could provide "add-ons" to the voucher to purchase more expensive education for their children. Obviously, wealthier families and those with fewer children would benefit most from this arrangement, so it would be likely to have highly inegalitarian consequences relative to present approaches and to attempts in recent years to provide greater equality of educational expenditures.[7] In contrast, the voucher proposal that was to be the basis of the OEO experiment emphasized compensatory vouchers where children in low income families would receive larger vouchers than those in less poor ones. In addition, add-ons by parents or subsidies and charitable contributions were not permitted, since they would represent ways of circumventing egalitarian intentions of the plan.[8]

Finally, the 1979 California Initiative stated that the legislature may take into account a variety of factors when setting the dollar value of educational vouchers, including such factors as grade level, curriculum, bilingualism, special needs and handicaps, variations in local cost, need to encourage racial desegregation, and other factors deemed important by the legislature. However, these deviations are purely optional on the part of the legislature and would have depended on the politics of the situation. In contrast, according to the language of the initiative, schools would have been permitted to charge higher fees or add-ons to the voucher from wealthier parents without any legislative intervention. Further, there was no prohibition in the California Initiative against "contributions" to the schools that one's children attend or to subsidies from sponsoring churches or other organizations. The result is that richer groups of parents could have augmented vouchers with other resources to obtain far superior education for their children than those parents whose resources and institutional affiliations would limit them to the basic voucher provided by the state. Since these privileges of the wealthy would have been mandated constitutionally, they could not have been altered by legislative action. Rather, they would have required a new constitutional initiative in order to be repealed.

Financial provision for transportation is also an important consideration, since the number of educational alternatives available to families will surely depend upon ability to obtain geographical access to different schools. Even in the absence of subsidies for transportation, higher income families will likely have little difficulty in providing access for their offspring to schools over a large geographical area. The use of both public and private transportation facilities is heavily contingent on one's income. However, the poor typically lack such advantages because of inadequate resources, so without transportation subsidies they would be extremely limited with respect to geographical access. (It should be borne in mind that even a trivial cost of $1 a day for public transportation would amount to almost $200 a year for each child enrolled in school.)

The Friedman plan makes no allowance for transportation, since it would permit the voucher to be applied only toward tuition. The OEO plan would make adequate transportation freely available for all students who were included in the experiment. The California Initiative would have required arrangements for transportation "in accord with reasonable conditions and limits upon cost to be fixed by law." Since the legislature would decide how to interpret this provision, it is not clear what arrangements would be made for student transport under the initiative. However, the relatively high cost of transportation for small groups of students who will be distributed ideosyncratically among schools does not suggest optimism in terms of transportation allowances. Even minimal cab fare or minibus fares of $2.50 each way would amount to about $900 a year per child.

Regulation

Although the voucher approach represents a shift from government production of educational services to the marketplace, that market would be regulated by the eligibility requirements established for schools to redeem vouchers. Just as different financial arrangements of voucher plans will create different educational outcomes, so will differences in regulation. Among major areas of regulation are those of curriculum content, personnel, and admissions standards.

The present system of public education provides a highly detailed and articulated set of curriculum requirements with respect to areas in which instruction must be provided and students must have instructional experiences. In addition, there are numerous areas in which teaching is prohibited, the most notable being that of religious instruction. In contrast, different voucher plans vary with respect to curriculum requirements.

Friedman is not specific about curriculum requirements under his plan, but it is apparent that they would be minimal, with emphasis on instruction in basic skills and a common set of civic values. The OEO voucher plan is somewhat more detailed, but it also lacks specifics (with the expectation that the plan would have to meet requirements of the state in which the experiment would take place). However, it does require that schools provide standardized test results for their students for purposes of evaluation, for parental information, and for use of prospective clientele. The California Initiative would also have had minimal curriculum requirements, limiting them to those required of private schools at present.

Further, the Friedman plan and the California Initiative would encourage a large diversity of schools with respect to political, religious, philosophical, and ideological sponsorship and offerings. The state would not intervene or attempt to regulate instructional content in these areas, except to assure that no laws were being violated. Presumably, Nazi schools could teach white supremacy and hatred of blacks, and black nationalist schools could teach racist doctrines as well, as long as neither school advocated interference with the civil rights of others.[9] That is, the state would be able to subsidize the teaching of divisive social views within the limits of existing laws. The Office of Economic Opportunity voucher plan would have proscribed many of these options, although exact regulations on these issues were never clarified because of the failure to implement a voucher experiment.

Personnel requirements of voucher plans also can differ. The Friedman approach would impose no standards, but would let schools and parents make decisions of whether or not personnel were qualified. The OEO approach would have been limited primarily to teachers who were qualified on the basis of the existing licensing practices of the states in which the voucher experiment was attempted. The California Initiative relied on existing personnel requirements for private schools, and these are considerably more liberal than those for the public schools with respect to training and licensing.[10]

Regulation of admission practices shows similar diversity among voucher plans. Friedman would permit schools to have complete rein in setting admissions policies. The OEO would set fairly detailed requirements, including nondiscriminatory practices, possible quotas for racial composition, and a lottery approach to choosing some portion of the student body for schools that had more applications than places. The California Initiative also would have prohibited discrimination in admissions on the basis of race, religion, or gender, but it would not require any particular composition of enrollments. That is, if a particular religious school received no applicants from other religions, it could remain religiously segregated. Obviously, schools that emphasized a particular political or ideological point of view could also be completely segregated even without discriminating against applicants of other views, so long as they did not appeal to parents with other viewpoints.

Clearly, depending on permissible curriculum offerings, personnel requirements, and admissions standards, different voucher plans will generate different outcomes with respect to what is learned in school as well as degree of segregation according to students' gender, religious, political, ideological, and social class lines. Any review of the implications of a particular voucher approach must be based upon an examination of specifics with respect to regulation. Such an analysis should extend beyond the few basic dimensions that have been discussed here to all dimensions of the curriculum, personnel requirements, admissions requirements, health and safety standards, rights of student to transfer to another school, and procedures of due process and adjudication in cases of conflict between schools and parents.

Information

The final dimension for comparing voucher plans and their implications is the nature of the system for providing information on educational alternatives to prospective clientele.[11] Two facets of information are of particular importance. First, education represents a rather complex service that cannot be easily summarized in ways that will reflect accurately the nature of the educational experience that a particular child might face. Second, methods of providing appropriate information on a large number of educational alternatives to a wide variety of audiences is likely to be costly and problematic, particularly with respect to the least-advantaged persons such as those who are not well-educated, who are not English speaking, and who tend to move frequently because of the marginality in job and housing markets.

In the first case, it is possible to provide information on such major distinctions as those of a religious, political, or ideological nature. If a school is sponsored by Reverend Moon, the Catholic church, Seventh Day Adventists, or the Jewish Community Center, religious orientations will be obvious. Further, if the school is characterized as a military academy, a learning collective, a Ku Klux Klan school, or a Black Panther school, types of indoctrination will also be straightforward, and voucher advocates would argue that parents could choose according to their preferences. Even schools that emphasized particular curricula such as the arts, sciences, sports, and "human potential" could be presented in such a way that parents could make choices among distinctions.

However, qualitative aspects of education are much more difficult to characterize. Anyone who reads college catalogs will be impressed with the fact that the majority of institutions in higher education claim to seek academic "excellence" and have distinguished faculties. That is, it is much more difficult to ascertain how well institutions carry out their mission educationally and to present that in a usable format than to read self-serving claims. Further, if schools with various political or religious orientations tend to use clandestine approaches to obtain converts and adherents, as has been reported for certain religious groups, there will be an incentive to distort information in the direction of those descriptions that will secure clientele. Of course, advertising and promotional abuses can occur for other types of schools as well (see U.S. Federal Trade Commission 1976).

The second problem is that persons from the most disadvantaged backgrounds are the ones who may need information services the most. Such persons are characterized by low educational attainments, higher probabilities of being non–English speaking, and higher incidences of neighborhood mobility because of their lack of housing and job stability. In essence, they will have to be apprised in adequate depth of available alternatives in their native tongues or in a form in which the information may be comprehensible to them. Also, one must bear in mind that within any state there will be virtually hundreds of local educational markets, each with its own unique information and dynamics.

This means that the system for providing information must be highly decentralized, with information agencies and counselors available in every community—factors that are likely to be costly. Even with the extensive bilingual information campaign that saturated the Alum Rock School District in which the OEO modified voucher demonstration was tried, a surprising proportion of the population was not even familiar with the existence of the plan (Bridge 1978: 514–16). Despite use of newspapers, mailing, radio announcements, neighborhood meetings, and information counselors, one-quarter of the residents were unfamiliar with even the existence of the voucher demonstration over a four year period. As might be expected, those with lower educational attainments and non-English-speaking backgrounds showed the highest levels of ignorance. More problematic is the fact that it is highly unlikely that any ongoing voucher plan could afford the obviously high costs of the OEO "saturation" approach.

While the Friedman plan makes no direct provision for information and the OEO plan provided for an extensive arrangement, the California Initiative specified that reasonable requirements of disclosure be established by law with respect to curriculum and teaching methods, qualifications of teachers, and resource use, as well as the possible requirement of standardized test results. This information would be made available through sources independent of schools, and nonliterate parents and others with special information needs would receive a grant redeemable for the services of independent education counselors. Also, deliberate provision of false or misleading information by schools would be forbidden. These information requirements appear to be extensive and responsive to the needs of disadvantaged families. However, the fact that no details were given in the initiative for implementing their specifics (and that the budget provided for these services is miniscule, as will be described in a later section) leaves them open to a variety of interpretations with respect to the form and comprehensiveness of the information plan.

Summary of Voucher Arrangements

In summary, an attempt to understand the nature and implications of educational vouchers can only be attained by examining and analyzing specific attributes of particular voucher plans, rather than generalizing about the approach. Different specifics can lead to radically different results. Of special importance are arrangements for financing, regulating, and providing information for the educational marketplace. Clearly a voucher plan with "compensatory" vouchers for the poor, no add-ons, an extensive information system, and regulation of admissions to assure participation of the poor will have vastly different consequences than one that provides a uniform voucher with parental add-ons, a poor information system, and a laissez-faire approach to admissions. In short, any debate over desirability or unattractiveness of vouchers should be based upon a discussion of specific details and their possible consequences rather than assuming that conclusions can be drawn in a vacuum by addressing the voucher concept.

One additional, but central, conclusion that can be derived from this discussion is that claims for voucher plans may or may not be supported by their details. For example, the California Initiative asserted that one purpose is "To protect freedom of religion, but aid no religion." This statement is obviously designed to give the impression that church-sponsored or related schools are not eligible for vouchers. While the initiative required that such schools incorporate as separate entities for purposes of being eligible for vouchers, a careful reading of the initiative makes clear that such schools would certainly be eligible for vouchers. Indeed, since they enroll the vast majority of children in the independent schools of California, they most likely would have been the primary recipients of the shift to vouchers.[12]

Authors of the California Initiative (Coons and Sugarman 1978) responded that the voucher aids no religion by drawing legalistic distinctions. First, they would state that it is children who would receive voucher benefits, not institutions. Second, they argued that the requirement that schools incorporate as separate legal entities will divide the schools from their religious sponsors, despite the obvious content and intentions of the curriculum and instruction. These attempts to create legal technicalities that are likely to mislead average citizens are unfortunate, for it is clear that a major intention and impact of the initiative was to aid religious schools and to subsidize religious instruction.

The California Initiative also called for decentralization of the public administration of education through the marketplace, but it did not mention that the shift to vouchers will also centralize many functions of schools from the local to the state level. At present, the state must coordinate and monitor the financing and educational offerings of California's 1040 local school districts. In turn, those districts address educational needs of the children within their jurisdictions, including monitoring attendance and compliance with compulsory attendance laws.

Under the voucher system, the state would need to monitor attendance patterns and enrollments of almost five million youngsters as well as to ascertain their eligibility for vouchers and the appropriate amount of the voucher. That is, the state would have to ascertain whether each of the five million students is enrolled in an approved school as well as diagnose the educational characteristics of each child in order to ascertain how large the voucher should be. Recall that the California Initiative would have awarded different voucher dollar amounts according to grade level, curriculum, bilingualism, special needs and handicaps, variations in local costs, need to encourage racial desegregation, and other factors. Presumably, each child would have to be located by the state and screened for voucher eligibility. Further, the state would have had to establish relations with individual schools rather than school districts in order to determine whether a school was eligible to redeem vouchers. The state would have had to provide information services in every community as well as means of adjudicating complaints and conflicts between parents and schools. In short, many of the present functions of schools that are carried out at local levels would have become functions of the state and administered centrally at that level.

Moreover, the California Initiative would have limited state expenditures on such functions to no more than 0.5 percent of the total public cost of education. Using the present level of expenditure in California, the initiative would have limited annual state expenditures on all of these functions to less than $10 per child. Precisely how the state would conduct the extensive functions implied by the initiative and create an extensive information system, screen children for voucher eligibility, certify schools, and handle complaints for less than $10 a year per child is not addressed. What is clear is that either the state would perform these services in only the most perfunctory manner or costs would be considerably higher. Of course, one could question whether the state has the administrative and technical capacity to handle these functions for five million students at any cost. Experiences with government regulatory agencies hardly suggest cause for optimism.

Finally, the California Initiative argued that it would limit costs by mandating that expenditures not rise beyond those costs associated with school age population and the consumer price index. However, by absorbing an additional half million students presently in private schools who would become eligible for vouchers, the state would become responsible for another $1 billion a year in additional costs under the initiative. Over the next decade, total costs of public schools might have become at least $10 billion higher, even without increases in the consumer price index, by underwriting the 10 percent of California's elementary and secondary students who presently are in private schools.[13]

Clearly, if voucher initiatives are put before voters, the nature and intentions of the details ought to be clear rather than obfuscatory. The California Initiative had been constructed in such a way that citizen debate is likely to be highly misinformed on each of the above-mentioned issues. While some of these points will be obvious to persons who are familiar with the educational system, others will be obscure to all but the most careful and knowledgeable analysts on the subject. Unfortunately, few of the "true" provisions will be apparent to the average citizen who is being asked to vote on the initiative.

VOUCHERS AND SOCIAL DILEMMAS

Perhaps the greatest social dilemma with respect to vouchers is raised by the potential divergence between private choices and social benefits of education. Presumably, the reason that so much of our social resources are devoted to education is that reproduction of our social, economic, and political system depends heavily on preparing the young to understand and participate in that system. Even Friedman (1962: 86) argues that the state ought to pay for the cost of basic education because of its important role in providing common values and knowledge necessary for an effectively functioning democracy.

This concern is composed of at least two major dimensions. First, schools are expected to provide students with an understanding of the role and functioning of our democratic system of government as well as to prepare them for participating in such a system. Second, schools are expected to create and sustain a system of social mobility in which a child's income and occupational status are not linked inextricably to those of his or her parents. Schools are expected more nearly to equalize adult opportunities among youngsters born into different racial, social, and economic circumstances. In this section, we explore the probable impact of the voucher mechanism on these two social goals of schools.

Vouchers and Preparation for Democracy

A major function of public schools is the transmission of a common language, heritage, set of values, and knowledge necessary for appropriate political functioning in our democratic society. To a large degree schools attempt to reproduce these traits through a common curriculum and an attempt to provide heterogeneous enrollments. That is, it is presumed that exposure to a variety of students from different backgrounds as well as a common curriculum with respect to social studies and civic content will prepare students adequately to participate in democratic institutions.[14]

In almost every respect, the voucher approach would violate these premises by encouraging separation and stratification of students according to parental commitments and orientations and by tailoring curricula to appeal to and reinforce these parental concerns. While neighborhood residential patterns in America prevent complete heterogeneity in student attendance patterns even within most neighborhoods, there are different religions, political viewpoints, ethnic backgrounds, and ideologies represented. Further, there is some degree of racial heterogeneity in a large number of public schools, even though the overall picture on racial integration is not a happy one. The voucher approach would systematize allocation of youngsters to schools according to family background and identity to an incomparably greater extent than even the more segregated of our present neighborhood-based schools.

Indeed, the appeal of vouchers is that parents can choose the type of education that they desire for their children by simply selecting a school that matches their needs most closely. While it is true that parents might wish to choose schools that emphasize arts, sciences, sports, basic skills, or humanistic objectives to a greater degree than present schools, these are differences that can be sought and attained through a variety of arrangements in the public school system. We return to this matter in a later section. However, what makes the voucher approach unique is that parents will be able to send their children to schools that will reinforce in the most restrictive fashion the family's political, ideological, and religious views. That is, school will be treated as a strict extension of the home, with little opportunity for students to experience the diversity of backgrounds and viewpoints that contributes to the democratic process.

The importance of being exposed to conflicting positions in forming democratic values cannot be overstated. This fact is illustrated by a recent study of attitudes toward dissent among West German youth (see Weiler 1971; Stiefbold and Weiler 1970). The central finding of those studies is that youth who display high tolerance for viewpoints that differed from the majority ones on specific subjects had been exposed to controversy or conflict to a greater extent than those who had little tolerance for dissenting views. Even more to the point, the greater the reported frequency with which controversial topics had been entertained in classrooms, the higher students' tolerance toward dissenting viewpoints.

If we consider that under a voucher approach parents will tend to select schools that reinforce their own views, opportunities for exposure to constructive conflict and controversy will be significantly narrowed for their offspring. It is highly dubious that Catholic schools will or should promote discussions about the pros and cons of birth control and abortion or that Ku Klux Klan schools will provide anything but the most negative stereotypes of blacks, while Black Panther schools perform similarly for whites. John Birch schools are not likely to expose students to a debate on the virtues of medicare and public assistance under monopoly capitalism, and Maoist schools are not likely to find any virtues in the political institutions of America. This situation is hardly one that is likely to have salubrious consequences for a democracy in which controversial issues must be addressed and resolved continually.

Vouchers and Equality

As we indicated previously, the way in which a voucher approach is financed and regulated and information about it is provided will have an important impact on how egalitarian will be its consequences. However, even though there will be differences from plan to plan, vouchers will tend to create greater transmission of inequalities from generation to generation than the present public schools. This problem tends to assert itself because parents seem to pursue child-rearing patterns that are consistent and reinforce their own values and class position in the society (see Kohn 1969; Bowles and Gintis 1976). This can best be understood by considering what these values are and how they might affect the choice of school.

Let us assume that parents wish to select the school that they believe will have the most chance of making their child a success in life. Clearly, rules for success differ according to where parents are situated in the productive and occupational hierarchy. Kohn (1969) has shown that working class families seem to emphasize conformity in their children (obedience to rules), while parents in relatively higher occupational positions stress independence and the ability to choose among available alternatives. Research of Hess (Hess, Shipman, and Jackson 1965) on maternal interactions also tends to substantiate these differences, with lower class mothers stressing a "do as I tell you" approach in teaching their children while middle class mothers seem to follow a more heuristic approach. Obviously, conformity and "do as I tell you" are ingredients for success in working class occupations. Such·occupations require workers to report to work on time, follow orders of superiors, carry out repetitive tasks, and obey rules and regulations of the firm in order to succeed.[15] Individuals in these occupations who do not conform are not rewarded with steady work and job promotions. Thus, research on behavior of working class parents suggests that they will select highly structured schools for their children that emphasize a high degree of discipline, concentration on basic skills, and following orders.

In contrast, occupational experiences of upper middle class parents suggest that independence and mastery of principles or concepts breed success. Managerial and professional roles require ability to consider alternative production techniques, products, marketing strategies, and personnel; to create rules and regulations that define the work organization; to maintain relatively great flexibility in personal work schedules depending on individual needs; and to have the ability to give even more than to take orders. Parents who derive from such occupational positions are more likely to stress freedom in the school environments of their children, with a heavy emphasis on student choice, flexible scheduling, few significant rules, and light enforcement of those that exist. They will expect the school to place a great deal of responsibility on the student in choosing and undertaking his or her educational experiences. While attainment of basic skills will be taken for granted, there will also be a much greater devotion of the curriculum to communicative skills in the form of both writing and discussion.

If parents choose those school environments that they believe will maximize probability of success as defined within the context of their experience, the working class child will be provided with schooling that will reinforce working class orientations while children from higher classes will attend schools that will orient them toward upper echelons of the occupational hierarchy. As Kohn has concluded from his study of the effect of parental occupation on values of children:

> The family then functions as a mechanism for perpetuating inequality. At lower levels of the stratification order, parents are likely to be ill-equipped and often will be ill-disposed to train their children in the skills needed at higher class levels. . . . No matter how dramatic the exceptions, it is usual that families prepare their offspring for the world as they know it and that the conditions of life eventually faced by the offspring are not very different from those for which they have been prepared. (1969: 200–201)

Vouchers would make this class stratification and socialization even more "efficient" by making it possible for parents to choose particular primary and secondary schooling environments based upon these values. Thus, differences in child socialization among classes in our highly stratified society would be augmented by a more perfect correspondence between the social class orientations of the parents and the schools they chose. In contrast with the present system, where at least some children find themselves in schools that do not necessarily reflect their parents' social origins, the voucher approach would streamline transmission of status from one generation to the next.

Further, to the degree that social class stratification increased, it would become easier to identify individuals for particular positions in the social class hierarchy by the school they attended. Each school would connote a different breeding or charter that would have a certification value in preparing individuals for further educational opportunities or positions in the labor market.[16] Even without identifying actual proficiencies of students as individuals, information connoted by the class orientation of schooling would tend to serve a stratification role for further opportunities.

The voucher approach to education represents a paradox. It seems reasonable to believe that the effects of greater choice among consumers and increased institutional responsiveness will enhance the welfare of society. At a rhetorical level, we would be improving ability to give families the education that they want for their children. However, as we have demonstrated, expansion of choices and market responsiveness will be much greater for upper income groups than for lower income and minority citizens, and the element of choice will lead insidiously to an even greater degree of class stratification and socialization than exists at present. The fact that these latter effects will be based upon individual "choices" and "preferences" means that exacerbation of social class differences in fortunes of children will be considered the responsibility of the parents who chose the schools rather than the class-oriented society that predetermined parents' values that led to the choices.

In summary, in two very important respects, the voucher approach would violate underlying premises of schooling in a democratic society. By segregating students in school environments that tend to reinforce values, prejudices, attitudes, and behaviors of their parents, the diversity of experiences and exposure to other viewpoints, which are at the base of the democratic process, will be largely eliminated from schools. Further, to the degree that parents will tend to choose schools that emphasize ingredients for success consistent with their niche in the occupational hierarchy, schools will tend to reproduce in children work values and orientations associated with parents' occupations. To a large degree, public support will be utilized to provide educational outcomes that conflict with the social purpose of schooling.

ARE THERE OTHER OPTIONS?

One of the unfortunate features of the current debate on vouchers is its tacit constriction of the range of options that are posited for improving American education. Advocates of both vouchers and the existing public schools tend to place the choice at two poles—a voucher system versus the present system of public education. Since it is voucher advocates who must provide a persuasive case for change, they pose the question in a way that is conducive to the answer that supports their case: Who should make the decisions about how each child will be educated? They then limit the answers in this multiple choice quiz to two possibilities—the family or the state.

The family is characterized as being deeply concerned with the educational needs of its children and anxious to make good decisions on their behalf. The state is characterized as an insensitive bureaucracy of functionaries whose concerns for children are relatively low on their schedule of priorities. We are then asked to choose one of these sources to make decisions for our children. Needless to say, most people would choose the family over this faceless bureaucratic state for making sensitive decisions in behalf of their own children.

However, the comparison is largely contrived. First, the state is hardly a monolith, but is composed of different levels and degrees of personal concern and citizen access. For the average parent, it is the personnel in a single school or a single classroom that have relevance, rather than an abstract notion of bureaucracy. Many teachers are deeply committed to the educational needs of children in their classes, and many are amenable to suggestions from parents. Other teachers are indifferent or worse. Of course, the same can be said for parents. Many parents are deeply committed to the educational needs of their children and will work with teachers, administrators, and other school personnel to try to fulfill those needs. In other cases, parents will be hard pressed by the demands of work, marital difficulties, poverty, or illness and will be unable to devote much time and attention to their children's educational needs. In other cases yet, parents will not have appropriate rapport with their children or understanding of their children's needs.

Given the relatively high rates of divorce and separation, alcoholism, and other stresses on family life in America, it is somewhat difficult to argue that families are always preoccupied with what is best for their children. The point is that one finds examples of both sensitivity and dereliction among both families and schools, and the real question is what overall arrangement can best contribute to the development of children in meeting both their individual needs and those of society. The answer to that question may suggest options that are ignored when the debate is limited to the existing public schools or vouchers.

A second artificial aspect of the voucher debate is the tendency of voucher advocates to ignore or denigrate any social purposes of schooling beyond those reflected in family choice. In general, these conclusions are reached by arguing: (1) there is no unanimity on the social purposes of schooling; or (2) schooling should not be concerned with social purposes, but only with individual needs; or (3) almost any voucher arrangement will meet the social purposes of schooling, whatever they are. Coons and Sugarman (1978) argue the first point, West (1965) asserts the second one, and Friedman (1962) seems to support the third point of view.[17]

Indeed, a large part of the explanation of why family choice should replace the existing system is predicated on arguing away the relevance of the social benefits of schooling. Yet if voucher advocates truly believe that schooling confers benefits on only those who choose and receive schooling, one must surely raise the question of why education should be funded from the public trough. That is, one must justify why government should raise tax revenues to provide families with vouchers that will be used to serve only their own personal desires with no important social benefits. In short, if schooling is designed to meet only the narrowest private desires of citizens, the basis for public funding is undermined. More to the point, without social purpose, the demand for public revenues from the state is indefensible.

In summary, voucher advocates tend to frame the debate on schools as one that can only be resolved by choosing between the existing public schools and a voucher approach. Thus, they intimate that if we are dissatisfied with public schools as they are constituted, vouchers represent the only alternative responsive to our needs. Moreover, this conclusion is reinforced by the tendency to ignore or dismiss social purposes of schooling, strengthening the family choice arguments. Unfortunately, they fail to point out that if schooling provides no social benefits beyond those received by the families and children receiving the schooling, there is no justification for public funding. Yet the dilemma remains. Given the legitimacy of many of the complaints about the existing public schools, are there other options besides vouchers? More specifically, is it possible to maintain the social purposes of the public schools with improvements in their responsiveness and diversity?

PUBLIC CHOICE APPROACHES

The purpose of a public choice approach to improving education is to capitalize on the social benefits that are conferred by the public production of education, while encouraging a greater degree of choice and diversity within that framework. These approaches are premised on the view that the virtues of utilizing public schools for preparing the young for democracy and social mobility do not obviate the need for greater educational diversity. Fortunately, there are public choice approaches that represent alternatives to both the existing public schools and vouchers. Paradoxically, at least two systems of public choice in education have developed as by-products of the quest for vouchers.

The OEO attempt to provide an experiment with educational vouchers was not successful in finding a state that would relax its educational code to accommodate the experiment, particularly with respect to use of public funds for private schools. After an extensive search for an appropriate site and a concerted effort to convince state legislators to pass enabling legislation for the experiment, the OEO finally decided to initiate a "modified voucher" experiment. In reality, the modified approach was not a voucher approach at all, but a system of public choice (see Cohen and Farrar [1977] for an overview). Participating schools in the Alum Rock (San Jose, California) School District were required to provide a minimum of three distinctive educational alternatives or minischools at each school site. Teachers at each school site joined forces with other teachers to create the minischools in which they wanted to teach. Personnel in each minischool had considerable discretion over the educational approach and curriculum, although they still had to meet curriculum requirements. They were also given a budget for acquisition of materials and other instructional needs (details are found in Weiler et al. 1974).

Each neighborhood school was converted into a complex of from three to five minischools, at least tripling the number of options that families had at their disposal. In addition, transportation was provided to minischools in other neighborhoods, so that the actual number of options was considerably larger, over fifty in the latter years of the demonstration. Particular orientations of minischools were quite diverse. Major categories included minischools emphasizing basic skills, fine and creative arts, multicultural activities, individualized learning, and innovative open classrooms (see Haggart, Rapp, and Wuchitech 1974). Parents were also provided with considerable information on the fifty or so alternatives, including availability of counselors with whom they could discuss their child's educational needs.

Early evaluations of this approach suggest fairly high levels of satisfaction among parents and participating teachers, and summary evaluations of the five year demonstration (which ended in 1977) will be available shortly (Weiler et al. 1974). From the perspective of a public choice model for education, the Alum Rock demonstration has a number of important virtues. First, it represents an approach that can be implemented in existing public schools with no alterations in state constitutions and or educational codes. Second, it enables the school system to preserve basic social objectives that can be expressed in curriculum policies and the composition of student enrollments. Third, the approach would minimize costs of monitoring student attendance and transportation in comparison with a state wide voucher program. Finally, there exist considerable evaluative data on Alum Rock that should be helpful in refining and improving the approach.

An alternative public choice approach is embodied in the Coons and Sugarman California Initiative, which specifies a category of public independent schools. These schools would be established as independent entities within school districts and would serve as alternative schools within the public sector. Without commenting on the specific provisions in the initiative for this class of schools, the overall idea has provocative consequences for establishing greater choice within the public schools. Moreover, the approach would not require modifying the state constitution, but would only require an action of the legislature to establish this new class of schools and the conditions under which they would operate.

A third option for greater public choice would be the establishment of somewhat greater decentralization in the governance of local schools. In many school districts the emphasis on uniform policies tends to homogenize educational offerings without taking account of the specific needs of student populations in particular school settings. A movement toward a more meaningful system of community involvement in the governance of local schools could improve the responsiveness of schools to the special concerns of students and parents. This emphasis on "community control" would also enhance democratic functioning of schools in that parents, students, and teachers would work together to define and implement the educational process in a democratic fashion. (For discussion of the concepts and some of the particulars, see Levin 1970.) Control over much of the curriculum, budget allocation, personnel selection, and managerial practices would be relegated to persons who are most closely affected by them.

CONCLUSION

In summary, there are a number of intriguing options for improving responsiveness of public schools while ensuring that they address their social purposes. If voucher proposals stimulate both the development of these public choice approaches and citizen awareness and political efforts to implement them, debate on vouchers will have performed an important service. Up to now, discourse on vouchers has tended to ignore other options by omitting them from consideration. Surely political initiatives to modify a state constitution on matters of such great importance as educational vouchers ought to be accompanied by an informed debate on all feasible options. It is hoped that this discussion has contributed to that goal.

NOTES TO CHAPTER 8

1. Data in this section are taken from Dearman and Plisko (1979).
2. For trends on the public evaluation of schools between 1969 and 1978, see Elam (1978). The job situation is reviewed in Freeman (1976).
3. Design for the ill-fated experiment is found in Center for the Study of Public Policy (1970).
4. An early evaluation is found in Weiler et al. (1974), and an overall assessment is contained in Cohen and Farrar (1977).
5. It is not clear what this qualification means. If a child is saturated educationally by a particular ideology, religion, or political view, it is reasonable to believe that the person has been socialized or indoctrinated by that point of view. This language seems to be deliberately evasive or misleading with respect to the main issue of whether a school would be permitted to indoctrinate a child politically, ideologically, or religiously. It is clear that the California Initiative would permit such indoctrination.

6. This analysis is set out in greater detail for postsecondary entitlements or vouchers in H. Levin (1977).

7. This is not to argue that there is some feasible approach to education that can provide perfect equality of educational resources among families. To the contrary, wealthier families have the ability to provide many types of educational experiences outside of the schools that families from less-advantaged backgrounds cannot provide for their children. However, different educational approaches can reinforce these inequalities or attempt to reduce them. Voucher plans also have these possibilities according to their specific provisions, although we will suggest below that even the most egalitarian voucher plan will tend to generate inequalities of a magnitude that is less likely than those associated with the existing public schools or public choice approaches to schooling.

8. The OEO Preliminary Report discussed seven alternative economic models and their consequences (see Center for the Study of Public Policy 1970: ch. 2). The specific details of the recommended model for the OEO experiment is found in Ibid., ch. 5.

9. That such schools would be eligible for subsidies does not mean that a high proportion of parents would choose such extremes. However, there is little doubt that the purpose of the initiative would permit such alternatives. At a public forum at San Francisco State University on April 24, 1979, Professor Coons was asked by a member of the audience whether such groups could sponsor schools that would be eligible for vouchers. His response was: "They pay taxes, don't they?"

10. In most cases there are neither educational nor licensing requirements. The school must be staffed by persons capable of teaching, but this is not defined clearly. See Cal. Educ. Code §48222.

11. Bridge (1978) and Klees (1974) provide thoughtful analyses of information requirements under voucher plans.

12. For example, in 1976 about four-fifths of students attending private schools in California were enrolled in church-affiliated schools (California State Department of Education 1978: 14).

13. This interpretation is based upon the ambiguities and contradictions among a number of passages in the initiative. For example, paragraph 4 states that: "For school years 1980–81 through 1986–87, the total public costs of elementary and secondary education in all common schools shall not exceed the total public costs of elementary and secondary education in 1979–80 adjusted and compounded for changes in the consumer price index and total school age population." I have interpreted this as meaning that adjustments will be made for the number of students who become eligible for common school support. Since this number would increase under the initiative, the total school age population would rise.

Others have interpreted this as a demographic phenomenon. However, if this were the case, then the age categories would have to be specified in order to obtain a precise classification. For example, if the compulsory attendance laws were used to define "school age population," students below the age of 5.75 years and above the age of 16 years would not be calculated in the measure. Accordingly, I have interpreted this as the number of children who will actually be attending the newly defined common schools, since any age criterion that does not specify the particular age range is ambiguous.

There is a further point of ambiguity in interpretation. If the initiative intends that the budget will not rise to accommodate additional students who become eligible for public support by shifting from existing private schools to "independent public and family choice schools," then how will the additional financial obligations be covered? Paragraph 15 provides for educational expenditures in support of students enrolling in independent public and family choice schools at 90 percent of that cost in public schools. But only if all students enrolled in independent public and family choice schools would total costs be contained while absorbing almost half a million additional students. As long as students choose to stay in public schools, then real educational expenditures for each public school would decline within the total expenditure limit in order to accommodate the new students who become eligible for public support in the independent schools.

14. The major treatise on this subject is John Dewey (1961). It is important to emphasize that these arguments are not germane to the postsecondary educational sector, where the emphasis must be on other goals. Rather it pertains to the compulsory portion of education.

15. The basis for these distinctions in the occupational hierarchy is found in R. C. Edwards (1978).

16. Meyer (1970) develops a theory of "charter" effects of education. Thurow (1975) explains how a job queue of educationally certified workers can explain the behavior of U.S. labor markets and the distribution of earned income.

17. Note that "voucher advocates" can be quite diverse in their philosophies. In California it appears that at least one other voucher initiative will be proposed and possibly two more. Jack Hickey is sponsoring a voucher approach in which parents would receive cash for their children meeting certain prespecified test scores performances, regardless of how the standards were achieved. That is, a parent could attempt to meet the standards through schools; home study using computers, audio cassettes, and programmed instruction; parental or professional tutorials; and so on. However the domains for the tests and their measures as well as other crucial details are omitted from the initiative.

REFERENCES

Bowles, Samuel, and Herb Gintis. 1976. *Schooling in Capitalist America.* New York: Basic Books, Inc.

Bridge, Gary. 1978. "Information Imperfections: The Achilles' Heel of Entitlement Plans." *School Review* 86, no. 3 (May): 504–29.

California State Department of Education. 1978. *1976–77 California Public Schools Selected Statistics.* Sacramento.

Catterall, J., and T. Thresher. 1979. "Proposition 13: The Campaign, the Vote, and the Immediate Aftereffects for California Schools." Program Report 79–B5. Stanford, California: Institute for Research on Educational Finance and Governance, Stanford University.

Center for the Study of Public Policy. 1970. *Education Vouchers. A Report on Financing Elementary Education by Grants to Parents.* Cambridge, Massachusetts, December.

Cohen, David K., and Eleanor Farrar. 1977."Power to the Parents? –The Story of Educational Vouchers." *Public Interest* 48 (Summer): 72–97.

Coons, John E., and Stephen D. Sugarman. 1978. *Education By Choice.* Berkeley: University of California Press.

Dearman, Nancy B., and Valena W. Plisko. 1979. *The Condition of Education.* Washington, D.C.: U.S. Department of Health, Education and Welfare. National Center for Educational Statistics.

Dewey, John. 1961. *Democracy and Education.* New York: The MacMillan Co.

Downs, Anthony. 1970. "Competition and Community Schools." In Henry M. Levin, ed., *Community Control of Schools*, pp. 219–49. Washington, D.C.: The Brookings Institution.

Elam, S.M. 1978. *A Decade of Gallup Polls of Attitudes Toward Education 1969–1978*, Bloomington, Indiana: Phi Delta Kappan.

Edwards, Richard C. 1978. *Contested Terrain: The Transformation of the Workplace in the 20th Century.* New York: Basic Books.

Freeman, Richard B. 1976. *The Over-Educated American.* New York: Academic Press.

Friedman, Milton. 1955. "The Role of Government in Education." In Robert A. Solo, ed., *Economics and the Public Interest.* New Brunswick, New Jersey: Rutgers University Press.

_____ . 1962. "The Role of Government in Education." In *Capitalism and Freedom*, ch. VI. Chicago: University of Chicago Press.

Haggart, S,; M. Rapp; and J. Wuchitech. 1974. *Instructional Aspects of the 1972–73 Mini-School Programs in the Alum Rock Voucher Demonstration.* Santa Monica, California: The Rand Corporation.

Hess, R.D.; V. Shipman; and D. Jackson. 1965. "Early Experience and the Socialization of Cognitive Modes in Children." *Child Development* 36: 869–86.

Institute of Economic Affairs. 1967. *Education: A Framework for Choice.* London.

Jencks, Christopher. 1966. "Is the Public School Obsolete?" *The Public Interest* 2 (Winter): 18–27.

Klees, Steven. 1974. "The Role of Information in the Market for Educational Services." Occasional Papers on Economics and Politics of Education, 74–1. Stanford, California: Stanford University School of Education.

Kohn, Melvin L. 1969. *Class and Conformity.* Homewood, Illinois: The Dorsey Press.

Levin, Henry M., ed. 1970. *Community Control of Schools.* Washington, D.C.: The Brookings Institution.

_____. 1975. "Educational Vouchers and Educational Equality." In Martin Carnoy, ed., *Schooling in a Corporate Society* (2nd ed.) pp. 293–309. New York: David McKay Company, Inc.

_____. 1977. "Postsecondary Entitlements—An Exploration." In N. Kurland, ed., *Entitlement Studies,* NIE Papers in Education and Work, No. 4, ch. 1. Washington, D.C.: National Institute of Education.

Meyer, John W. 1970. "The Charter: Conditions of Diffuse Socialization in Schools." In W.R. Scott, ed., *Social Processes and Social Structures.* New York: Holt, Rinehart, and Winston, Inc.

Smith, Adam. 1937. *The Wealth of Nations.* Modern Library Edition. New York: Random House.

Stiefbold, R.P., and H.N. Weiler. 1970. "Political Socialization in West Germany: Tolerance of Conflict and Dissent." Paper presented at 1970 Annual Meeting of the American Political Science Association, Los Angeles, September.

Thurow, Lester. 1975. *Generating Inequality.* New York: Basic Books.

U.S. Federal Trade Commission. 1976. *Proprietary Vocational and Home Study Schools.* Bureau of Consumer Protection. Washington, D.C.: Government Printing Office.

Weiler, Daniel et al. 1974. *A Public School Voucher Demonstration: The First Year at Alum Rock.* Santa Monica, California: The Rand Corporation, June.

Weiler, H.N. 1971. "Schools and the Learning of Dissent Norms: A Study of West German Youths." Paper presented at the 1971 Annual Meeting of the American Political Science Association, Chicago, September.

West, E.G. 1965. *Education and the State.* London: The Institute of Economic Affairs.

_____. 1967. "Tom Paine's Voucher Scheme for Public Education." *Southern Economic Journal* 33 (January): 378–82.

INDEX

ABOUT THE CONTRIBUTORS

Charles S. Benson is a professor in the School of Education, University of California, Berkeley. He is also principal investigator of the Children's Time Study, Schools of Education and Law, University of California, Berkeley. He is the author of *The Economics of Education.*

Stuart Buckley is research sociologist for the Children's Time Study. He holds degrees in philosophy, economics, and politics from Oxford University, England, and an M.A. in sociology from the University of California, Berkeley. He is currently a third year law student at the University of California, Berkeley.

John E. Coons is a professor of law, Boalt Hall, University of California, Berkeley. He is the principal author of *Private Wealth and Public Education* and, with Sugarman, has written *Education By Choice.*

Walter I. Garms is dean and professor, School of Education, University of Rochester. He specializes in school finance, higher education finance, educational business services, and computer simulations. He has authored, with Guthrie and Pierce, *School Finance: The Economics and Politics of Public Education.*

273

James W. Guthrie is a professor in the Graduate School of Education, University of California, Berkeley. He instructs courses and conducts research on the politics of education, school governance, and school finance. He has twice been elected to four year terms as a director of the Berkeley Unified School District. His other major publications include *New Models for American Education* and, with Garms and Pierce, *School Finance: The Economics and Politics of Public Education.*

H. Thomas James is president of the Spencer Foundation in Chicago. His professional experience includes secondary school teaching; supervising principal, district, and city school superintendencies; assistant state superintendent for finance and research in Wisconsin; and professorships at the University of Chicago and Stanford University, where he was dean of the School of Education from 1966 to 1970. His teaching assignments included courses in school administration, school finance, and school law; and his research and publications include a series of studies of school financing.

K. Forbis Jordan currently conducts legislative analyses for the U.S. Congress as senior specialist in education with the Congressional Research Service of the Library of Congress. Previous professional experience includes service as a faculty member in educational administration at Indiana University and the University of Florida and research and consulting activities in school finance.

Michael W. Kirst is professor of education, Stanford University, and president of the California State Board of Education. His research interests center upon school finance, educational policy, and the politics of education.

Henry M. Levin is a professor of education and affiliated faculty, Department of Economics, at Stanford University. He is also the director of the Institute for Research on Educational Finance and Governance. His fields of interest include the economics of education and human resources, educational finance, economics of evaluation, and the economics of workplace democracy.

Mary P. McKeown is a finance analyst with the Maryland State Board for Higher Education. Previous professional positions include finance analyst for the Illinois State Board of Education and faculty member at Sangamon State University, University of Illinois, and Eastern Michigan University. Research and consulting interests include school transportation programs, management information systems, and systems analysis.

Elliott A. Medrich, co-principal investigator and director of the Children's Time Study, Schools of Education and Law, University of California, Berkeley, holds a Ph.D. in city and regional planning from the University of California, Berkeley.

Jacob B. Michaelsen is a professor of economics at the University of California, Santa Cruz. He served as an elected trustee and president of the Santa Cruz Board of Education. As a consequence of this service he became interested in using economic theory to develop a comprehensive analysis of decisionmaking in school districts capable of contributing to the formulation of sound public policy toward the schools. He has published a number of articles with this focus.

J. Alan Thomas completed his Ph.D. in educational administration and school finance at Stanford. He participated in several school finance studies and authored *School Finance and Educational Opportunity in Michigan*. His interests in resource allocation resulted in the book *The Productive School* and more recently in a report to the National Institute of Education entitled "Resource Allocation in Classrooms." He is currently professor of educational administration at the University of Chicago.

AMERICAN EDUCATION FINANCE ASSOCIATION OFFICERS 1979–1981

President 1979–1980	Allan Odden
President 1980–1981	Richard Rossmiller
President Elect 1981–1982	Edwin A. Steinbrecher
Secretary-Treasurer 1979–1980	Dewey H. Stollar
Secretary-Treasurer 1980–1981	George Babigian
Ex-officio	James E. Gibbs

Directors

Kern Alexander	Bernard Gifford	James Kirkpatrick
Jerald Anderson	Margaret E. Goertz	John T. McGarigal
Roderick Bickert	James W. Guthrie	Dexter A. Magers
Fred Bradshaw	James Hale	Esther O. Tron
Robert Brischetto	Michael Hodge	Cynthia Ward
Nelda Cambron	C. Cole Hudson	Lillian Dean Webb
Joseph O. Garcia	Jack Jennings	William Wilken
Walter I. Garms	James A. Kelly	

Sustaining Members

National Education Association
American Association of School Administrators

277